Dancing
with the Pole

Dancing with the Pole

A Stripper's Diary

BUGS B

authorHOUSE®

AuthorHouse™ LLC
1663 Liberty Drive
Bloomington, IN 47403
www.authorhouse.com
Phone: 1-800-839-8640

Published by AuthorHouse   08/14/2014

ISBN: 978-1-4969-3450-5 (sc)
ISBN: 978-1-4969-3451-2 (e)

INTRODUCTION

Hello everyone! I know some of you love to read stories about peoples' personal lives. I'm sure a lot of you enjoyed my other book, "My Black Men", talking about my past relationships. I enjoyed talking about that because it gave me a chance to express myself, my feelings, and thoughts about the things I experienced as a woman while being with those men. Not too many women get the chance to do that nor do they want to talk about it openly. Let alone are comfortable in doing such a thing. It takes a certain kind of nerve to let something so personal leave from your comfort zone. And I have a few of those nerves.

I am one of those people who have lived a very interesting life so far. I am also comfortable with talking about my interesting life because as an adult, it is important to remember where you came from and to remember how you got where you are now. Some people will treat life as if it was given to them and they didn't have to struggle to get by. They do this to hide the part of their past that they are embarrassed to talk about. Everybody has something about them they would love to never hear about again. Truth is, in some cases, that's the best part about the person you are today. Your past shapes the person you become. That's why the subject of History is so important.

I am a firm believer that at some point in a person's life they have gone through a tough time for whatever reason. Things seem to be going good and right when you're about to make a power move. BAM! Something unexpected happens and knocks you down to the ground. Now you have to start over or your plans are put on hold till you don't know when. Don't you just hate that? There is no real expressive way to put it than, "This sh#t f*cking blows!"

I remember when I first heard that expression used, I was in Georgia for a summer college program. We were on a large campus walking all around that thing to the different classes. This Hispanic kid was pissed about something. I think it was the fact that we had to walk so far in the heat. He was fussing for the longest and out of no where he just came out and said, "Man this f*cking blows!" All of us who heard him busted out laughing in tears! It still tickles me even after 13 years. I wonder where he is and what he's up to? I just hope things are going smooth for him.

So, what are some of the things you have done when things didn't work out for you when you find yourself in a pickle? Can you picture this. . .

You have two part time jobs. One is in the morning and one is at night. You have these jobs because the first one at night pays you peanuts, stresses you the Hell out, and was the only thing you could get when you really needed a job. So you set out to get another job hoping it can replace the dead-end job you already have. Instead of replacing it with full time hours, the company only has part time hours with a little higher pay. Seventy five cents higher. You take it because the hours are early in the morning and will work with the other job schedule.

Here you are with two part time jobs. You're working and getting by. Then you go out to party one night with friends and on the way home you have a bad car accident that totals your car because the drunk person you hit wasn't suppose to be driving at all. How do you fall asleep on the freeway with no lights on? So without a car you can't deliver pizzas for one job and you can't get to the far away city for the other job. You end up loosing what you had.

Mean while, you still have rent to pay, bills, and kids to take care of. You're looking for another job but no one is calling you for an interview and if they do, they don't call you back to hire you. Time is going by and all you want to do is get another job and be happy. That just doesn't work out for you when you really need it to work out. If you were in this situation, what would you do?

This is what my situation was at the beginning on 2013. It happened in the beginning of February. I was feeling stuck and almost hopeless. So many thoughts were running through my head that I told myself, since I'm tired of stressing, I'm just gonna get through this the best way I can.

Before all this madness happened with my car accident one of my close friends, who will be known as Bubbles, had asked me to take part in a money maker with her. She was working a job she did not like and wanted to make extra money on the side. She asked me to dance with her because she didn't want to do it alone. I had actually thought about dancing some years ago but never had a serious need to get into it. This was not the same situation. It was time for momma to use that sex appeal to bring money into the house.

I do not remember when it was that Bubbles and I first went to a strip club/bikini bar to check it out. She went online and found this one place that was near us to go check out. The bar was not full nude because it serves alcohol. And in California there are strict rules concerning that. That's why she choose the place because you got to keep your clothes on and that was more comfortable for her. We went in one night during the middle of the week. There was a nice little crowd inside and the atmosphere was great. There were several stages for the girls to rotate and dance on. That's what we liked most. We went back a second time and it was still cool. This was the place for us.

Yes, I did spend time looking for another job. No. I did not find one. I still had rent, bills, kids, and other expenses to cover, so going with the plan was a must. It was a choice. Keep looking for a job with no money coming in, or keep looking for a job while bringing money in from dancing. What would you do? My point exactly. I'm confident in myself and with my body. I get a lot of compliments from men and women. Might as well test the waters and see if what people had been telling me all these past years would hold up in a bikini bar. Boy were they right.

The first time I got up on that stage my whole body was shaking. But I had watched and learned a few things from scoping out the club and dancers the first few times her and I went. While I was on the stage, it felt like so much was going through my head and at the same time my mind felt blank. I was putting my all into the dancing that I forgot the fact that I still had three more stages to dance on. My legs were already sore to the max from the bending and squatting. When I was walking off the third stage I thought I was going to collapse before I made it to the dressing room to sit down! I had a lot of ones in my bag, thank God. Bubbles was more happy that the whole thing was over. The only part she enjoyed was counting the money she got on stage. She was so scared and nervous that she kept wanting drinks from the bar to ease her nerves. I didn't need none of that to perform. This was serious business for me and my kids.

After a while I decided to start a diary of my experiences as a dancer so that I can share with the world what it is like for someone like me in this situation. It was scary at first, but when you play the book by the rules, you are making it a safe situation for yourself. Don't ever let one of these customers bend you to get what they want. If they do it once, they will feel empowered to do it again. And what is there to stop them after the first time? This book is just to share one person's life as a dancer/entertainer at a bikini bar in California.

SEPTEMBER 30, 2013

High Horse Riders

Today I woke up feeling different. I'm trying to fight off a cold I feel creeping up. I can feel it in my sinuses and my throat. I been taking Alka-Seltzer Plus. Orange Zest. Ugh! But I'm not taking it for the pleasurable taste. I'm trying not to get sick so I can still work and make that money. Can't do it right when your nose is running off your face and your head hurts. That's not sexy.

I had a difficult time getting to work because there was traffic on the freeway. Some how a huge piece of concrete got in the lanes. Guess it fell off some type of construction truck. Then after that Cal Trans was cleaning the shoulder of the freeway with the street sweepers. My thirty minute drive was forty five minutes. Glad I left an hour early. They be fussing at the job about being late but don't get started till thirty minutes later.

When I got to work there were a few girls there. About five of them were in the dressing room I was getting dressed in. I don't know about the other two dressing rooms. I never been inside them but I think they are tiny. After about an hour or two I was sitting at the bar waiting for more customers to come in. I was also watching whoever got on the stage to dance. A customer who was an electrician was walking by me coming from the bathroom. He wanted me to come to his table. He was there with two co-workers having drinks and playing pool. They already had two other girls at the table. I don't know or talk to any of them but they were cool.

Now. This person I'm about to talk about is the main person who is an ass to me. She get on my nerves in so many ways! I will call her Miss Stiffie. The first time I saw her dance I thought she was made out of glass. She dance like she's gonna break something if she don't move slowly, stiff, and gently. I don't know how old she is but man. She don't have it like she used to. Anyway, she came over because she's a waitress and a dancer, and had to see if anyone needed any drinks. The guy who wanted me to come to the table bought drinks for everyone. Even her. She even got some nice tips from the men too.

We all were sitting at this little table but I was sitting closer to the stage we were next to. Girls had started coming to the stage to dance once

1

they were finished dancing on the main stage. Miss Stiffie had already seen me sitting at the stage before she went up to dance. I was facing my party. I heard her say something while she was dancing but couldn't hear her clearly. After the security guard seen her throwing a temper tantrum like a two year old, he came over and moved me from "her" stage, two feet over so that I was actually sitting at the table.

Apparently, we as dancers cannot sit at the stage if we are not tipping. It was some B.S. about me taking her tip money from her because the guys will be paying attention to me and not her. For one, there was not a lot of customers there. So it's not like I was messing up her chances of making money. And I didn't see a group of people breaking their necks and falling over chairs to grab a seat and watch her dance either. Unless she seen some people I didn't.

I was annoyed when this happened. Even the security guard didn't want to say anything to me because he knew we were all over there together having fun and entertaining the customers. There seems to always be that one B-word making a fuss about some little crap like that. I don't know what's wrong with her but I'm so done. This is not the first time she acted prissy with me while on her high horse.

A few weeks ago I showed up trying to work on a Friday. There were a lot of girls there that day for the day shift. I was trying to find a place to put my bag so that I could start getting dressed. I had a Gatorade bottle that I sat on top of a black trunk. The cap was clearly screwed on and closed. I didn't know who's trunk it was and didn't think it mattered. It wasn't going to stay there for long.

Miss Stiffie was sitting across from the trunk. Matter of fact, I think she was sitting on someone else's trunk. She says to me, "Can you move your drink off my trunk. I don't want it to spill and get my things wet." I looked at the bottle sitting on the trunk with the top closed, as if to say, "If it did spill, how would your stuff get wet?" I moved the bottle and put it on the floor.

I heard her talking the other day about how she don't like people putting their things on her trunk. Do you know, that after you go home, all kinds of stuff go on top of that dam trunk? It's a trunk! It was made to be tough. That chick has some evil ways. I don't see how someone can work in such a small environment and act like there's miles and miles of room for everybody.

October 8, 2013

I. Am. So. Very Tired.

This weekend has been very busy for me because of the fact that I worked a double this past Saturday. One of the managers asked me the week before if I could do a double. I guess he doesn't have enough girls sometimes on the night shift. Hard to believe. I said that I could this one time. Boy. What a night!

To make things better, I had a pole class that Tuesday before that really put me in a lot of pain. The class was Inversion Virgin. It teaches you how to do upside down moves on the pole. I was real excited about it. That's one of the main things that I want to learn how to do. I know you gotta use your legs to hold and grip the pole. And you have to be strong enough in your arms to hold yourself upside down while holding onto the pole with your hands.

For the most part, things went good during the class. I was able to do two kinds of hand stands and a third that's a little different. There were three moves that I could not do successfully. They required me to have that arm strength and be able to kick my legs up to the pole, gracefully. Nope. I was not forcing it. The bruises I earned on my inner arm and left leg were satisfactory enough.

Come Saturday, I was unsure about dancing. I just told myself that I would dance to slow songs and take my time. When I got on stage I did just that. I like to flex my back, body and move sexy when I dance. I was testing my back and it felt pretty much okay. I was able to do my normal moves but I had a curiosity about my signature move. I spread my legs a little, bend my knees, reach for the floor behind me, then arch my back so my stomach is up in the air, and I'm looking like an upside down "U." Then I bend my knees and arms at the same time to show off more flexibility. The guys love it cause I'm the only one who does it.

Yes, I was able to do my move! But my back was still hurting a little. For the most part I was good to dance and entertain. Great news. Because I knew I was gonna be there all day and night, I took it slow. I wasn't approaching customers like I normally do. I was taking my time or letting them come to me while I sat down checking out the scene. Long as I can get on stage and dance I'm good with the making money part.

When six o'clock came around, things kind of slowed down. Not that many customers were there. But man, did it pick up big time as the night went on! There were not a lot of girls there. Some from the day shift stayed over too because they were asked. We made good money that night. Those men were throwing that money on the stage. I might start working doubles on the first Saturday of the month just to rake it in. But it did take a toll on me the next day. And going out staying up late Friday night did not help me either. Lesson learned.

Now the funny part about that following Sunday, there were only four dancers that showed up. I guess they said, "Screw going to work! I got enough money!" Me, I wanted to add on to what I made the night before. So I was there to do the math. The female bartender was called into action. She was put into rotation and got up on stage and did her thing. Plus, she's a rocker chick. It was nice to hear different music that I like listening to, and watch a different, interesting style of dancing. Not many girls get on stage and fist themselves in front of men. Well, she's the only one.

That was actually a slow day. Wasn't too many customers there. I guess that was a good thing. It's better when it's a nice amount of customers vs. the amount of girls. For one, the less girls there are, the sooner you have to dance on the stage. Even if each girl dances to two songs, you will be back on stage in no time. Then second, if there are a lot of dudes and a few girls, that means there will be a lot of pulling and waiting for the girls. Men will be trying to get a girl to talk to and spend time with. No break time. Only money time.

OCTOBER 17, 2013

What a Wednesday Night!

So yesterday was the Wet T Shirt contest. Every Wednesday night, girls who work at the club and girls who don't work there will participate in the contest. I don't know what the prize is but it's fun to watch all of them dance. If you want to try out at working there or get your feet wet at dancing, then Wednesday night is the right time for you. Things have changed since I started going months ago. For one, the girls that show up to dance have changed. There was a mixture of White, Mexican, and Black girls showing up. Now there's a lot of Black chicks that look a mess. I guess the word is spreading around about Wednesday night.

The weird thing about last night was the prostitution going on. There were chicks that looked like street walkers and men going around making offers for sex. I couldn't believe it. Even my friend who wanted to go was approached by a Hispanic man who asked her how much for everything. She sat there laughing. I didn't see how it was that funny for her to keep laughing. It's a shame that he didn't waste time getting at her like that without a simple conversation first. But it's the ones out there encouraging this type of activity by accepting the offers.

Now when I first got there and was trying to use the bathroom, there were three girls in the little two stall bathroom styling their hair to dance on stage. One of them was explaining how she worked there before and got fired for fighting. I left because it was hot in there and I didn't want to keep waiting in there. I would just come back later.

I went back to the dressing room to wait for my friend to finish getting ready. When she was done we went to the bathroom. The girls were still there. A stall was open so my friend went in first and I waited for her to come out so I could go in after her. There is a Black waitress who came in to use the bathroom. She seen that both stall doors were closed but that didn't mean anyone was inside them. She asked a question about anyone being in the stalls. One of the girls who was styling her hair answered, but it wasn't nicely.

Let me fill you in. The waitress knows the girl who was fired for fighting. She remembers her from the last time and she apparently has a smart mouth and that's how stuff got started. She was the same one who answered the waitress in a rude manner. She said, "Obviously since both the doors are closed." Rude, isn't she?

This started a huge argument between the two. I only have one question: If you are trying to go back to work at the same place you got fired from for fighting, why would you start some mess to get yourself kicked out? The girl talked a lot of trash and did nothing. Her friends held her back. The waitress said what she had to, left the bathroom, and went to tell one of the managers what happened. The girls were then told to leave. To add, how you gonna be in the club's bathroom with a huge bottle of alcohol, that you didn't get from the club? Oh you done messed up now!

The waitress apologized to me later on for her behavior. I told her there was no reason to. We don't need any girls like that here. There's enough nasty attitudes going on around here as it is. One less is better than one added. She obviously hadn't changed and did not need to be back here. The place is too small for all that trouble.

The best part of the night was not when home girl slipped and fell on her butt. It was when chickka was drunk out her mind and got on stage to dance. The contest had started. She was the first to go. She had on her white t shirt on and it was cut in the front and tied with a knot. She had long curly hair, jean jeggings, some one inch black heels, and a huge gut. She looked like she might have been in her forties. Anyway, when she got on that stage, before the music started playing, she just knew she was the queen of the night. She got up there and did things I couldn't believe. She drug herself across the floor on he knees like a dog dragging its butt across the carpet. She laid on her back near the pole, kicked her feet up into the air and shook her legs. She was pulling the back of her pants down and they wouldn't stay down. They kept going back up. She was really feeling herself. Then when she got to the last stage and was bending over, her boobs fell out her shirt. I started screaming.

One of the girls I'm cool with went over to the stage while she was dancing and gave her a dollar as she cheered her on. It was so funny to see but I'm not sure the chick knew she was being made fun of. There were some other new people who got on stage and did their thing. I don't want to go to another Wednesday night. I'll stick to the other nights. It's much more safer.

At the end of the night I was happy that everything was over. It was so crazy yet entertaining. I was happy that I had a fan who was tipping me as I went to the different stages. He was dark skinned, sexy, short hair cut, and claimed he was from Nigeria, but had no kind of accent. He didn't want my bottom in his face. He wanted to see my face and talk with me. He kept balling up the bills and throwing them on the stage. Just toss them, why ball them up? They don't have to be right beside me. He wanted to exchange numbers but it never happened. It's a nice change when a man wants to admire your beauty by looking at you while tipping. It's hard when they want to look for free while taking up your time. Those are the ones who don't get much attention from the girls.

This Saturday I'm excited about working a double. I have a new outfit I want to wear. But I have to ask the manager if it's okay to wear with the pasties. It's a black top with strings crossing over my boobs. It is so dam cute but I gotta make sure I can wear it and not get told to put something else on. I'll wear it for the night shift and hopefully I'll make big bucks wearing it. Some girls believe that what you wear help influence the money you make. I believe it plays a part. And I will test it out. Can't hardly wait!

October 22, 2013

Gimmie That Money!

I will now say that this past weekend was awesome! Today is Tuesday. I have been so tired from my double Saturday. It was worth it. I made sure that I did not stay out all night. I came home and got some sleep. Well, as much sleep as I could get. When I went n to start my shift I told myself to pace myself and take a nice flow to last throughout the entire day.

The awesome part about Saturday was the fact that it started off great. There were only four girls who started the shift. They were not doing much as far as dancing goes. I was the only black chick there. When I was going on stage I choose a slow song so that I wouldn't break a sweat. There wasn't too many men in there and I didn't want to mess up my freshly flat ironed hair that I did that afternoon. I actually wore my own hair instead of a wig. The girls were shocked to see how long my hair was.

To my surprise, when I got out there and started dancing, some men actually came to the stage and sat down to watch and tip me. I made good money from four main dudes. Two were really enjoying themselves. They did not want to miss me dancing. Then there were two others who were there for over eight hours. Drinking, tipping, laughing with each other at the TV. It was a White and Black guy. The Black guy was tipping me good because he really liked me. He wanted me to come sit and talk with him after awhile. I did. And I loved that $20 he gave me.

When the night shift started, it was eighteen girls. I couldn't believe it. I thought there would be like six or eight girls. The night was still good cause there was one dude who liked me and tipped me good. Funny thing is, he started off tipping two dollar bills. Ain't that funny to have happen at a bikini bar? Money is money. Plus I collect them for my son to keep. A little hobby of mine. I also like to collect the gold dollar coins for myself.

I was able to finish the night at 1:30 am. I was running on fumes. There were still people who wanted to talk to me, but my ass was tired. I was sleepy and ready to go home. I still had to come to work the next day at 1:30 pm. When I'm tired, things don't too much matter. I value my rest and don't want to miss too much of it.

That Sunday I felt rested enough when I went back to work. I was very happy about the 400 plus dollars I made. I put that money up. I need to build my money up to move into another apartment. I wanna make sure if I need to bribe the landlord with money, I'll have enough for the job.

OCTOBER 24, 2013

That Was Cool

Yesterday I went to work for the day shift to make up for not being able to work Monday. I had no idea how a Wednesday would be. The first thing I noticed was the amount of girls that were there. Even though I got there early at 11:30 am there were already five girls there and more on the way. I was shocked. I got dressed, ate my fast food, and went out on the floor.

The first thing I didn't like was the security guard that was working. It wasn't the normal guy. It was his day off. The one hat was there likes me. The spot where I like to sit by the door was where he stayed talking to me the whole time. I mean non stop talking. OMG.

During out conversation I told him I was getting ready to get my nipples and private area pierced. I like piercing a lot. He made a deal that if he came to watch me get the piercing, he would pay for it himself. I accepted it hoping that he would pay for them. I wasn't to confident in it happening. I wasn't all that sure if I wanted him to see me like that, then he think he can get a little closer to me. Nope. Not interested. Whatever. I have the money and don't mind paying for it myself.

I did good with making money that day. And a new girl started. She dances okay. The guys liked her. I didn't talk to her but I think she'll be fine. I didn't have any annoying people bothering me. That was nice. And I didn't see that one Mexican who gets drunk and wants me to kiss him on the lips. Ugh! I haven't seen him in a while and I don't miss him either. Actually, Wednesday went by real fast. The only time I went to the dressing room was to change my outfit and to eat. Other than that, I was on the floor.

October 27, 2013
Better Than I Thought

Yesterday was one of those days that you have no idea how it's going to turn out. Then it turns out too good to be true. I was mentally prepared for it to be a odd day because it was only four girls at the club and I wasn't sure if any other girls would show up. Then out of no where about five of them walked in late. I remember when I walked in late it was a crime.

The first thing that made me happy was when one of my regular customers walked in. He's an older Hispanic guy with his own company. When he comes in, he likes to hug, kiss, and buy me a drink, and cop a couple of feels. He tips nice. A good $40 or more. I was just pouring ones into my purple Michael Kors purse. Great start.

Then when I had to go up on stage I caught the attention of someone who likes big booties. He was tipping me good and followed me to the third and fourth stages. He was enjoying my dancing and I was enjoying his tipping. Then when I sat down to talk to him he kept putting money in my top. I got more money from him than from my regular customer. I sat and talked with him till he had to leave. There was a party he had to go to.

The rest of the shift was smooth. There was an ok crowd there. They enjoyed themselves. Some of the girls, two or three, had dressed up in costumes for Halloween. I guess the night shift had a lot of girls dressed up. It might have really went down that night. I'm good. I'd rather take my kids Trick or Treating then go home.

Now today is Football Sunday. The club will either be kind of empty or occupied with football fans watching the game and not the dancers. Today I won't be breaking any sweats trying to impress anyone. I'll be playing around on stage seeing what new tricks I can do with the pole. Save my energy for something else. Like the drive home.

I do hope that today goes by fast. The DJ for today doesn't play our songs. He acts like the internet don't work so he can play his oldies. I can't stand his ass. I have to use my phone or music CDs to dance to the music I want. And then he has a friend who comes every time he works. He likes to tip me a few dollars and cop some feels and try to get off by standing behind me real close. I found out one day he's short of workers upstairs in the main building. If you know what I mean.

(Drum roll please)

Today went good. I walked out with a solid $100. And that dam sho is better than $40. Thank God the 49ers game was earlier. I hate it when people come in to watch the game and they don't pay attention to us dancing or tip us. Take your stupid self to a regular bar! Us like men with money!

We had eight girls, I believe it was. We had to dance to two songs. Before it was started I sat at the bar and watched one of the games on TV with the manager, security, and one of the girls that get on my nerves. She was annoying me with her comments. You know how you sit with people and talk. And you're not talking to that one annoying person, but they keep talking to you? That's what was going on. And to add to my delight, she was sitting next to me.

When it was time for the show to start I changed seats and sat where I normally sit by the door. There was one guy a seat away from me who kept looking my way. After a while he finally asked me if I wanted a drink. I told him yes and moved one seat over so that I was sitting next to him. It was nice having a conversation with him. When he went to the bathroom, a guy in overalls walked by coming from the bathroom asked when I was going up. I had one person a head of me and he was happy about that.

As I was getting ready to go on stage, there were four men who took a seat at the stage to watch me dance. I was surprised because I wasn't expecting anyone to come sit at the stage to watch me dance. Sometimes no one comes. They all sit in the "cheap seats" as some men call them. The cheap seats are the seats at the table on the floor away from the stage. You watch the dancer without tipping them.

I was the only Black girl for the day shift today. I had no problem with it either. It just meant that when I got on stage, there was different music played. Like Hip Hop, Rap, or R&B. The others like that alternative or something almost like Country music. Some will dance to Hip Hop but not all the time. I had two customers asking me to dance to certain songs for them. No problem. You want to feel special, I can do that for you.

Before I go to bed, I just want to tell you about the funny thing that happened today. There was a new girl that started yesterday. She had dreads. One thing about this situation, I always think it's weird when I see a White person with dreads. I think to myself, "What would possess you to do such a thing to your straight hair?" But that's what it is. She has dreads and dances. One customer said she's a hippie. I'll believe that.

You can tell that she is new to dancing because she doesn't have dancing shoes yet. She has regular heels and they don't look like they have that much needed grip at the bottom like dancer shoes. Plus she looked as if she was high as Hell, or drunk as a skunk. While she was dancing on the pole before it was time to leave, she did a move and her foot slipped. Thank God she was holding onto the pole. Cause she would of fell hard in the worst way on the edge of the stage. She rolled around the pole and it looked cute as she slowly slid down till she was sitting still on the stage. As usual, I did not laugh. But my mouth did drop open.

OCTOBER 28, 2013
Not Bad For A Monday

So I went to work thinking that today would be slow. I thought that there wouldn't be too many people in the club tipping. I just wanted to make whatever amount I could and be happy with it. Anything to add to what I already have.

I got there and quickly seen that I was the only Black chick there again. Yes! Happy face! The customers who like Black girls will like me. I'm the only plus I have the long hair and big booty. I got dressed and ready fast. I wore my hair straight. There was one dude who was sitting at the bar when I came out. He looked like a cute twenty something year old. I think he was Mexican but he kept holding his hand up to his mouth. He was smoking and didn't want me to smell his breath.

The first thing I noticed was that he was sitting next to the seat I love to sit in by the door. I sat in my seat right next to him anyway. He kept acting like he wanted to say something to me. But I just kept on with my normal programming. I mentioned about the Warriors vs. Lakers game coming up. He turned around and started talking about it. He likes the Lakers.

When it was my time to get up on stage, guess who came over and tipped me? When I was done dancing, I went back to my seat and started talking with him. He told me that he's in the streets, one of his baby momma's is Black, and if he had more money with him he would of tipped me more. Heck, I'm happy that you gave me something! Thanks.

There was one gentleman who tipped me $20. I had a few 10s and 5s as well. I enjoyed today. It went smooth and there were no problems and the girls did good. Well, I hope they did good. Then it got real good when my regular customer came in and draped me in money. I still can't stand to see him sometimes. But he's a good tipper. He'll be known as Hairy. Notice the way I spelled it. He asked me one time if he could talk to my friend who comes with me on Wednesday nights. I told him sure he could, but he wasn't going to continue talking to me. Leave me alone because she is a close friend, and we don't play that. I guess he thought he was gonna have it his way. No way buddy.

OCTOBER 29, 2013

Not What I Thought

Tuesday, Tuesday, Tuesday. I went to work after going to bed late. My son wanted to go to that midnight release of a video game. I promptly went to sleep when we got home. When I woke up I wasn't too tired. When I got to work, there it started.

There were a few girls there. More than six. The one weird Black girl was there. She is the one who danced to country music the whole shift. Oh boy was that nerve wracking. I don't know if it's a customer who pays her to dance to dance to it, or if she's trying to dance to what she thinks the White customers will tip her to. It's common for girls to dance to Mexican music if there's a lot of Hispanics in the club. And there was some other Black girl I hadn't seen before.

When the shift started it was clear that there was not anyone there to tip us. The four people there were drinking beer, watching TV, and watching us. There also were a lot of people eating inside the club from the restaurant. After getting their plate of food, they came and sat down to watch us dance. A lot of times, that's all they're doing.

I was not going to break a sweat for nothing. I'd rather take my time and not tire myself out too fast. I dance to slow music when I think it's going to be slow. That's one of my early shift tricks. As I danced on stage I was also watching TV. A recap of the game usually be on and I catch a glimpse or two of a good pass or tackle. There was no need to get worked up over nothing. But the shift didn't stay like this. Thank God.

After a while, when I was sitting down at my chair, one of the older Black guys who comes in often came over and asked me to sit with him. Really, he was sitting with Miss Stiffie but wanted me to sit and talk with his friend. I had no problem doing that. It was an interesting conversation we had. Both men were tipping me and the guy who brought me over kept coming to tickle my feet. Yes, I'm ticklish.

When it was time for me to dance again, I noticed that a dark skinned dude with dreads had placed some money on the table for me as I danced. When I was done dancing it took a while before I went over to sit and talk with him. Now tell me, why was Miss Stiffie sitting at the table talking with his light skinned friend? That was so dam annoying for me. I don't even know why she was at the table talking to him, when the Black dude she was talking to at first was still there. And he had just told me he was waiting for her to come back to him. Ain't that something?

Then there was this one customer who comes in often. He was petting my face like I was a kitten. I don't know what his deal was but it was crazy. I was happy to get up and leave. I was getting worried about what he would do next. He rubbed his left hand over my back and looked like something was wrong. He then asked me if I had been in a car accident. I told him no, but clearly forgot about my car accident in February. Now why would he ask me a question like that? I was nervous about asking him that and seeing what he would say.

When I noticed it was almost 5:30 pm I decided that I wanted to go home early. I wasn't gonna be called to dance on stage again. And I wanted to get in that heavy traffic and get home sooner than later. The manager said I could leave. So I turned in my ones for twenties and went to change my clothes. On the way out one of the girls I'm becoming cool with was sitting at the table with the two dudes I was sitting with earlier.

She wasn't dressed yet. Looked like she had just got there and started talking. As I was telling the dread head bye, she said hi to me. She's a pretty girl. A pretty mix of Mexican and Black. Her mom is Mexican and dad is Black. She asked me if I was doing a double. I told her I was going to do one Saturday coming up. I had to get ready mentally for that. Then she stood up and said, "I want the titles for your books." Talk about being floored. I would never expect one of the girls to ask about my books. And the fact that she knew about them. How did she hear? I just reached into my purse and gave her a bookmark for the first one and explained how to find the others. I felt kindda good about myself walking away. Someone asked me about my books.

November 3, 2013
Leg Status: Pain And Soreness

Since last Tuesday I haven't been doing much to prepare for my double on Saturday except rest and think about it. Wednesday I went to get my nipples and private area pierced. I love them! Although my nipples hurt like something awful. They're done and I missed them so!

I didn't know what to expect about Saturday. I was only hoping that it would turn out great. It's the beginning of the month. People will have their beginning of the month money. So whoever comes in should be tipping nicely. Of course I paced myself so I wouldn't run out of gas before time to go home. The day shift was starting out real slow. There were more men there watching and drinking than tipping. One girl left early cause she claimed she had her boyfriend's car and had to go pick him up from work. I think she just wanted to leave early because it was slow.

But even when it's slow you can still make some money. But I think what her problem is, she comes in and takes her sweet time getting ready. She has this long weave she has to comb and when she comes out to dance she don't really do nothing. Then when she don't get any tips on the stage, she'll go back to the dressing room. I don't really see her talking to any customers. So how do she expect to make money? Things are always different for me that I have to treat everyday different. I already know not to expect much from these men. You just have to keep at it.

Nothing special happened during the day shift. There was one cute twenty one year old who still had breast milk dripping from his chin. I'm not sure if it was his dad he was there with. I was able to get some tips from dancing for them on stage. They were playing pool by the third stage and took a seat when I went over there. They seemed pretty entertained with me. They didn't stay long. I think they were just passing through.

Now, Miss Stiffie started something with one of the girls before I left. Apparently the blonde haired girl who was in the dressing room has a habit of quitting then coming back to work. Miss Stiffie was getting in her business as if once you leave, you shouldn't come back. They started arguing fast. She even went as far as to tell the girl, "You shouldn't say you're quitting then come back. It makes you look stupid." She got her dam nerves! If a person has to leave because of whatever reason then decides to come back for whatever reason, they can do that. I couldn't believe she was attacking her like that. What's it to her? And I know for a fact that last night was not a good night for Stiffie. She wasn't getting any tips on stage, especially for the night shift. She stayed in the dressing room. With her lazy dancing self.

The thing that really got on my nerves during the night shift is when men wanna talk and be all up in your face, but ain't giving no money. Why are you asking me what I want, while making it seem like you can take care of me if I was to be your girlfriend? Stupid. That's why my day shift customer got treated the way I treated him. He wanted me to come to the bar and sit on his lap. I told him to pull out some money first. He gave me a stupid look when I asked him how much money was in his hand, because it looked like $3. I was not in the mood for his B.S. He did give me money over the time period I sat with him. And I asked him to buy me a drink. When we went into the night shift I didn't go back over to him. He wanted me to touch him and I didn't want to.

I decided to do something different. Instead of counting my money at the end of or half way through the shift, I decided to wait till the end of Monday's shift to count it. Some of the girls were talking in the dressing room about how they don't cash in their ones till days or weeks later. I decided to wait till I have a few days off to count them all. But I'm gonna have my boo count them. When we went out Halloween night to a club, I heard a song the DJ was playing that was talking about letting "her count my money." So, I'm gonna let him count my money. I have all the rubber bands he'll need too.

So now, my legs are sore. I'm gonna stretch some and hopefully that will make them feel better for later. But before I leave for work today, I will be taking a Motrin for the pain.

November 4, 2013
So You Mean To Tell Me

This whole time I was thinking wrong. I was thinking, first of the month = money, money, money! No. Far from it. One of the girls in the dressing room explained to me that it's slow at the end and beginning of the month because of rent. I totally did not think of that one. Wow. And to add, this weekend was bad for everyone else too. Except for a few.

So yes. Sunday's day shift was slow. There was not a lot of action going on. Girls would get on stage and dance. Few, if any tips were given. Plus the fact that it was Sunday football. The guys that do come in be glued to the TVs and beers. I was shocked when I seen a few dollars on the stage my first time dancing. I still remember that one time I sat at a table with some guys that came in and was watching a baseball game. They completely ignored my attempt at a conversation. That's why now, when I see them watching TV, I do not bother to talk to them.

Then one of my regular came in. Hairy. He gets on my nerves now. Always talking about how bad he wants to have sex with me. I do not want to hear that. I was so happy to tell him I can't have sex for the next few weeks. That way he'll stop asking me. Then after that I'll tell him I'm in a relationship and can't have sex with him cause I want to be faithful. That way, I'm breaking it to him gently. He didn't get it when I told him I don't have time for him anymore.

The one thing that made me smile as I left Sunday night was Miss Stiffie getting into it with one of the girls. I don't think I know her, but when she walked in, her hair was tied up like a slave's back in the day and her face looked like she just killed her boyfriend after catching him in bed with another woman. She was not a happy camper. She had put one of her bags on the steps that goes up to the mini stage in the dressing room. Miss Stiffie walked in and couldn't walk up the steps to sit in her normal spot.

This is where things went wrong. She asked "Who's sh#t is this?" The angry chick looked at her and said "Mines." Miss Stiffie asked her to move it so she could get by. Angry chick picked up the bag and put it right where Stiffie was planning on sitting. Stiffie was like, "Oh no. That's not going to work." She picked up the bag and tossed it to the floor and sat down.

Angry chick looked at her for a few seconds then asked her if she was drunk. Stiffie said no, then the other girl got pissed.

"Now, I would be wrong if I slapped the sh#t out of you for throwing my bag like that. Don't touch my sh#t!" Everyone was very quiet in that dressing room. Stiffie said ok and was doing something with her phone. I can't believe she threw her bag like that. It was too much.

Now today was a better day. The only time I started making money is when two of my regulars came in and tipped me while talking at the bar. I hope this coming weekend will be better. The good news is that my period started today, so these next few days I'm not working, I don't have to worry about dancing while on my period. That is such a pain as a dancer. Constantly worrying if any blood is leaking. Thinking if the flow feels heavy or not. And the worst one. If the dam string is hanging for everyone to see. I'm just glad that it's happening now. But I could of sworn I had a period a few weeks ago. This is happening too soon but I guess it's okay to have it again than to not have it at all.

When I go back to work Saturday, I have some new songs I want to dance to. And I'm gonna try my little trick when I throw my feet into the air and spin around the pole as I'm sliding down. I would have been did it but the pole is not long. My short self be feeling like I'll kick the low ceiling above the stage! Some of the other girls are taller than me and they do it with no problem. I need to practice more. I can't wait till I can get my own pole!

November 10, 2013
A Better Saturday Than Last

Going to work yesterday was nice. I went in happy and left happy. The thing that was different about this past Saturday was the fact that I spent more time talking to customers. I met some new ones and they were nice. Tipped me some good money.

The funny part was when I had two drinks back to back, then got on stage to dance. I did fine at the first stage. It was the next stage that I was doing a move that required me to bend backwards. I was doing it with one hand when I should have been using two. I lost my grip and fell down on the back of my head. I was alright. I even laughed when it happened. But it was still okay after it happened.

After I got to work I thought it was going to be one of those ticking time bomb days, when you're waiting for something exciting to happen. The DJ came into the dressing room looking disturbed. There was this one dancer who would take girls home with her when they're drunk so they could have sex with her husband. She would take the girls' phones, snap a picture of them with her husband, then send the picture to the parents of the girls. Ain't that something?

The part that kindda upset me was hearing that this one Asian chick might have been a victim of this woman. I was wondering where she was because I haven't seen her in a while. I liked her. I first met her when I was coming on amateur nights. I even worked with her a few times after I got hired. This is a perfect example of why I don't talk to chicks there now. I don't have much trust.

As far as money, I did pretty good. Not as good as I wanted to do but I made over $100 like I like. Today I will talk to customers more and hopefully I'll come out with more than yesterday. Since it's Sunday I only have four hours to make some money. I don't want to stay. I might if the money is coming in nice, and I'm not too tired. I might be able to stay till 1:30 am.

Soooooo today was not too bad. I did have a good feeling when I started the shift. The security guard asked me how I was feeling today. I told him I was feeling pretty good. We had a good amount of girls today and an okay crowd. The 49er game was on and they lost to the Carolina Panthers.

I did good dancing on the stages. I even started out wearing my white boots. I bought some garment tape so my boobs wouldn't fall out the white and purple one piece I have. That worked great. I had some cool tips from people. And I was wearing my curly hair. I washed it and let it air dry before I went to work. It was cute.

There was an older man who came when I was dancing on the stage. When I was done dancing I went to go sit and talk with him. I couldn't understand too good what he was saying. He had a strong accent. I started getting tired of him after a while. He was doing that annoying mess I hate. When you want to leave to go to the bathroom or get away, he acted like he was gonna block me. I don't have to be tied down to anyone. I might want to talk to someone else.

Then the annoying dude showed up to be with his DJ friend. He took the hint that I don't want to be bothered with him anymore. He tried to talk to me but I ignored him. I didn't want to hear what he had to say. Then the other annoying customer came in. Hairy. He didn't say anything to me and I was happy about that.

In the dressing room the girls were talking about how slow the shifts have been lately. I guess the holiday season isn't good for dancers. One chick said that no one made over $20 the night before. I find that hard to believe. Sometimes one or two people will score better than the group. That's why it's important to have a nice relationship with your regular customers. They'll come back for you.

I actually did good the last stage I danced at right before I left. There were three men sitting at the stage. When the music started I went in doing what I do. A lot of booty dances. They really enjoyed what they seen. One man even said, "That's what we came to see!" I guess it was between my dancing and my pierced nipples. They were Raiders fans too.

Tomorrow I plan on going fishing with my mom. I might go to work after we get back but it don't look like it. I'll go Tuesday.

November 11, 2013
Happy Verteran's Day!

My plans for today was not to go to work. Go out like my mom and I used to. Mom and daughter. Catching fish. Talking one on one about things. Getting excited when one of us has a fish on the line. Oh yeah. We would have had that time. But she couldn't get a person at the store to sell her the fishing licenses. She waited for someone to come help her and no one showed up. So she wasn't able to get them. This morning she didn't want to go anymore. So I went to work.

When I pulled up the parking lot was empty. When I got inside the joint was empty. No problem. Don't mean it will be like that all day. I put my clothes on and waited for things to get started. People started coming in slowly. There was a cool little crowd. For my first dance I didn't have faith of anyone sitting at my stage. So I danced to Boy George, The Crying Game. Then I danced to a song that was a little faster. I was having fun up there.

As time went on, I caught the attention of these two Hispanic men sitting at the bar. They enjoyed my company when I was done dancing. One didn't speak English that good so his friend had to translate. The one who couldn't speak English started getting on my nerves. He wanted me to go outside with him to his van. I don't think so buddy. I don't do that kind of work.

After that I had to get back on stage to dance. That's when I caught another man's eye. He was heavy set, older, with size 52D cup man boobs. He wanted me to come sit and talk with him after I was done dancing. I did. The awesome part about him was the three $20 bills he tipped me. He might have been a teacher but he had better money to give than others. It was clear that he liked Black women. There was another Black chick there he was spending time with before me. And after me he helped tutor her in Math at the bar.

Hairy came in AGAIN today. I was sitting with heavy set dude when he came in. It looked like he got off work early and stopped by. Guess he was looking for something to get into before going home. I ignored him when he came in. Even when I got on stage I didn't look at him. I didn't want to see that stupid look on his face. I just wanted to dance, move to the next stage, dance, then get ready to leave.

Before I went to the back to get ready to go, the one White dude who really took a liking to me and came to all my stages was there. He was sitting at the bar near the bathrooms. He said something to me as I was walking by. I didn't notice him cause his back was facing me. When I say that man shocked me when I turned around so he could put money on me, I had no idea he was putting two stacks on both sides of me. And by stacks, I mean he gave me two stacks of over ten ones.

When I went in the dressing room to get ready to leave, there was only two people in there. One was the chick I saw when my friend and I first came to the club. She has huge boobs. I'm talking about balloons filled to the max! She was getting dressed. Another girl walked in complaining about a customer. I guess what happened was, he was giving someone else attention and not her. Miss Stiffie had to explain to her that any man who comes in here is not just for one girl. She was really upset about whatever happened.

Then she walks over to the chick with the big boobs and ask her how many CCs does she have. She said eight. So the other girl says that she wants six CCs. I turn around, they're standing in front of the mirror looking at each other's boobs. Wow. I thought they were real! Nope. There are CCs. I just hope that these girls who get a boob job are seriously making more money with them. I know a lot of men like boobs, others don't care if they're fake, and a lot just want boobs in their face. I'll pass. The only thing fake on me I'll accept is a broken nail. Nothing else.

I did want to stay and do a double but something told me to go home. I think I would of did real nice by doing a double. But I'll come a few extra days this week. I'm thinking about going tomorrow night then maybe Wednesday night. And then maybe Thursday night. We'll see what happens.

November 13, 2013

Tuesday Night Rocked!

I liked working Tuesday night. I left my house a little after 4 pm and the traffic, for the most part, was smooth. Next time I can leave a little later and should be okay. When I got there I left my bag in the car and got some Mexican food from the little restaurant next door. Then I went inside and watched the girls finish up the day shift while I ate my food.

There was about twelve girls working on the night shift. They were cool. The shift started out awesome. It was a challenge at first because this table of men, drunk men, acted like I HAD to sit with them because they were attracted to me. One of them kept trying to get me to exchange numbers with him, and it was not happening. And I know he was wasted because he kept repeating questions he already asked me. I hate that. When I couldn't take it anymore I went to the bathroom and hung out near the other side of the bar till it was time for me to dance on stage. That's when they left. I think something happened and they were asked to leave. Yes.

One of the times I was avoiding the rowdy table of drunk men, I was talking to two Indian men at the bar. The conversation was nice. They had hot tea with honey while I had a pink Moscato. They were two men who got off work and came to hang out. There were no open chairs left so I just stood in between them. One asked me if I could go to the bathroom and wash the perfume off my chest. Hell no. This is Victoria Secret. You don't wash this off after you just sprayed it on. If it's too much for you, I will leave. And that's just what I did.

The funny part was when I was talking to one dude at the bar and another was sitting next to me watching. Like he wanted to talk to me too. So when the other dude finally left, I looked at the little Indian dude who had been watching me and asked him if he wanted some company. He said yes, so I scooted over into the chair next to him and started talking to him. He bought me my second pink Moscato. We had a nice time talking till he had to leave. That's when I seen another guy looking at me.

He was a timid White guy with glasses. Remind me of Revenge of The Nerds. He was cute though. It was funny when he told me how he goes to another bikini bar where he gets lap dances, and gets nervous when he gets "excited". He be ready for the girl to stop because she's doing a really good job at giving him the dance. But she keeps going. It was his first time at my club and I gave him a very good impression. I don't know if anyone else talked to him but I took care of that. And he loved touching on my booty.

When he left I sat back and chilled. I didn't want to talk to anyone else for a while. My girl was there that I hadn't seen in a while. The one who started on a Saturday day shift, and I was the only one who reached out to her. I'ma call her Curly, cause she has long curly hair. She done got used to things now. I guess she only work at night since she also work at a hair salon. She scared me when I went in the dressing room to put my clothes on to leave. I didn't know she was in there laying down. She was drunk. I do think sometimes she has one too many drinks. But she still knows how to carry herself like a lady.

The night went smooth. I found a $20 at the last stage when I went to it. It was in a corner of the stage. I picked it up and put it in my purse. I made $20 when I was dancing for these two Asian dudes. One was getting ready to leave to the Middle East. He's in the army. I hope he comes back in good health and one piece. Nice that he stopped by to see us first before he leaves this weekend.

The girls had fun. I made over $100 and that was good for me. When I was in the back during half the shift counting how much I had so far, one of the other girls who's a better dancer than me was talking about how she hadn't made close to $100 yet. At the time I had over $60. I didn't feel too bad about what I had. It's nice sometimes to know if someone is experiencing the same as you or not.

Tuesday night was a good night to work. I met some new people and enjoyed their conversation. I plan on working Thursday day shift and see how that goes. I have to get as close to $1,600 as I can incase I get approved for the apartment. I'm almost there. I'm not gonna rush them either. I'll wait and work on building my moving money. What else do I have to do besides make money?

November 17, 2013

Counting

Yesterday was awesome. I love doing a double in the middle of the month. So much money to count. I got to the club super early because I wanted to put a bunch of curls in my hair. One thing the girls know about me, I don't waste time getting dressed and ready. I don't want no one coming at me about not being ready or none of that.

When I was dressed I went by the door and talked with the guard. There wasn't too many people there yet so I was chilling. Then Hairy walked in. I guess he thought I was gonna come sit with him at the bar. Nope. I stayed where I was. Another customer came in that I usually talk to but he was going through some personal things and didn't want to talk. I was okay with that. But don't turn around days later trying to tell me what happened. I'm not gonna care then.

Day shift started out pretty good. I caught the attention of a customer when I was at the last stage. He liked my booty. He came over and tipped me. Then I went and sat down with him. He was cool. He was on his way to buy shoes. Sneaker head. But stopped by the club first. He was giving me 5s. Then that one Hispanic customer who gets drunk off beers and starts repeating himself and asking for kisses showed up. He was expecting me to see him and come over to him. Nope. Wasn't in the mood. He was talking to other girls and I was happy about that.

When he did get my attention, it was because I was dancing on stage and he came and sat at my stage. Then later on I went over to him to see what he had to say. He was drunk. And talking about how he don't have anymore money because he gave it away to the other girls. Okay. I'm not mad. I'll just walk away since there's no good reason to stick around and be annoyed by you. He left shortly after.

As 6 pm came closer more people showed up. I decided to stay because I hadn't made my minimum happy mark of $100. Night shift was awesome. I even had some fans. A guy and two girls. I was sitting at the bar and when my name was called to go up and dance, this guy rushed up to me and asked if I was about to go up. I told him yes and he smiled. I noticed him and two girls taking seats at the stage. They enjoyed the show. When I went around to the other stages, they followed. They enjoyed my dancing.

There was a lot of birthday celebrations too. The one girl mixed with Black and Mexican gave a few of them. They really liked her dancing. Then the White girl with the dreads gave a birthday dance. She was high out her mind with whatever she was drinking. She almost fell on her ass a few times trying to dance around all cute. And can you believe she had the nerves to change her stage name by the time night shift came around? It was something stupid. She named herself after a flower. Like _____ Flower. The things drugs do to people.

November 22, 2013
Boy Was This A Nice Thursday

Today I decided to go in on a Thursday night and see how I would do. I had flat ironed my hair the night before and felt that I wanted to wear my wig. I even cut it short because I didn't like how long it was. I got to work with about forty minutes till the night shift started. I kindda hung around watching to see who and what was in the building. When I got dressed and came out, I was wearing my wig and a grey two piece outfit I got from Miami.

The first thing that happened was me going to the bar to have a seat. I heard someone calling my stage name. I looked and seen a dark skinned dude straight across from me in the distance. He called me over. So I went to see who he was and what he wanted. As I got closer, I heard him telling his friend that I have two bald heads. He wanted to put the money on me and watch me walk away. The guy was talking about my butt. I let him put the money on me, then let them watch me walk back to my seat. That was easy money.

When I sat down at the bar, I was trying to sit close to the seat I normally sit at by the door to see who comes in. There was this white guy who was sitting there in the seat next to me. He was so drunk, he kept repeating himself. And I wasn't even asking him a lot of questions. I was not ready too talk with the drunk that early today. I kept walking away from him till he finally got up and left. I don't need to hear about your wife when I'm not trying to do anything with you in the first place.

This night was not a fast and eventful night. There were more girls than customers! I was kicking back. I did see my regular customer, the lawyer. I didn't think he recognized me with my wig on. He was sitting at the stage watching another girl dance when I noticed him. I squeezed his shoulder from behind to say "hi", and he looked at me like he wasn't sure who I was.

When I got on stage there was this Black guy from New York who came over and watched me danced. It was funny because I did a new move where I lay on my back with my head hanging over the edge of the stage, and I put my feet in the air then touch the table with my toes as I bend my legs back towards me. Since I was laying on my wig it pulled it off but it didn't hit the ground. It was hanging. I just pulled it back on and got up the finish dancing. He came to all the other stages I danced at and I sat down to talk with him.

We had a fun conversation, but for some reason he felt that I had to call him A.S.A.P. I do not do those. I don't want a relationship with a customer outside of the club. No no and more no. When he left things became real slow. I just sat down watching people and looking to see who I could talk to. This one White guy obviously did not like me. I looked at him and he gave me a dirty look. Then when he was sitting at the stage and I got up to dance, he got up to walk away. So. I'm not here just for you. And I'm still making my money.

The lawyer was there again. I was shocked to see him. Seems like he's always there now. He said he came cause he thought he heard me say I was going to come. Yeah right. Whatever. I got some money from him. Talked for a while till I had to dance. He was my only regular customer I saw there. I'm glad Hairy wasn't there. He gets on my nerves.

The one thing I'm starting to hate is when the men come in there high on drugs. I had a Colombian tell me that he and his friends had took coke. And the whole time he stood in front of me swaying side to side, I wanted to get up and walk away. I do like that. I have no idea if something small will set of a trigger and they flip out on me. He kept coming back to where I was sitting to talk and was not tipping me. That's another thing I can't stand. Stop talking to me, if you're not paying me.

Another guy with a tight sweater on was talking to me and didn't understand that I didn't want him putting his hand down my panties. What do people be thinking? Then after a while he starts bothering me about going to the back seat of his car. What? Really? No way. I don't care how cute I am to you, I'm tired of telling you I'm not having sex with you. That's why a lot of times I'll sit at the bar and not go talk to anyone. I don't want them making such proposals for me.

One girl I had never talked to before told me she's from the same city as me, and pays someone $60 to get dropped off and picked up. She works three nights out the week. Who ever is doing her like that needs to be horse whipped. And she needs to find something better. That don't make sense at all. She can't carpool with me cause I don't work nights like that. I work days on the weekends. I can't help her.

Now, one of the bartenders got messed up from drinking too much and fell asleep. The security pulled him to the back in the kitchen and let him sleep on the desk. He came up to me and asked if I was wearing a wig earlier. He wanted to put it on the bartender and take a picture of him. When I got to where he was sleeping, it looked like he was sucking his thumb at first. But his tongue was rolling around in his mouth. We got the picture. Don't know how much he'll like it when he see it.

Yeah, it was a good night. Not sure about working Thursday night again, but I will do a Tuesday night again.

NOVEMBER 24, 2013
I Liked This Saturday

As I was on my way out the door for work, my mom asked me if I was going to do a double. I told her I wasn't sure but I'd let her know if I decided to. I took some money with me so that I could go to the clothes store before work and get my daughter a dress for ThankgsGiving. When I walked into the store I had to check out the purses first. That's when I seen her. A beautiful Jessica Simpson purse! Of course I walked away and bought my daughter's dress. I didn't have enough for both. I told myself I'd come back for her.

When I got to work, there wasn't too many girls there. But as usual, more will come later. I was happy because I wasn't feeling tired. I didn't go out the night before so I had got enough sleep. The started out looking like it was going to be dead. People started to come like an hour later.

The girl who comes in and takes her time getting dressed and ready, then leaves early when she don't make money on the stage walked in late. I don't know why she comes in sometimes. She should spend more time on the floor instead of in the dressing room, and maybe she would make more money than what she does. She dances nice. She just needs to not give in so easy.

I was one of the last girls on the list for dancing because I didn't pay my stage fee when I got there. I didn't think the DJ had change for a 20 dollar bill, so I wanted to wait. When I did pay it made me last. So I had the pleasure of watching everyone else dance to their two songs. As I was waiting to be called, an older guy came up to me and sat down to talk. He was nice. That's when I seen the dark skinned dude from New York that comes in sometimes. He's cool. He works two jobs and have a son back in NY.

When I was called to the stage, I was shocked that the older guy and an older White guy with missing front teeth came to sit and watch. I did my thing and made money. I went to the next stage and made more. The shift was going good. I made most of my money, if not half, from some Mexicans hat came in from a construction job down the street.

As I was walking by their table to go to the next stage, they called me over to tip me. Since they like my big booty, I would bend over and shake

32

it for them. Then I would tell them to spank it, cause I could see that's what they wanted to do. So if they had a dollar to put in the side of my panties, they could spank me three times. Oh yeah, my butt was on fire but my purse was filled with dollas. Then later on one of them asked me to come over and sit with them. I sat and talked and made more money as one wanted to rub on my nipple. He would put money on my every couple of minutes. They got mad at their friend because the beer was getting to him, and he was getting out of line. He got on my nerves trying to stick his dirty fingers where they didn't belong. Bastard.

While my customer from New York was there I sat and spent some time with him. He came in before he had to go to work. Drank a couple of beers, played some pool with the girls, and hung out with his friends that walked in later on. He didn't want to leave because things were getting good but he went on to work.

I had a slipping incident on stage. While I was at the bar, a customer had brought in a box of Sees candy. We were eating it. One of the girls had dropped a piece on the floor and I stepped on it. I didn't know that I had stepped on a couple of pieces. I was doing good with the dancing when I got on stage. I think it was my last time dancing on stage for the day. I was just about done with the song when I was turning around the pole and my right foot slipped. I was holding onto the pole so I didn't fall. I just laughed and kept dancing like nothing happened. I was cool. Not too embarrassed. It happens.

Hairy walked in before I got on stage. I looked at him and kept walking cause my name had just been called. I think he took the hint that I don't want to be bothered with him anymore. When I went to the last stage, I could see him watching me in the fun house mirrors that's by the stage. I don't even want him looking at me. I want it to be like we never met and never will.

When I was getting ready to leave I was happy to see my home girl, who got into a car accident last week. Her car was totaled and I was worried about her being able to get to work. She can't get another car if she's not making money. But she was there! I was happy.

I did want to stay and work a double but I really wanted to leave and go buy that purse! And I decided that I wanted to take my daughter out to eat so that we could have some time together. My son was with his uncle and cousins so I wanted to do something for just her and I. It was nice and we enjoyed it.

November 25, 2013

I Enjoyed That Sunday

Yesterday, Sunday, I was a little irritated that morning trying to get a new tire for my car and couldn't because of traffic going into the flea market. I was calm after arriving to work. There was a nice number of girls there so I got dressed while eating the food I had just bought. When I went out onto the floor there were a few guy there already sitting at the bar. I seen the Mexican sitting at the other end that be wanting me to sit on his lap. I wasn't in the mood for him so when he walked by me getting my attention, I kept watching the girl dancing on the stage. Even when I walked by he was trying to get me to come sit with him but I pointed to the stage and told him I have to dance and kept walking. I should of went and got his money, but he don't be giving enough money to tolerate him. Maybe next time.

I was the fourth girl on the list for dancing. Since the lousy DJ who acts like the internet is down so that he can play the oldies was there, the girls ahead of me were dancing to slow oldies music. I was about to fall asleep from the music. When it was my time to go up and dance I pulled out my MP3 player and plugged it into the system. There was a heavy set Mexican sitting at the end of the stage. I started dancing for him to some rap, and later on another person came and sat on the other side of the stage. I felt good dancing to something faster. I even did my upside down trick and it felt good.

The second time I went on stage I was playing some Webbie and people really got juiced after that. This one dude that walked in with a hoodie and pajama pants came to the stage and threw a lot of money at me. I had the booty shaking and he loved it. Some other men that I met before came to the stage going crazy They got tired of seeing the girls dancing to slow stuff. Time for a change.

This one chick I'm cool with told me before I went on stage to leave some money for her. I told her, sometimes I feel like the black sleep. I can't even get $2 on stage from my dancing half the time. She was one of the girls dancing to the oldies. She made a good amount of money after I got done dancing. I ran to the stage and pointed to the pile of money she had on the floor from the customers tipping her, and I said "Look! You got enough money? You need some help picking up your money?" She laughed and was happy about her earnings.

She has one of those really small and slim frame. Looks like she's a size 0 or 1 in pants. Straight up and down. No shape. She dances good and is pretty when her hair is down and curled. And there has been plenty of times she got more money than me from dancing. So what's the difference? It's different for everybody at times. I was just having my moment but it will not always be like today.

Before I left I met this older White man at the bar who bought me a drink before I went on stage. I went and sat to talk with him since I had twenty minutes left. Then the lady who sells the dancing outfits came in and she showed me a white outfit with silver little shiny pieces on it. I told her I'd get it tomorrow. Then the man bought me a bottom piece and I appreieciated it. He was nice and I enjoyed his conversation.

This week I will work more days than usual. The girls have been hyping up Wednesday, so I'm looking forward to see how it turns out. The customers might fill the place the place up trying to celebrate before ThanksGiving. We'll see how it turns out. I won't be disappointed if it don't turn out good. It will still be extra money for me. My friend will probably be mad that I'm not going to the contest that night, but she has to do that on her own. I have other plans. I have to twist my son's dreads that night so he can look nice for Thursday.

One of the girls who does pole tricks good was crying when I went in the dressing room. I almost didn't see her sitting to the side, but the glimpse I caught of her, she was trying to hold in a cry. Looked like she might have been on the phone but she wasn't talking. She was just fine standing in front of me talking to one of the other girls. I didn't say nothing to her. I went to her friend and told her she was crying and to go check on her. I felt that it would be better for one of her friends to talk and comfort her instead of someone she don't know. Plus I didn't want to know what her problem was.

Sunday was good. I didn't see my regulars. I might see them today. It's Monday. I usually see two of them. I might try to stay an extra hour till the traffic dies down. Gotta see if the manager will allow me to do that. Just wait for the traffic to get smooth so I'm not sitting in it going crazy. The manager who works the night shift today is pretty cool. I'll ask him and see what he says.

I Want Sunday Back!

Monday. Day shift. Sucked! It was a slow shift. Not as many people there as Sunday. Certainly not as many people tipping on stage as Sunday. But I still did good. My regular customer, the lawyer, came in. All smiles. This is how things went.

When I hit the floor there was this Mexican who kept giving me the eye. When I did go and talk to him it was difficult. You know how you try to talk to someone you don't know, and the conversation don't go smooth? It became akward to him cause I wasn't sure if he really understand English. He gave me a weird vibe and I walked away from him and went to sit back down. Then this older White guy came over and asked me to come sit with him.

It didn't take long before he got on my nerves. I hate it when men want me to stand right in there face hella close. For one, who reassured you that your breath didn't stink? What makes you think I enjoy it when you talk to me, and I feel you spitting on my face? And why the Hell do you think I want you all up in my face? It got to the point that I was dying for the DJ to call my name to go up on stage. Boy was I happy when she did.

Dancing on stage today was not energetic. I made it look good though. It always helps when you know someone is interested in what you're doing. I had some fans who sat at the other stages. Can't be too down.

What I learned from yesterday, guys have different and serious feelings about things. Two dudes I was spending time with yesterday had rules about tipping girls dancing on stage. One had a rule that he just like to watch from a distance, not sit at the stage. You know what that screams to me? I am shy. I don't like people looking at me. One of the girls that was dancing on stage had his attention. He wanted to give her some money but acted scared. I yelled at him to go put the money on the table. When he did, he kindda ran away. She was dancing on the table and I told him to sit down and enjoy the show. He finally sat down and enjoyed himself. Then when I got on stage to dance, him and his friend were both at the table. How funny.

The security guard told me that a lot of guys come to places like a bikini bar or strip club, because they're not able to approach a girl anywhere else. I believe that for the most part. Half the guys I met at work were too shy to wave or speak. Other guys want to look at half naked girls and wish they could have them. Or they have a wife or girlfriend but wants to enjoy someone with a more lively personality. People like them, give people like us good jobs.

Hairy brought himself to the club. When I got off the stage I saw his sorry looking behind at the bar. I waved at him and went straight to the bathroom. When I came out I went to sit with a customer who wanted my time. It was cool with him because he didn't want to be all up in my face, and I was getting tipped every few minutes. At that point the drinks I had started to really kick in. But not too much. I also got that white two piece outfit I wanted yesterday. Wish I could have had someone buy it for me, but I still got it. That's all that matters.

November 27, 2013
I'm Tired And Happy!

I'm at home from a very hard and fun day at work. The day before Thanksgiving. Before I talk about today I have to talk about yesterday. Tuesday November 26, 2013. I went to the night shift. The dressing room was empty when I got there around 5:30 pm. I got dressed and went to the floor to get a head start on making money.

The whole shift was extremely slow. There were more empty seats than people sitting in them. Dancing on stage was no better. I still found a few people to talk to and make money from. There was one Black dude that came in and sat at the stage as I was starting to dance. He kept smiling at me and came to my stages. When I walked past him as I was going to the last stage, he asked me if I was gonna come sit and talk with him.

I explained that I can't sit and talk with him while he's at the stage and a girl is dancing. So he got up and came to my last stage and watched me dance. Then we went and sat at a table and talked. There were a few girls who were trying their hardest to get in his eye because he was clearly the only man there with money to spend. I didn't mind cause I was still getting mine. He told me that one of his friends told him there was a red bone at the club that be working it. Guess it was me he was looking for and found. I am the only one who be shaking it.

Some of us started to play around or huddle up in groups to talk. We wasn't tripping off the customers because they weren't worth out time. They wanted to watch us dance for free and drink. We were so ready to go home but the manager that was working don't like to let the girls go early. Even with five customers and twelve girls. Shame.

The customer I was sitting and talking with had a Hukka. One of those cigar like things that you can add flavor to. I had never tried one before. The first time he let me try it, I didn't know that you had to push the button on it to turn it on to taste the flavor. The second time I tried it I took it in too hard. Dam near choked and killed myself! The vanilla was so strong when I took it in hard. I laughed and tried it a few more times till I got it right. I enjoyed it.

Now today was much different. When I pulled up to the club there were so many cars already there. Girls were piled into the dressing room. I found a little space and got dressed. The stage was almost filled with people sitting down watching. I spent a lot of time talking with people. Even some of my regular customers showed up. It was so fun. I enjoyed myself.

I even had a customer ask me to dance to a song for him. I told him no problem, even though I already had a song I wanted to dance to. But since he tipped me good I was happy to do it for him. Even Hairy showed up. Boy I tell you, that man really has nothing else to do with his time. But come to the club to try to get any kind of affection. Hey, that's what bikini bars are for!

The one thing that was different about today was my interaction with two of the girls that I never talked with before. One was that girl who comes in and leaves early when she doesn't make money from dancing on stage. The other is her friend who hasn't been there in a few weeks since she got a check for a few thousand. I was getting ready to walk past them as they were talking with customers, and the short one who leaves early had money in her panties. I lightly pinched her booty with my nails and tried to run away, but she called me back to show of my booty to the customers. It was fun and entertaining, but I didn't want to get too comfortable. I just wanted to pass by.

There was one girl who came for the night shift that hadn't been there in about six months. She was a BIG girl. Big as in tall. The girl that leaves early was telling her she seen her at the club early. The big girl was saying something to her about it wasn't her. I don't know what it was all about but I wasn't trippin. When the big girl was called to get on stage and dance, her friend got up there with her. I don't think she can perform on her own. I don't care how long it's been since you danced, you shouldn't be dancing at every stage with your friend. So does that mean, you're only gonna work when she work? I don't like it when people can't stand on their own.

There were a few customers I thought would have been there but wasn't. But I was busy with so many others that I may not of had the time to spend them. The day shift was still awesome and everyone had fun. There were no big problems as far as I know. Things went smooth. I don't know how the night shift went and don't care. That contest was probably crazy with all the girls working and amateurs that showed up. One of the Black girls that started last week was there to work the night shift. She got on stage to dance before I left. Just to show some support, I went to her stage and threw her some dollars. She was dancing to a slow song. I told her to just take her time and go with the flow. She did good.

Again, I had more drinks than I should of. I spread them out over the hours and I didn't have any problems with dancing. It was fun. I'm glad I went to work today. It was so worth it. Saturday I'm not sure how it will go. One of the girls was telling me to work Saturday night, but it depends on how things go that day during the day shift. I might just take a break and work the day shift. Work a double in a week or two.

November 30, 2013
Saturday After ThanksGiving

Today started off like any other day. I went to get something to eat before going to work. When I pulled up in the parking lot there was one car in the front. When I got inside there was two customers inside. I sat down to eat my food and watched some of the college football game that was on TV. I thought I was gonna be sick before things started because when I was eating my food, I didn't have nothing to drink with it. Normally I do but nobody was at the bar so I couldn't get some water. After I got dressed and ready I had the strongest feeling in my stomach that I was starving. I asked for the water, then had a feeling like I was about to throw up. I ran to the bathroom and took deep breaths. I was able to stop the throwing up feeling from the deep breathing, then slowly drunk the water. I was fine after that. Never again will I eat a meal without water.

It was close to 12:30 pm by the time the DJ realized what time it was. So the show started late. The girl that comes and takes forever to get ready then be ready to leave after one dance on stage walked in almost close to 1:00, talking bout things not being started yet. I looked at her crazy, cause what do she care? She don't be getting here to be ready on time anyway. Plus she was the last person to dance so what difference did it make?

I was the third girl to dance. I was thinking about dancing to some old 80s music. Some "Crying Game" or "Send Me An Angel". But when it got closer to my turn to dance, there were a few more people who had arrived. So I danced to some of the regular up to date music I normally do. There were people sitting at the stage tipping so things started out nice for everyone.

The dark skinned dude from NY walked in. I sat and talked with him till I had to dance. While I was talking to him a regular of mine walked in and sat at the bar. When NY went outside to smoke I went and sat with the customer and made some money till he came back in. He was watching the Alabama vs. Auburn game. He had bet that Alabama would win, but apparently it didn't happen like that. He left once he seen they were not winning.

Later on the lawyer came in. He rode his motorcycle because he gave his helmet to the guard at the door when he walked in. I gave him a few minutes before I went over to him. We talked a little bit then watched the game. When this one girl was dancing on stage, he wanted to go sit and watch her dance. I went by the guard and counted my money till it was my turn to dance. He didn't come to the stage and watch me dance. I dance for some dudes and an old guy. Then I went to the next stage and danced. No one was sitting to watch me, so I played around till a customer came up at the end of the song to watch me. I didn't know he was there till he whistled at me. I was looking at the screen next to the stage showing recaps of the game.

When I was done he asked me, "Where do I tip you at?" I told him I would come around to him. His eyes lit up. I got off stage and went over so her could tip me. Then I sat down and talked with him till he left. He was there with a friend. They are in a rehabilitation center for drinkers. They were given a pass for the day and came here. How nice of them.

I was funny to me because one lady was dancing on stage. He told me he didn't like her. Didn't find her attractive. Then proceeded to tell me that he don't like White women. I laughed. He's a White man who don't like White women. Sound like a Black man who don't like Black women. I never heard a White man say that before. But I know it's some out there that do feel like that. I think he said it because I told him I wrote a book talking about my past relationships with Black men, because that's all I've dated. So I guess he was sharing.

The shift went good. By 3:00 pm I had already made my minimum of $100 for the day. I was happy. I was ready to chill but there was another customer who wanted to talk to me. He came over to where I was sitting. I had my foot up on a chair stretching it out. He asked if I was saving it for someone. I told him no and let him sit down. I had one last dance before the end of day shift, and I couldn't wait to go on stage. He was starting to get on my nerves trying to reference him and I having sex. I do not care about how strong a man he is, or what he can do. That is no concern to me.

Right before I went on stage, one of the girls I'm cool with came up to me to ask for some feminine wipes. She is the same one that the customer was saying that she was trying to over shadow me when we were dancing on stage together. She went out and got a dark colored lip stick like the one I be wearing. I was not surprised. She's taking in what she sees from others. Still learning. And still not a competition for me. As some would be concerned about.

I liked today. It went by fast and was fun. I kind of wanted to stay because there seemed to be a lot of people coming in for the night shift. But I was ready to go home and rest. I'll do a double some other time. I'm not worried about it. I need some rest. And I can't wait for the new silver shoes I ordered yesterday to arrive. I wanted some silver one to better match my clothes. I might get some other colored ones. I seen some purple ones I like but I have no purple. Oh well.

December 1, 2013

This Ish Sucks!

Today was a very disappointing day for me and a lot of other girls who worked today. Mainly because it's the first and people had rent to pay as well as bills. I was expecting a slow first of the month. No surprises this time. I went into work happy knowing, or at least thinking that I would end my night having dinner eating seafood with my boo. But as the day went on, I developed an attitude.

It looked like it was going to be a good day. Football game was on. Niners won. I was one of the last girls on the list to dance, so I was sittin back watching the game. There was no one that I wanted to talk to. I really just wanted to sit on my butt all day. I had no real reason to walk around and try to talk to people. No one was coming to the stage to sit and watch me dance. Well, two people did, but they didn't stay and watch me. The people there were focused on the game and their beer.

After the second time on stage I didn't care much about dancing. I was just moving around the pole. Hell, I was watching the TV myself. I didn't care. You don't want to watch me or tip me, I won't put on a good show. Why waste my energy? This one customer even came over to me and asked why was I sitting by myself not socializing with anyone? I was happy sitting by myself. I wasn't feeling lonely.

Then one time I was playing around on the third stage, I got down to move to the last one. As I'm walking threw the tables where people were sitting, one guy in a Niners jersey called me over to him. You know what that bastard said to me? "Sorry I was too lazy to get up and tip you." I had to force a smile on my face because I really wanted to give him a dirty look and walk away before he could put the money on me.

As a dancer, it pisses me off to hear stupid garbage like that. You wasn't too lazy to get dressed, leave the house, and come here were you? I wasn't too lazy to walk over here to this table was I? Some men are so sorry when it comes to certain situations. Just like the guy worrying about why I'm sitting by myself. He didn't tip me, so why was he so dam worried bout what I'm doing and not doing? That's why I'd rather spend most of my time sitting down relaxing till someone lets me know they want my time.

When I was on strike in the dressing room, I was talking to this one girl who drives two and a half hours to work at this club where I'm at. She's one of those girls who dances to slow music. She told me that she hadn't even made $20 yet! And it was past 3:00 pm. I couldn't believe it. I knew she had made more money than me because she always had some one going to her stage. I'm still trying to figure out how I made thirty something dollars. Cause I sho didn't get that much love.

Then that special dude who's friends with the DJ came. I almost cussed him out. I was sitting at the bar minding my own business eating a candy cane when he came over. He got real close to me trying to push against me. He asked me for change, so he could have twenty ones. I don't give him change anymore because it's not like he's gonna give me the twenty ones. He'll just give me two or three. He can get change from the bartender, cause I'm tired of his mess. Then the fool was taking forever to put $2 in my top. He don't even know how to be slick and cop a quick feel. And he had the nerves to try to put his nasty fingers inside my panties. I pushed his hand away and told him no. He walked away, thank God.

Since my daughter will be home tomorrow, I'm going to work the night shift. Hopefully it will turn out better than today, Or I'm going home early. If it's gonna be slow like this, I can stay home and put my time to better use. Hopefully my package comes at the end of this week. I can't wait to try on my shoes and wear them on stage! I might go back online and order those other shoes I liked. They were black with large rhinestones and eight inches high. They were real nice looking.

December 3, 2013
What A Bummer Monday

Since I wasn't able to go to work Monday morning, I went in that night. I knew not to expect much, but Dam! That was bad as Sunday. The good thing was that the cool manager was working tonight. He don't be trippin if you want to leave early when it's slow.

When the shift started there were only a tiny handful of people there. There about five or seven that I could see. I went to the back, got dressed, put some curls in my hair, and went out to the floor. When I went on stage the first time, I was tipped by two Hispanic guys. One didn't speak English and had the nerves to try to ask me for sex. No, no, no, no, and more no. And he did not look clean. He looked dirty. Like, "I need a hot bath and a lot of soap" dirty. EWE!

The first annoying thing about last night was Hairy showing up. He walked in when the night shift started and went sat in the back where the bathroom was. I hate when he sits there. I had to go to the bathroom before going on stage and there he was. No one was sitting with him so he was just out in the open when I walked by fast. I knew I couldn't ignore him like I wanted to, so I just smiled and waved. He tried to say something to me but I kept walking. I waited in the bathroom for my name to be called. I knew I didn't have long so I just killed time till then. When my name was called, I made a straight bee line to the stage.

I enjoyed the first half of the shift. The place was dead so I made it fun for me. I even danced to Prince's "Beautiful Ones" and loved it! But then when dudes started coming in and still wasn't tipping, I was like, time to go home. One dude went to the bar, got a hundred ones, and still wasn't tipping. So what the Hell is he going to do with the ones? One girl told me that when she was dancing on the third stage, four guys were sitting there watching her, but only tipped her $2. What sense does that make? And who sits at the stage and don't tip?

I was not feeling it. I did not want to sit there and watch all that madness go on. And there were a lot of groups of White men there. I really felt the strong presence of racial preference. Some men will sit and watch every girl dance and tip. Others will only go to watch the White girls.

Hispanics will go for Hispanic girls. This doesn't happen like this all the time but it was clear last night. It was no big problem, but if that's how people were feeling last night, I'd rather take my tired behind home and eat some Gumbo then go to bed. I can wait for things to get better and get out of this slow spell. I want to be productive with my time. Sure, it might have gotten better the later it got. I just didn't want to wait for it. I already knew it was gonna be slow. I can accept that. Wasting time, I can't.

I did talk more with one of the girls. Her normal group of friends were not there so it was me she choose to talk to. When the shift started she asked me if I smoked, and wanted me to go to the back smoking area with her while she smoked. I said yes. She looked like she wanted some company. I went to the back with her and talked. She had a customer she wanted to get away from because he was tipping her a dollar at a time. And his hands were super rough as he touched her. She tried to get me to sit with him so she could escape him. What good would he do me, if that's how he was doing you? When we went back to the floor she seen Hairy sitting by himself still, so she sat with him. Great!

I want my period to hurry up and start so when I go back to work Saturday it will either be over or almost over. I hate dancing when it's time for redness. One girl told me earlier that when her period is getting ready to start, she breaks out in pimples. Down there. Wow. I'd rather keep having my discharge a few days before it start. That sounds a lot better than acne in the soft spot. Next week I have a wax appointment so I really need it to hurry up and come. Gotta keep my grass low as possible.

I noticed that when Miss Stiffie works her doubles at night, she tends to get real drunk. Drunk like she can barely walk by herself. I know she lives close, but that is a very bad look. She stayed in the DJ booth taking shots. She already wasn't making any money. So you're gonna get pissy drunk too? At least get drunk while you're making money. I think she was messing around with the DJ. She looked like she was trying to be all over him. Ewe. She might be older than him. I know she's having problems with money. She should get a regular job. That way she will some guaranteed money coming. If her rent is $2,000 a month, I have no idea how she's making it. I know Sunday she went to a football game with a customer. It was nice to not see her.

NY came in today. I sat at the bar and talked with him. We were laughing at how some f the girls were dancing. It was great entertainment. He mentioned how one girl was still and boring. She really didn't do nothing except move around the pole. There was another girl that was big. Like wide load big. She had an okay shape, but was filled out. She was another slow dancer. It was just something to do for the time being. Hey, I know people talk about me. But I can't help the way I move, and the same goes for them.

December 7, 2013
A Nice Cold Saturday

I went to work expecting the day to be real slow. Expecting to get on stage and have people stare at me while they sit in their chairs. There were a few girls already in the dressing room by 11:30 am. I got my hair braided Wednesday so I didn't have to worry about doing my hair. I went in, put my bags down, and started eating my chili. When I got dressed I put my grey jacket on because I knew it was going to be cold out on the floor, and I wasn't in the mood. It's gonna start getting colder in there and I can't take it.

It looked like it was going to be super slow, but after 1:15 pm rolled around that's when people started to come. A lot of men who got off work in construction made up a large amount of those people. I know they were shocked to walk in and see the Christmas lights and the real tree we have. I don't help with the decorations. The DJ and some of the girls help out with that.

There was no problem making money today. Even the girl who does one dance and be ready to go made some doe. I know she was happy. But she was still hanging out in the dressing room. I went back there to change outfits and she was laid down sleep. Guess she had a busy night.

A lot of the guys were really enjoying my show of my licking my pierced nipples with my pierced tongue. It's nice to have something no one else does. Makes a signature that people will remember and others can't duplicate. That's why I tell girls to do what comes natural to them cause someone will like it. I have another move I wanna try one day. Maybe when I do a double. Or maybe tomorrow.

Now today was very different. Hairy came in. I didn't pay him no mind. I was doing my normal thing dancing on stage, talking with customers, and not talking to him. When my customer I was talking to had to leave, I was sitting at the bar putting my ones in order so that I could count them. The female bartender came over and asked me if I wanted something to drink. I knew that meant someone wanted to buy me a drink. I asked her who was buying it and she said the guy in the corner. When I looked, it was Hairy.

I rolled my eyes and told her what kind of drink I wanted. When she brought it to me I went and sat with him to say thank you. He just had to ask why I don't like him no more. Why do people really wanna know stuff like that? What difference will it make? You're not going to change any of the feelings that I have. Closure? Do people still want/need closure now days? Just move on and keep going!

We sat and talked. It was an okay conversation. I told him I didn't want to hang out with him anymore and he understood it. He was trying to talk me into at least having dinner with him at a French restaurant. No thank you, I'll pass. He feels that I'm the only girl that has his attention and the only girl he wants to deal with. Okay, you got feelings. You need to go see a doctor about that.

The main thing that I hated about today was the fact that my period started late. It was suppose to start Monday. I was happy thinking that it would be over by Saturday. Nope. This mess started Thursday. Hopefully it will be over tomorrow, but I plan to work Monday and maybe Tuesday. I'll do Tuesday if it's over by then.

There was a cute Asian dude playing pool that really likes me. He gave me a huge and had a hard time letting me go. He was kissing on my neck and squeezing on my booty. He comes in often. As far as I know he comes in at least once a week. But from what he said to me today, he comes in more but don't always see me. It's okay. See me when you can!

Sunday. I wonder how that will be. The DJ will be playing oldies and whoever don't have their own music will be stranded to play what he has. I hope that more girls start bringing their own so I don't have to hear all that old crap. It gets tiring. But it's a short day. I might stay a little longer since the manager closing is cool. I'll see how things go.

Sunday Night Football!

Last night was real fun. The whole day was fun! The main thing that made it great was the change of DJs. Our usual DJ was out for whatever reason. Thank you God! I was sitting at the bar eating my food and watching one of the football games. The night DJ came walking in and we were looking at him like, are you here to pick up a check or here to work? Soon as he asked about his time card, the celebration was on!

I was the first person to jump up and get excited. I felt that I was going to have an attitude the whole day listening to all that 80s music. Too much. But this was going to be great day to enjoy. I was even drinking Bacardi 151 with pineapple.

The day shift went good. I don't remember spending too much time sitting down by myself. I was either dancing on stage or talking with a customer. It felt like they had the heater on too so that was a nice feeling. And I wasn't sweating like I normally do. I'm so happy my hair is braided.

This one customer came up to me and asked about his friend getting a lap dance for his birthday from me. I told him to just talk to the DJ so he can set it up for him. When I was at the bar with a customer, I saw the security put the chair on stage and the guy get called up to the stage, but another girl was called up to give him a dance. I think the birthday boy didn't want me to give him his dance. Well, I hope he enjoyed the dance he got.

When it got close to 6 pm, I was debating on whether I should stay longer or go home. People was still coming in because their favorite team won the football game. So there was a lot of red and white jerseys in the place. I asked the manager about staying for a few extra hours but leaving early. He said the earliest I could leave would be at midnight. I decided. To stay and make more money. Glad I did.

There was a group with chicks that came in with some dudes. They really liked my booty and was showering me with money. I enjoyed it. People were coming in happy that their team won or that they won the bet. So they were coming in with money to spend.

One dude was telling me how he had spent about $150. I think it was really on drinks because he always had a drink in his hand whenever I saw him. But he was tipping so there was no problem with him from me. He was a cool guy. He was freaking out because I was teasing him. I was rubbing my boob on his chin and hugging him. It was funny. After I was done driving him crazy I walked away so he could calm back down.

There was this one Hispanic dude I was talking to that got real drunk and had to be put out. At first he was all over me. He bought he a drink and I sat at the bar talking with him. Then I had to go on stage to dance. That's when he started tripping about something. Next thing I know he was put out. He tried to come back in but security pushed him back out. It was crazy.

As it got closer to midnight things started to get slow on the stages. I wasn't tripping cause I had made enough money to go home happy with. And plus I was still enjoying my night. I didn't have any annoying people bothering me. I did buy a cute outfit from the lady who makes and sells them. It's white and silver with red lining. I asked her to make me a two piece outfit with purple velvet and silver lining. These two outfits will be great with my silver shoes when I get them! Hopefully they will come tomorrow. I'm so excited. And one of the girls I'm cool with got her some new shoes. They're all black and look like they're eight or nine inches tall. She was working them too. But I think they're the same as another girl's shoes.

What I might start doing is staying for a few hours after the day shift ends on Sundays, if the Forty Niners win a game. Things seem to go a lot better with people celebrating. Only if I'm not too tired.

DECEMBER 11, 2013

Just Like I Thought

Since I didn't go in to work Monday, I told myself that I'll do it Tuesday night. I'm still trying to get back to how that first Tuesday night went. Super good! But I'm having a hard time doing that.

I got to work and there was a nice amount of girls working. I think it was about twelve or more. Soon as I walked into the joint Hairy was sitting there at the bar. I didn't really notice it was him at first till I left the bathroom and made my way to the dressing room. I wasn't paying anyone any attention. When I got dressed and came out onto the floor, all I wanted to do was drink my hot apple cider and relax before I even thought about trying to talk to anyone.

When I came out and went to the bar, he was still sitting there. Looking at me all stupid and stuff. I really think he be trying to give me a puppy dog face, which I don't fall for. At all. I spoke to him but don't think he heard me. Later on when I was relaxing and taking in the scene, he sent the bartender over to ask me if I wanted a drink. Yes, I did.

I sat and talked with him for a while. I became annoyed because one of the girls, who I think is really trying to take some of my style, came and sat right next to me. She was eating her food and talking, but I think she was waiting for me to leave so that she could talk to Hairy and get some money. Cause usually she be walking around looking for someone to talk to. Instead, she was sitting right next to me.

When I was called on stage to dance, I knew that she was going to take over. So I didn't trip. I had my drink and some money on me from him. I wasn't trippin. I went and danced on stage then sat at the door with security talking to him. The night was okay. Two guys walked in, a Black and Asian. I heard the Black dude tell security that this was his first time being here. After security was done giving them a quick fill in with the rules, they went and sat down at a table. Security turned and told me I better get him, he's a newbie.

I wasn't in the mood. I looked dude over and told security that I'd rather talk to the Asian guy, cause the Black dude might like White women. The way he walked in with his bald head, shirt collar all turned up to his ears. It was a mean thought but I couldn't help it. I just wasn't in the spirit.

When I did go to the table it was because one of the girls was talking to the Black dude, and the Asian was sitting there being a third wheel. I felt like that was my chance to go talk to him. He was in a bad situation where his fiancé just left him for a total looser. And I mean, dude has a temp job paying $10, and he's an illegal alien. Asian dude was a manager, well settled and well paid. That's her lose. We talked about his problems and he felt much better about it. Black dude kept buttin in our conversation like he wasn't still talking to the other girl. How rude of him.

Now the night got real good for some girls when this large group of Hispanics came in throwing money around. I didn't go over to be a part of it, cause like I said. They were throwing money around. So how do you know what's yours, and what's hers on the floor? I do not like that at all! I'd rather be by myself with a customer than to be with a bunch of girls. I did not even try to be apart of that. I pass. They stayed for some hours.

After a while, like around ten or eleven, a lot of girls were ready to go home because it was dying out. People had stopped tipping on the stage and it was cold as ice in there. Even I stayed in the dressing room for the last hour and a half with my clothes on waiting to leave. Others girls were just leaving early. I think they were tipping the manager and that's how they left. I am not tipping him. If I am ready to leave and you tell me that I have to stay, I will not tip you, because you are not doing me any favors. That is how I feel. You want me to tip you, but why? Managers at regular jobs don't tip their managers, and you have not done anything special for me. I was so happy to leave.

The one thing that irritated me when I was dressed and ready to leave was this one dude trying to have a conversation with me when I was on my way to the door. He was some of the last people that came in. My last time dancing on the stage, I did not put much effort into it. It was clear that the people standing there at the bar was going to look and that's it. So I was up there just walking around the pole, doing little things. As I'm walking to the door with my bag so I can leave, this guy calls me over to tell me I did a nice job up there. Okay, and you're telling me thing because. . . .

The time before my last dance on stage, there were four white guys sitting at the stage when I started dancing. They had these faces that were blank and looked as if they were not entertained. So I smiled at them and told them to smile. How am I suppose to dance and look at you, when you're looking at me like you want to push me off stage? So I shook my head, got up from in front of them, and went to dance on the other side of the stage where I didn't have to see them. I would have been happier for them to get up and leave so they wouldn't be sitting there like dummies.

When I left I had $60 in my purse. That's $60 I didn't have. This week I'm not working anymore night shifts. I'll work Thursday and maybe Friday day shift. If it's gonna be slow like this for the rest of the month for me, I'll stick to days when I know the manager will let me leave. I can be happy about that.

December 12, 2013

Much Better, Much Better

I want to say that today was much better. Even though there were about twelve girls, there was a nice number of customers tipping. I think this was my first Thursday working day shift. So we had to do a review. That's when all the girls get on stage when the shift starts so that the manager can see who's working, who paid their stage fee, and the customers can get an eye full of us.

A lot of the girls went to the side stages. I went to the main stage and it was just me and one other girl. Then another girl came and stood at the back of the stage with the other one. No one was dancing or moving around. I was the only one at least moving around the pole, letting people know I was awake.

There were a number of guys who went and got them a plate of food to eat and came sat in the club. They ate their food and watched us dance. I don't know about everyone else, but I was tipped a dollar each from three men. I was surprised. I wasn't expecting them to tip me, I thought they would have just there and ate.

While I was sitting at the bar, there was this one customer who came over to talk. He looked like the one guy I was talking to when I first started my shift that Wednesday before ThanksGiving. I went to where he was sitting and talked with him. Before I went to go dance again, he had tipped me $20. I think he really likes me. I even gave him one of my book stubs for my first book to download onto his phone. I can't wait for him to finish reading it and give me feed back.

The rest of the girls had a good time. There were no incidents and I didn't hear any complaints. I did enjoy the Bacardi 151 with pineapple. I wish I would have ate more before I drunk it. I didn't get sick. I was just feeling REALLY good. I could still walk straight and dance the way I wanted to.

I want to add something that Miss Stiffie said while in the dressing room. I think it was from the other night. She was explaining how she was dancing n stage and a group of young guys in the club were laughing at her as she was dancing on stage. She was made and refused to dance till they left. That sucks. I really do think she would be better off getting a job. Seriously.

December 13, 2013
I Like This Friday The 13th!

I almost didn't make it to work today. Today was the last day to pick up your layaway at the store. I waited an hour for them to bring my items out. That messed up my plans for today. I had some things to do before that I couldn't do. Plus, I didn't get my shoes that was suppose to come today. I wanted to dance in them. Hopefully they come tomorrow or I'll be pissed.

I made it just in time for the review. There were a lot of girls again. So Thursdays and Friday are busy on the day shift. Good to know. The girls were all packed in the dressing room I use. Putting their makeup on and curling their hair in the mirror. I'm glad that all I had to do was put clothes on and perfume. My hair is still braided so I was out of there fast.

There was a cool number of customers in the club. A few of them got food from the restaurant and came to sit and eat in the club. Things started out slow at first then picked up later. I was on my second go around on the stages and was on the last one. I was just playing around because I didn't think no one was paying me any attention. But hen I looked in the mirror there was someone sitting at the stage. So I turned around and danced for him. He was a big, handsome Black guy with an accent. He's from the Caribbean. Nice. He tipped me a lot of ones so I sat and talked with him at the bar. He's the manager for a construction company. His employees call him the Grim Reaper because he fired about sixty people from the site.

I talked with him till he had to go. His employees were asking about leaving early, and he had their checks. He stopped at the club on his way back to work because he's heard about the place. I was shocked when I seen that he went home, cleaned up, and came back before he went to a meeting in the city. It was perfect timing because the lady who makes the outfits had showed up with the purple and silver two piece I wanted. I asked him if her could buy it for me, and he did. I was happy it didn't have to come out of my pocket!

There were a few people that liked me and I had conversations with. It was nice. One creep I had to run away from because he wanted to go sit in the restaurant area, where there was nobody. He was trying to get fresh with me. Pulling on my top and bottom to see what was underneath.

When he had a call, I lied about going to see where my name was on the list. I knew, but wanted to get away from him. I told security that he was back there and I wasn't comfortable being there with him. Security went and told him he had to leave because the place was closed. I started talking with another customer. Then one of the girls told me he was annoying her. Yeah, it is annoying when men want "stuff" from you, but don't tip.

It was a cool day. I left at 6:00 pm. I was getting tired and people were starting to leave. The main stage didn't have people sitting at it anymore. The night shift girls were coming in. Most of the day shift girls had left. It was a good day that you made enough money to be happy with and leave. I'm glad I made it for work. It was worth it.

The customer who I normally sit with was there. The lawyer. The one who I was going to sit with yesterday but he was waiting for the other girl. She wasn't there today and I didn't go over to talk to him either. He came to my stage to watch me dance and I didn't ask him about sitting with him. Two guys ran over and threw money at me before I got off stage. So I went and sat with them.

Sometimes things start off slow, or not how you would expect them to. That's why I still don't go there with expectations. I'd rather get there then see how things go. It makes for a better work experience to be surprised later on. That's why when things are early I don't worry bout things. I'll sit around and relax till the men get comfortable and the liquor get threw their system. That's my plan.

I think my new thing will be to work Thursdays and Fridays. With the amount of people that were in there, that will be a good turn out for me as they get used to seeing me there. It was fun. I did think a fight was going to break out, but security ran over there by the pool tables so fast, the guys calmed down. I didn't want a fight to happen. Not on my shift. Don't want anything to spoil the party.

December 14, 2013
A Nice Saturday At Work

I was able to get my shoes from the post office today. Yay! I went to work happy. There were a few girls there already getting dressed. I was one of the last to get there and still got ready before everyone. When I walked out to the floor, I was eating my bag of hot chips and drinking my sports drink with ice. Making sure I was hydrated. I went and sat at the bar. There were three men sitting there. They were attracted to my black fish net dress I had just got.

Today the guy who's family owns the club showed up and was paying a visit. He talked to me for a bit and explained how he used to work as a manager for twelve years. He don't miss it as much. Then some guys came in. It was about ten of them. It looked like they were on lunch break. Still dressed in their uniforms. They were some nice tippers. They left so fast. One of the girls was made when they left because she didn't get a chance to dance for them.

I just told myself that she would have had a chance to dance for them if she wasn't last on the list all the time. She comes late and takes all dam day to get dressed, do her hair, then get out on the floor. She also complained when the girl after her was playing music she didn't want to dance to when she had to move to the next stage. I didn't say nothing to her. I left it alone. If she really wanted to fix it, she would talk to the DJ about it.

So, that same customer was there again today that I haven't been sitting with like I normally would. And the girl that he was choosing over me wasn't there. I spent my time with other customers. I didn't even say hi to him. I'm shocked that he's been coming so often. But there's men that come every single day. Yup. Must be nice to be a dude with a bikini bar close to your house.

I was surprised when I was dancing on stage and seen a customer come to the stage and fill a corner of the stage with money. When I looked again it was the customer from yesterday. The manager of the construction company who had his employees' checks with him. He was dressed regularly. I was happy to see him. He's cool to talk to. When I was done dancing I went to sit and talk with him. I stayed with him till it was time for me to leave.

I think everyone had a good day. It was kind of busy today. A nice crowd was in the club. I did pretty good in my shoes. I need to find some leg warmers of a grey or silver color to dance in. My shoes are silver and I need matching leg warmers so I can still look good. I don't want to show my legs or get the black spots on my knees. I hate that. Need more leg warmers other than my black ones. Other than that, I like them. I gotta break them in. I'm going to dance in them again tomorrow and see if I can get better at them. They are higher than what I'm used to but that's fine. I do want some higher shoes. I want to get some eight inchers too.

I am developing a nice working relationship with the girls. I notice some girls let other get to them and they feel the need to separate themselves. That's why I say, I didn't come here to make friends. As long as no one is giving me trouble, I can take it. I know there are some that has things to say about me, but who doesn't have something to say about someone? People need to get over it. Not everything can be avoided. I'd be a happier person if that was the case.

And I found out today that the Sunday DJ is not going to be able to work tomorrow because he has to work his other job. That means that the night DJ will probably be working again. Super! Another Sunday without 80s music all day. I can't wait to come to work and enjoy myself. I wonder how many girls will come in tomorrow? I hope not too many. I hate when it's a lot of girls. Seems like it takes forever for the next time you have to dance on stage.

DECEMBER 15, 2013

Sad Face, But Not Sad

Today started off like any other day. Parking lot was empty. No one was in the club. Well, I did get there early to eat. The girls started coming in close to 2:00 pm. The DJ I like showed up and things became fun. I told myself that today I was gonna switch up the music and enjoy myself a little.

When the show started I was the third girl to dance on the stage. There wasn't too many customers and the tips were non existent for me. The money I did make was from three people. And my new fan favorite came in today. That man really enjoys being around me. He was on his way to a company party and stopped by to see me. He was dressed in his black suit looking like a million bucks. It was nice to see him again.

He said he wish he could come see me tomorrow but he has to work in a different city. I plan on staying home anyway because I have things to do. And I want a break. Maybe after this month is over things will be better. If they don't get better, things will still be alright. I have my good days and bad days.

The shift did go by pretty fast. It wasn't too cold in the club. I almost wanted to stay for a little bit to see if it would get better later on but my son wanted me to get donuts. So I left and told myself I'll put in extra work this weekend. I'll go around talking to customers and see what happens. Get a couple of rejections.

December 20, 2013
This Way To The ATM

So yesterday was a little different for me. I was the first person to dance on stage, so with the amount of girls that was there, it was a long wait for me to dance again. I got on stage and danced for the four or five customers that were there. No tips. I sat at the bar chilling and seeing who was there. There wasn't too many people.

As the people slowly came the girls were spending time talking with them. Almost every customer was talking to a girl. After a while I went to go change my outfit and when I came back out onto the floor, the dude who likes me from NY and knows all the girls was sitting at the bar. Feeling too good! I went and talked to him for a while because he had to go to work soon.

The one thing that got on my nerves is the fact that I was sitting right next to him and girls were coming up hugging and leaning on him like we were not talking. Just rude. I just put a fake smile on my face and looked around. I don't know why they think that's cool. They do it every time.

Later on I was sitting at the bar on my phone and the customer next to me was drinking a beer. He asked me a question about what he's suppose to do because this was his first time at a bikini bar. I told him what the dos and don'ts were, then we had our own conversation. He started handing over money after the conversation got good. He got more beers and that's when it happened.

He pulled out his debit card and asked how can he get more money. I pointed to the ATM in the corner and told him he gets the money from there, then gets the ones from the bartenders. He went to the machine then came back because he was too drunk to do it himself. So I went over and showed him how to slide his card in right. He asked me how much should her get and I told how ever much he wants to get. He got a hundred out. And yes, it was all mine.

I know he was probably lying when he said that all the girls there were disgusting. He don't like white girls and he like big booties. But there had to have been some other girls there besides me who he liked. One girl that was dancing n stage caught his attention. He was going to go tip her but changed his mind. He felt that he only wanted to give me his money. I'm okay with that!

I had a few customers who wanted to tip me because of my booty. It was the Mexicans. They love it when I walk around showing off my goods. My lovely lady lumps. And I did make an attempt to talk to more customers yesterday. One dude didn't speak English that good. Another dude said I caught him at the wrong time. He was eating a bag of chips. Then another dude just wasn't tipping. But I was happy that I tried. I do need to walk around more and put more effort into it. I just get tired of the ones who aren't fun to talk to. Or the ones you can't talk to cause they don't speak my language! But hey, it's part of the job. I did good when it was time to go home. Thank God.

So today was a good Friday. I showed up feeling good. Things started out slow because the customers were still coming in. But once things got started it was all good. They were tipping on the stage and I actually felt liked. There were some guys who came in while on lunch. A few came to the stage while I was dancing. One followed me to the second stage and third stage. He really liked my dancing. I tried to talk with him when I was done, but he still wanted to sit at the stage and watch other girls. So I went and sat at the bar.

Then a Indian guy kept walking past me wanting to talk. He remembered me from the last time we talked. This time he was getting on my nerves. He was telling me that he's going to Vegas with his family and was asking me a bunch of questions so that he would know what to expect. I had already told him what to expect. He wanted to know and kept asking me stuff. I didn't nothing more to say, so after a while I told him I was going to back to change and I didn't go back to him. He was getting annoying.

I got happy when I seen one of my regulars in the club. I was dancing on the last stage and he was walking out the door. He waved at me and said he was going to come back in. I had a customer waiting for me to finish dancing, but I wanted to talk to my regular. I went and told the customer that I was going to say to someone and I'd be back.

Now picture this. I'm standing right in front of the guy. He's sitting in the chair. We were close to each other because the space was small. This other chick that I never seen before till last week walked up and started hugging on leaning on him as if I wasn't there. Why do females do that?! Hella rude! And yes, she was going to stand there and have a conversation with him as if I wasn't there. The guy explained to her that he's occupied at the moment because I beat her to him and she'll have to come back later. She took her time leaving. I think I don't like her now.

When I had to go to the bathroom, I told him that I know when I walk away someone was going to run up to him. So I said my goodbyes in case I didn't get a second chance to talk to him again. When I came out the bathroom, guess who was all in his face? Yup. She wasted no time. I understand the man tips 20s, but don't disrespect others.

There was a group of three Black dudes that came in. They were just standing around watching and looking. When I was called to dance on stage the little dude asked if I was going up next. He got happy when I said I was. I danced on stage and he didn't miss a step. He didn't tip me either. He followed me to the second stage to tell me that he wanted to talk to me when I was done. He did not take his eyes off me the whole time I danced on the stages. I gave him some time to talk, and bottom line, he's a fan of my dancing. He wants to be cool with me, and see if I can be in a video with him. I didn't buy it. Most of the time, that's a evolved pick up line.

I enjoyed dancing on the stages today. There were customers watching and they looked like they enjoyed me entertaining them. There were still some that looked like they didn't like me, so I just danced in front of the ones who looked happy. I might have to start dancing on Fridays.

Even when I was leaving there was still a large number of girls for the night shift. I was like wow. Tomorrow I'm going to do a double if I'm not too tired. I hope it be just as busy or even more busy. I'm glad things picked up and started to turn out good. I didn't hear too many complaints from the girls on the day shift.

And let me not forget about the special event that happened today. Miss Stiffie's birthday party was today. I have no clue how old she turned. She had on a very nice red outfit. Very sexy. She got wasted. She was escorted to the dressing room and laid down. She has a blue blanket to keep her warm. She was laid out and covered up in that.

She was called to the stage and they lit the candles on her little cute cake. She blew out the candles then that one girl I now don't like, pushed her back and laid on top of her. So disgusting! Then they made it rain on her. I don't know how much money it was but they showered her with money. She loved it. I'm happy she enjoyed herself. Now I wonder if she's gonna come in to work tomorrow. . .

Since the grey leg warmers I ordered came today while I was shaking it, I'm going to wear my new shoes and hopefully get used to them. I washed my outfits that will go with them so I'm ready for tomorrow. Yup. Like Spongebob would say. "I'm ready! I'm ready!"

December 22, 2013

Just The Saturday I Needed

I'm still tired from yesterday but not like I normally be. The day started out good. People were coming in, getting food from the restaurant, tipping. There were a lot of different people to talk to. For most of the day shift I was talking to customers.

After a while I sat at a table with this heavy set guy who was nice and kept tipping me. I might as well spend time with him and collect his money he had to give. He made me laugh with his sense of humor. His friend was funny too. They talked about the dancers they weren't too fond of.

They really talked about Miss Stiffie bad. When it was her turn to get on stage to dance I told them about how she had a birthday party on Friday. The guy I was sitting next to asked me how old she turned. I tried not to laugh because I had no idea, and of course no one was talking about it. I wouldn't even be able to guess how old she is. The way she look, there's no telling how much work she had done to her body over the years. Even her skin look weird. Like those mannequins in the retail stores with the clothes on. It don't look natural.

They were cracking jokes about going over to the stage to tip her. The dude I was sitting with had his hair in a pony tail. His friend had a bald head. Pony tail suggested that he go tip Miss Stiffie. He looked at the stage and said, "Yeah, I'll go over there and piss on the stage." We all started laughing. And at the same time she was sitting down on her knees while on the stage.

When she was done with the main stage she moved to the next stage. Just so happens that we were sitting next to it. There were some extra people who were sitting at the stage so we had to push back to the stage behind us. Now, him and I were not sitting at he stage, facing the dancer. We had out backs to the dancer but the backs of our chairs was touching the stage. I was holding my drink sipping on it. Pony tail had his arm around me.

As soon as I heard the hard stomping of a foot, I knew it was her. I looked back and she was pointing to us. Security came over to see what her problem was. Yup, she wanted us to move from "her" stage. We scooted up five inches. Pony tail looked around and asked what did he do and the waitress told him that it's her. He really went crazy then.

The dumb part of the situation was, by the time she got to the stage to dance, the song was going off. So she made a scene at the end of a song when all she had to do was wait. Wasn't like she was doing a lot anyway. But the waitress also told pony tail that she got mad at a customer for sitting at her stage and not tipping her. She went off on him. Cussing him out and flipping him off. I asked myself, where was I when this went down? I wanted to see it!

When she moved to the last stage, they really went in talking about her. Pony tail said that she looks like one of the characters from the Simpsons. I died laughing. I was trying to imagine in my head which character she would be. They cannot stand that women. I guess she was having a bad day. Oh well.

I almost told one of the girls something real mean. I was sitting at the bar talking with a customer. And one of the girls just walked up and started talking like I wasn't there. I just looked at her because how rude can this tramp be? When I got tired of her standing by me, I got out of my chair and said, "Well since we were so rudely interrupted, I'm gonna go change my clothes." She tried to play that stupid roll, "Oh I'm sorry!" Oh go screw yourself.

There were eighteen girls and things went pretty good. When the night shift came around, things were still busy and money was still going around. There was a table with Mexicans next to the stage. They liked me but kept trying to talk to me while I was dancing on stage. I told them they can't touch me while I'm dancing so that security didn't have to walk over and say something to them. They still was reaching over the table.

I didn't get tired till it got close to midnight. There were some people there celebrating a birthday. One side of the main stage had about ten females that were not tipping. I can't stand that. Move from the stage if you're not going to tip the dancer. I was happy when the manager said that I could leave early at 1:30. The money had dried up for me and it was time to leave. I did real good at the end of the day. I'm thankful for that.

One thing that was messed up, this Black girl was dancing. To me, she is very ugly. She's not pretty in the face. Has a huge gap in her teeth. And is bald on her sides. She wears a long weave to. So when she dances and her hair is swinging around, it looks like she's wearing a wig that's about to fly off. It don't look right to me. She was dancing on stage and a customer tipped her a dollar. She reached inside her bra and played with her boob. The customer that was standing next to me didn't like her doing that.

He explained to me that he spent hundreds of dollars on her, and she never showed him her boob. But she can show it to a "fat woman for a dollar." Those were the words he used. I turned around and told the bartender, who heard what he said, "Hell, I get excited when I see a ten or twenty dollar bill. I be wanting to show more!" We all laughed. But yes, the girl did that wrong. You don't do more less. He did deserve to see a little boob f he spent hundreds of dollars.

I think it was later on, the DJ came in the dressing room to talk to the same girl. What happened was, there was a customer who was filling her up. And the DJ didn't think it was worth her letting him touch her the way he was. You know what her reply was? "As long as he was giving me money, he could touch all the booty he wanted." Really? These people!

Now today was completely different from yesterday. This Sunday was super slow. People didn't start coming in till around 4:30 pm. I already told myself this was not going to be a good. I was still tired from the day before and didn't want to do the whole dance my butt off for nothing thing. The DJ that I like showed up so I was happy about that. We only had to dance to one song on one stage. Other stages were optional. I was so happy about that. I wouldn't have done much of anything if I would have had to dance on other stages.

It was cool at first. There were three customers sitting at the stage for the first two rounds of dancing. Then when they left no one was really tipping. Certain girls had customers come to the stage to watch them. Not I. They either sat and watched from the tables or talked with the girls at the tables. Like I said, I'm used to it. That's why I don't do much when this happens.

I sat down the whole shift. I didn't try to talk to anyone not once and I didn't give much eye contact either. There was one customer that came in that was there yesterday. I wanted him to come sit at the stage so I could dance for him. He shook his head no cause he was waiting on the waitress to bring him some ones. He also might be the type that don't like to sit at the stage. There are some men like that.

When it was 5:15 I couldn't stop looking at the time. I was more than ready to go. I was sitting next to security and he noticed that one guy that came in with a small group kept looking at me. The guy had a scarf on. He told me that the guy kept trying to get my attention, and that's why he kept looking at me. I was on my phone trying to kill time with social media. I did notice one time I felt that I was being watched, but I thought he was just looking in my direction and not at me. So I didn't bother to look at him. I wasn't in the mood to talk.

I had a chance to dance one last time before leaving. I went to the DJ booth when it was my turn. He was looking at something on his phone. I stood next to him just waiting. When he was done with his phone I kept waiting. I wasn't in a rush to give him a song. Then the girl who was after me walks up to the booth. I got excited and asked her if she wanted to dance next. She said yes so I was out. I didn't care if there were more people in the club. Didn't mean that I was going to benefit from it. And I was okay with that.

December 26, 2013
Day After Christmas

So, I didn't go to work Tuesday because I got out of my doctor appointment late and there was a lot of traffic on the freeway. So I stayed home and got some rest and spent time with my kids. My daughter's birthday was awesome and I was ready to make some money today.

I already knew to expect it to be slow. Day after Christmas is not a fun, busy day. It is slow. I was on my way expecting that maybe there would be a lot of girls there like normal. But there were only a small handful of them there. Before I went to the job I got a salad, bowl of chili, and soda. I knew I would be hungry later so I got a little something to eat. I took my meds the doctor gave me and sat in the car to eat the salad. I noticed it had that funny looking cheese that look like cottage cheese. I ate it anyway.

It didn't take long for me to feel like crap. I wasn't sure if it was the meds or the salad. I felt like I wanted to throw up. I hate doing that. I told the DJ to make me the last girl while I try to feel better. My stomach wouldn't stop feeling like crap. So I decided the best thing to do was go throw up.

Soon as I did I felt much better. Still a little muddy in the stomach, but better. The amount of customers was like six. I really didn't dance on stage. I was stretching and playing around. Nothing serious. Then later these three drunk fools came in and were acting like they were in a party club. I didn't want no part of them. I kept dancing like I normally do on stage.

One of them, a short, Black dude had the nerve to come over to me at the bar and ask why I didn't show them any love when I was on stage. For one, they were talking with other girls while I was dancing. So why would I "show them love" when they're already getting it? And I don't show love unless I get love, or I want to show it. I also didn't want to be bothered with them creeps. All drunk and touchie touchie. I don't feel good. Leave me alone!

Today we danced two songs, one stage. I was happy about that. We had eight girls. I did okay at the end of the shift with $100. One of the girls came over to me and made me get up and come sit with her and some customers to make some money. I would of never expected that from her. She seems nice.

There was a large group of men sitting at two tables. Miss Stiffie got mad when she was dancing on stage because this blonde haired White girl was taking the attention away from her bouncing on a guy's lap. They must have been drunk to make all that noise for nothing. I understand she wants a fair shot at making money on stage, but like I said. Her dancing sucks. When she was done dancing some men went up and gave her some money. I guess they seen how upset she was and wanted to make her feel better.

Tomorrow it's a birthday party for one of the girls I don't know. I almost told myself I wasn't coming for her party but after being at Miss Stiffie's party, I know what to expect. I don't have to get her a gift. I don't have to go on stage when she gets her cake. I can stay away like I did for Stiffie's. This girl I don't know. She's another one I seen the first time I worked a Thursday.

I hope that tomorrow is busier. I will not spend more time sitting on my butt this weekend. I had a customer ask me if I was going back to my corner when I was going to the bathroom. He knows I sit in the same spot everyday. I didn't feel bad or embarrassed. I just feel that since next month is said to be real slow, I might as well put in the extra effort.

DECEMBER 27, 2013

The Last Friday of 2013

Today was not too bad. A lot more girls came and I was feeling much better. I got dressed and took my time getting into the mood. The customers were slowly coming in. We had to dance all four stages. That one stupid girl I can't stand was there. The DJ calls her Ms. K but that's not her name.

I did do my normal thing of sitting down at the bar. That's when the dude from Florida with the dreads walked in with his friend. I sat and talked with them for a while. His light skinned friend was getting ready to go out of town for vacation in a few hours so they came to enjoy themselves for a little.

When it was my turn to dance on stage, I noticed that some of the other girls had went to sit at the table with the dudes. I was not going back while they were there. Plus all the seats were taken. I'll just sit with someone else. And that's just what I did when I was done dancing.

I went and sat with the Black dude in a suit who came and tipped me at the third stage. I talked with him for a while and turns out he is frm the same area I grew up in. We might have crossed each other's path once or twice before. Ironic.

After a while I seen a guy sitting at the end of the bar that kept looking at me. So I went over and sat with him. He had an accent. I'm not sure if it was African or what. I didn't ask him either. I just enjoyed talking to him. After a while he told me he would have to leave soon to pick someone up from the airport. I was like, cool. That's when I looked and seen the manager of the construction company who gives me a lot of money. Haven't seen him in two weeks.

I excused myself from the guy I was talking with and ran over to him. He was just as happy to me, as I was him. And yes he had a lot of ones in his hand! He was there with one of his employees. They had just got off work and swung by. He's still working in the city. I figured that's why I haven't seen him. He was still wearing his orange work shirt. He said he had to work on Christmas. Wow. They must have a building to build that really needs to get built.

The girl who had her birthday party today enjoyed it for the most part. That girl I can't stand, Ms. K, made an announcement about everyone coming to the stage if you color you're down for the birthday girl. I stayed with my customer trying to get every last single dollar bill he had. I saw the wrapper that said $100 on the counter at the bar. I want ALL DAT! And I don't care nothing bout her. I'm here for money, not friends.

And the strangest thing happened today. The bald headed customer I don't sit with anymore sat the stage and watched me dance. I wasn't expecting that from him. The other girl he likes hasn't been there. I don't know if she went back home to wherever she came from or not. And that chick that had the dreads, I haven't seen her in a minute. Come to find out, she was homeless. I think she was the one that another girl was talking about. I knew something was weird about her.

One things the girls noticed about me is how I count my money at the end of the shift. I sit either on a chair or on the floor. I empty out my purse of all the ones on the floor. I'll pick them up one by one, facing money face up in the same direction. When I have a handful I'll start counting them off in a bundle of twenty then put the rubber band around it. Today I was sitting on the floor with a pile of money in front of me. One of the girls asked me why am I always on the floor. I told her cause I want to be closer to the money. She laughed. Sometimes if there is an available chair I'll sit in it to count the money, but I don't make a big fuss out of it. Long as I have pants on I'll sit on that floor and count money.

Well tomorrow is Saturday. No, I'm not working a double. I'm ready to go back to my three day work week. The extra days are fine, but I feel like I need a break. Soon as Tuesday come things will slow down and I can take a rest. My body needs it.

One thing I can say, I did enjoy being more active today. I will help me make more money and get more friendlier with the customers. They are more likely to tip when they know you. Guess I can work on building my fan base. I just don't want to get friendly with any creeps. Know what I mean?

DECEMBER 28, 2013
Last Saturday Of 2013

I was shocked to hear that Friday night was busy with a lot of customers. I hope the girls did real good. Sometimes, even if there are a lot of customers there, it doesn't mean that they're tipping. They'll come and hang out with their friends while drinking and having a great time.

When the shift started about fifteen minutes after start time, there was only four customers in the club. That was it. I was happy to see one of my regulars walk in. I went and sat with him. I was the second girl to dance. I danced to slow songs all day because that's how it was. I was not putting in too much effort. Most of my money came from that one customer. $80. I was happy.

Then Hairy came in. He makes me so sick. I was busy watching the college football game when he came in. I saw him in the mirror so I didn't have to look at him. He went and sat in that corner he like so much. I was still with my regular. I did not sit with him at all.

There was this one guy who was drunk out his mind. Whatever he was saying did not make one bit of sense. He was walking from the bathroom as I was sitting down talking with security. He stopped and started talking to him and was looking at the both of us as he talked. I didn't know what he was saying but his body language was hilarious! He was with a friend and even he knew he was drunk. The security told the guy that if he wanted to talk to me, he didn't have to act like he was talking to him. He could just ask if he could talk to me. I started laughing because I didn't feel that way. I felt that he was really trying to have a conversation with him.

Overall the day was okay. It didn't go bad. It was productive. Tomorrow I might not be able to go in since I don't have anybody to watch my daughter. We might go to the movies if there is something good out I want to watch.

December 30, 2013
Slow Monday Today

I did not go to work yesterday. I didn't have anyone to watch my daughter so I spent the Sunday with her. Today was a slow day. There wasn't too many people there for the day shift, but I was told by security that it was busy last night. Maybe if I would of came last night I would have had a good turn out.

I sat and talked with one of my regulars I haven't seen in a while. It was the one I tried to sit with and he turned me away because he was going through some things. I was walking to the bathroom and he was sitting at the bar. I looked at him but didn't recognize him cause he was wearing a hat and glasses. When I walked past him, he turned around and yelled "hey!" I looked at him and started laughing. It was funny talking to him because I had dug in my ear with my fingernail then looked at it. There wasn't any ear wax on my nail, but he thought it was disgusting that I did that. Well, I didn't dig in my nose.

When it was almost time to go, I was sitting by the front door playing on my phone. Watching the clock with forty minutes to go. This White guy came over to me and asked if I was the one he talked to last time he was here. I didn't recognize his face off top but I got up and went to sit where he was sitting and talked till it was time to go. We had a nice conversation. The thing that got me was, when I first looked up at him, he looked like Pee Wee Herman with long hair. He was cute.

While I was talking to him about something. It had to do with one of the girls coming from a far away city. His response was, "Yeah that girl is nasty." I was confused about who he was talking about because I knew we weren't talking about the same person. He was telling me about one of the girls who was wearing some fish net stockings with holes in them. And that's why she's nasty. I guess he didn't like the way she looked. He mentioned how she told him that no one liked her. He felt that the holey stockings had something to do with it.

At times what you wear has an effect on the customers. But just like when I have talked with a customer and they told me they didn't like White girls, they sometimes feel that way about others. Like Saturday when I was sitting with a customer who is a Black man, he was watching a Mexican girl dance on stage. She was laying down on the stage dancing and he asked me what was she doing. I told him she was dancing, and if he was Mexican, he would be able to see that.

I had to tell the DJ to not put me before one of the girls when she makes the dancing list. This girl is cool but I can't dance to the music she dances to. It is 100% White girl music that she dances to. I can't move to that! That's just as bad as dancing when this other girl is on stage dancing to Mexican music. Not everyone dances to that. Nor do they want to hear that in the club.

Now tomorrow I have no idea what to expect. But I will expect it to be slow and I will put more effort into talking with customers.

December 31, 2013

Success!!

The first thing I saw when I pulled up to the job was a few cars. I was happy about this. When I walked inside they had decorated the joint real nice. They had confetti on the floor with the little glasses and bottles. Streamers hanging from the ceiling. Balloons on the floor. It was real nice. I can't wait for them to take them dam Christmas lights down from the ceiling by the stage. They are annoying!

The main issue I had was when I had just put my first outfit on, I had started bleeding. It was light and I wasn't sure if my monthly was starting or not. I had put on a tampon to keep from messing up my bottoms but the regular wasn't good enough. When I had changed my bottoms to white (yes I know I was pushing it) the tampon wasn't good enough. Some had bypassed it and met up with my bottoms. I'm glad it wasn't all white. It had a shiny layer on the outside that was a soft pink.

When I was done dancing on stage, I ran to the bathroom and took off my bottoms to wash them in the sink with the soap. When I heard someone walking into the bathroom I tried to run back into the stall. I panicked. I wasn't sure if it was a customer or another dancer. I didn't want a customer to catch me with my bottoms off. Thankfully it was another dancer. I laughed and finished what I was doing and put my bottoms back on. Thy were still wet but I didn't wet all of it. Plus I was hot and sweating so the cold bottoms felt great to dance in. I had put a super tampon on and I was fine for the rest of the day.

There were a few customers inside. I went into the dressing room with my stuff and bag of food. When I got in the dressing room Miss Stiffie and another girl was in there. Come to find out there wasn't too many girls there. Just five. Great news to me!

We were in the dressing room talking. I expressed that I can't stand it when this one girl dances. She is so annoying when she dances, and guess what one of the other girls said. She doesn't like to dance after her because she done licked over everything! She sticks her tongue out A LOT when she dances. I thought it was funny. I understand that you're trying to get the customer's attention so that they'll tip you, but you look hella dumb at the same time.

Things started out smooth but had a nice pace to it. The men were tipping and the few conversations I had were good. One customer tipped me $20. He was a Black guy enjoying the rest of his day off. There wasn't too many people there but since it wasn't too many girls the men were pushing for our attention.

There was one time that I was dancing on stage and on one side was a group of dudes who were really entertained and full of energy. On the other side was this guy I was talking to before I went up. He was calling me to the other side of the stage to dance for him, but he wasn't tipping like the other side. So what was I to do?

I had sat on the edge of the stage and laid down on my back. I had on a shirt that was cut right below my breasts. When I laid on my back I lifted my shirt up so they could throw the money inside they had bald up into balls. He wanted my to come over to him and do the same. He gotta understand. In this place he entered, money gets attention.

There were two customers who's birthday was today. They wanted a birthday dance from me and one of the other girls. She really didn't want to do it but I did. Two chairs were put on the stage and we danced for them both. Then we switched guys and danced for them. It was fun. When we were done, we gathered up the money and I was getting ready to count and split the money between us. She wanted me to have all the money. She was that tired and didn't want to be bothered with the money. So. I put it in my purse after I told her thank you.

One think that really upset me was when I was getting ready to leave, one of the girls was dancing on stage. It's the same one I reached out to when she first started dancing. The same one who also got the same dark color lip gloss as me when she seen me wearing it. She was on stage with French braids in her hair. Can you believe that? Her hair was braided to the back. I have been the only one with braids for the past few weeks and now she gets braids. Watch what I do to my hair next week. I already have pans to get a flat iron. And I'm going to dye the front of my hair purple. And I'm going to get some more tatts on the other side of my booty. See how she likes that!

Now, something crazy happened today. While I was dancing on the last stage this stud came and sat to watch me dance. I have seen her around a few times. She wanted to talk to me when I was done dancing. I don't like girls but I didn't want to be rude to a regular customer who has been coming here for years. I sat down and had a cool conversation with her. She asked me about going out to eat with her. Oh my, no she didn't!

I know a lot of girls will not be happy that they didn't show up for work on the day shift. Too bad for them! I made my money and I'm very happy with that. Now the night shift was said to have four girls when I was about to leave. But I passed one girl who was coming in on my way out. I'm sure that a few others might have showed up. Oh well.

The one funny thing I want to point out, is what I noticed today. As I was talking with security while watching one of the girls dance on stage, I saw something new about her. It was the same girl that the White customer was talking about with the holes in her stockings. She was wearing new ones! I had to laugh because I was wondering if he really told her to her face about wearing holey stockings. That's why when I start getting two or more holes in mine, them suckers get thrown away fast. That don't look right. It looks like you don't make enough money to keep looking nice in stockings. Nobody wants to see that on a dancer that's trying to be sexy.

January 4 2014
Beginning Of The Month

As I have been saying, it's slow at the beginning of the month. Today proved it. When the day shift started, there were three customers inside. One was an old man that no one ever talks to. And two were regulars who were playing pool. So there wasn't anybody to dance for. I had danced to some old 80s music. I wasn't wasting any good songs on nothing. Even the girl who danced before me felt that she had wasted good songs when she danced. Well, if you look around, that should have told you what to expect.

The girl who was talked about by the customer because she had holey stockings was wearing some cute pink ones today. I guess she went and did some shopping because she was also wearing a cute outfit I had never seen her wear before. She was looking real cute today with her pink! Now if she would stop wearing that huge belt that hangs around her. I'll be real happy.

Hairy showed up today. I'm starting to catch on that he comes in every Saturday. Or on most Saturdays. I like it when he talks to the other girls because he leaves me alone. The last time I spoke with him, which was a few weeks ago, I was considering letting him take me to dinner. But then he wanted to squeeze in some sex. I told him no because he didn't want to use a condom. And I let that be the main reason for me to not want to talk to him. The man has a problem.

When a few people did start coming in, the tipping was still crappy. I was sitting in my spot watching the college football game. Chilling. My name was called, I went and danced. Then as I was moving to the other stage, one of the customer called out my name. I went over and talked to him. It was that one Black guy from a week ago who was staring at me from across the bar, and I went over to talk to him. He was happy to see me. The only thing that got on my nerve about him today was him trying to touch my piercing that's between my legs, by going inside my panties. I tell customers I don't like their dirty hands inside my panties. That's nasty.

A lot of the girls left early today. That's how bad it was. There were like eight girls for the day shift. I don't know how many there were for the night shift. In a week things should be better. I might not go back till Thursday. I'd rather be home than sitting there waiting for my name to be called. Go when the money is right.

January 9, 2014
Caught Beer Handed!

Today started off as another slow day. I thought that every Thursday day shift was jumping. Maybe that was just for December. There were I think sixteen girls at the club. The customers that were there, five, had gotten some food from the restaurant and was eating while watching us dance. People didn't start coming in till around 2:30.

My first round of dancing, I had went to two stages. We didn't have to dance on all four because there wasn't too many customers to dance for. As I was walking off the third stage, one customer who was sitting next to the second stage asked me if I was gonna dance on the second stage. I told him yes and danced for him and his friend. I wasn't even thinking about the second stage.

I really didn't talk to any customers today. I spent time sitting at the bar or talking with the security guard. I filled one of the girls in on the up coming trip to Miami. One of my thang thangs is going to be celebrating his birthday in April and wants me to come out there. Okay.

I had decided to get some nachos and sit down to eat. When I was finished one of the managers came over and told me that a guy at the other end wanted to buy me a drink. I got up and went over to him. We sat and talked. Then it was time for me to get back on stage to dance. He came over and sat down to watch. When I moved to the other stage he came over.

I went back to the bar to sit and talk with him. He told me that he was working across the freeway and got off work early. He came by himself to have some drinks and talk with some girls. Then he was telling me about his girlfriend and how she doesn't like to do certain things during sex. The whole time, we're sitting in our chairs with some distance between us. I have my clothes on and I'm drinking my second drink.

Out of no where, his girlfriend walks up with this horrid expression on her face. She was short, with glasses and looked like a geek. That's why he can't get the sexual satisfaction he wants from her. She's a dork! She was looking at him and wasn't really looking at me. She was very upset that he was there. She asked him what he was doing, and he told her, "I'm having a beer. Talking to a girl." She did not like that at all.

I asked her if she wanted to sit down, because she was just standing there. She said no. I just turned around and tried to hide my smile. The guy was calm the whole time, so she looked like the one over reacting. She asked him why he wasn't at work. He got off early. She told him he needs to leave now. He picked his money and phone up from off the bar, said he was sorry to me, and walked out with her.

Everyone who seen or heard what was happening started laughing when they walked out! They couldn't believe what happened. I was still sitting in the chair, smiling ear to ear. It was crazy. People came over to talk to me about what happened. The whole time I sat in the chair, I kept saying to myself, "Just don't touch me. Don't touch me." She was really pissed.

I heard later that when he went to his car, she was still yelling at him. Then someone else told me that she was hitting on him in the parking lot and he was pushing her away. Men be getting in trouble coming to the bikini bars. That was my first experience with that. It was funny and uncomfortable. Sitting with a man who gets busted by his girlfriend talking with a half naked woman. She was messing up my vibes. I'm just glad she didn't come in when I had my a$$ shaking in his face on the stage!

There was a customer sitting next to me when it happened. He was the first one to start laughing. I asked him if he was single, and he said, "No. I sent my wife to Africa." So I scooted my chair over towards him. It was funny. I talked with him for a little bit. Then he got a call that made him walk away. Or he seen someone he wanted to talk to.

I didn't even bother with counting my money today. I knew it wasn't going to be much. I left it in the purse so I can add to it tomorrow then feel better about counting it. I hope that more people come tomorrow. So I can at least feel like I'm not dancing for myself. I did pretty good with my hair being flat ironed. It didn't frizz up like it normally do. I did sweat a little but I had the fan on as much as I could to help against the sweat.

January 10, 2014
Good Friday For Me

Today was one of the girl's birthday party. The first thing that annoyed me were all the dam balloons tied to the chairs. How was the customers to see us dancing? And why did she, the DJ, put all the balloons up when she didn't do that for the other girls who recently had a birthday? Is this girl her favorite?

Anyways, when the shift started there was a lot of men coming in that was on break from work. Construction men. Tips were nice. When I was sitting at the bar as they were coming in, one sat next to me and we started talking. He told me that where he works, their foreman doesn't play. So they will be having a quick lunch break. It was funny since a lot of them be wanting to stay for a while.

When I was dancing on the last stage during my first round, I seen that one customer come in that I had stopped talking to because he was taking a liking to another girl. I seen he was sitting by himself and decided to go talk with him. He even brought up that it has been a minute since we've talked. I told him why. He laughed at it. He didn't stay long because he had to get back to work himself. That man has been coming to the club almost everyday! Wow.

I talked with a lot of customers today. They were excited when I was walking by their tables. There were a few Hispanics there. They love to whistle at us! And they were loving my booty. I would walk up to them, turn around, bend over, and shake it for them. I don't know how much money I made off doing that. But I was doing it to make that money.

One thing that had me upset was Miss Stiffie. I went to the dressing room about fifteen minutes before six to count my money. I was sitting down counting when one of the girls, who hasn't been working as often as she used to, walks in to start getting ready for the night shift. As she was getting ready Miss Stiffie walks in and sits down. The other girl was saying how she hasn't been sick, since a few other girls said they were sick. Miss Stiffie made a comment that she hasn't been working to get sick. The girl told her she has. So Stiffie told her she hasn't because she hasn't been seeing her.

The girl told her what days she worked then explained that she makes enough money in those couple of days to not have to work anymore. For some reason, Stiffie kept talking. I was looking at her like shut the Hell up! Just because you have to work everyday of the week and doubles everyday don't mean you can talk crap about others. I was only working three days a week because that was good enough for me. But I decided to maximize what I'm making and work two extra days. At least while I can.

I thought a serious argument was going to start because when things got quiet, Stiffie started up again. She asked the girl if she had seen her white bra. She wore it to work the day of her birthday. The same day she was pissy drunk and laid out in the dressing room. Now, I don't even think the girl was here that day. She told Stiffie no, she hasn't seen it.

This evil woman then says, "That bra was $100. And whoever stole it I hope they die." The girl told her that was a little extreme. Stiffie didn't think so. I feel that she might have lost her bra with no fault of anyone else. And why would she have a $100 bra? That makes no sense. Even my bra was $4 at Walmart. I don't need nothing but support. And she has fake boobs so why would she need such an expensive bra?

When she finally walked out the dressing room I was so happy. I was trying to figure out if she was drunk I noticed she has a habit of running her mouth to people like she knows better than them. She is not anyone's mother so she shouldn't worry herself as much as she do. These girls are grown and will do what they want.

When it was time for the birthday girl to blow the candles out on her cake, some of the girls went to stage to shower her with money and take pictures. That one girl I can't stand was on stage. She disgust me because every time it's a birthday party, she just has to climb on top of the girl and act like she's screwing her. Just nasty. I was sitting with a customer, as usual. Not interested in being in any pictures.

It was funny because when we got things started, one of the bartenders mentioned that the picture of the girl on the stage was not so flattering. It was a picture of her putting something in her mouth. Like a piece of banana or something. I busted out laughing because I felt the same way. It just didn't look right. And it was in black and white. Customers were thinking someone had died! Her colors were black and grey.

I spent about thirty minutes in the dressing room counting my money and putting it in rubber bands. I had over $400. Nice. I hope tomorrow will be the same. If not, I won't be mad. I might do a double next week.

Get this money while the getting is good. I have future plans and need money to pull them off! I'm in saving mode since I haven't moved into my freaking apartment yet.

What A Huge Difference

Today was not even close to yesterday. Most of the money I made was from one customer. Oh boy! There were ten girls today. The shift started off so slow. Everyone was dancing on one stage only. There wasn't a reason to go to the third or fourth stage. There were barely any customers to dance for.

I was sitting by the door talking with security when the few people did start to come in. I was in the middle of the list so when I went to dance the place was still pretty empty. While I was dancing on the first round, I noticed an Asian man put some money on the table for me. He went to the bathroom then came back and sat at the stage for my second song.

He wanted to buy me a drink so I went and sat with him and talked with him. He kept tipping me good so I stayed with him At some point I walked away to change my outfit and when I came out the dressing room another girl was talking to him. I didn't trip. I needed to go to the bathroom. When I came out, I went back to him. He really liked me. He was cool to talk to.

Other than that, I didn't get any tips on stage. That's how dry it was. But I'm used to it when I get on stage. Everyday is always different. What more can you expect? Now tomorrow, I already know that there will probably be a lot of customers for the football party. But one of the girls told me that last Sunday it was busy, but no one was tipping. So I'm ready to go in and see what money I can scrap up! No big deal. I'll just have to deal with all that dam 80s music from the DJ who's working tomorrow. ☒

When I first got to the dressing room, one of the girls was talking about the issue that one girl I can't stand was causing. The one who was very rude while I was standing in front of that one customer.

So the girl who was telling the story had stayed and worked a double yesterday. So for the night shift, there was one point of time that she was dancing on her stage making money. Ms. K was dancing on her own stage. But she wasn't making any money. So she went to the other girl's stage and started dancing. The girl was very confused and looked at her like she was trippin. You don't walk up on someone's stage if they didn't invite you to.

And the people who were watching her, obviously liked the way she was dancing better than the way Ms. K was dancing. The other girl is White and Ms. K is Black. Very big difference.

The girl was telling herself, she is NOT splitting her money with the other girl. Now the DJ for the day shift hadn't left yet and she saw what happened. She went over and told the girl to go back to her stage. They wasn't sure if she was drunk or what was going on with her. But the other girl said that one of the customers that was at her stage, was a customer that the other girl was trying to make money off of. She is a rude b#tch!

She was also saying that while she was sitting with a customer, the same girl was ordering drinks on the customer without his permission. The customer got up and walked out. The manager was pissed at her. I mean, some of these girls are serious about getting those drinks. I'd rather have the money, because my car don't run off of rum and pineapple. It runs off of gasoline. Know what I'm saying?

January 12, 2014

The Last Sunday

I am so done working Sundays! I am tired of going there and everybody is watching the games and not tipping me. I did get a few tips but the majority of people were so into the game. I'd rather stay home Sunday and work the days I know people are willing to tip me.

One of my regulars showed up before I left and I couldn't wait to go sit with him. I was sitting with one customer who tipped me at the last stage but while I was sitting and talking to him, he wasn't tipping me. So I decided to go sit with my regular that just walked in. I enjoy sitting with him.

There were twelve girls working today for the day shift. And it was just as many for the night shift too. Wednesday I plan to go work and see how the amateur night will be since I heard that a new strip club was opened tonight in the city I stay in. So I think a lot of the hood rats that come to my club will be trying to get in there for work. I hope so. They are so annoying and embarrassing!

One of the security guards who work on Wednesday nights told me how a girl, who was hella over weight, was wearing a sling shot. For those who don't know, it's an outfit that only covers the nipples and the front private part. The rest are strings that wrap around the body, making the female look almost completely naked. No person in their right mind should be wearing something not meant for their unattractive body size and horrible shape. I'm going to go and have some great stories to tell you!

January 13, 2014
Boring Monday

Talk about dancing for nothing. That joint was so dead today. The little money I made was from one of my regulars. Other than that, no one was tipping me on stage. The five people that were there just sat and watched. Towards the last hour, that's when I got tipped for dancing. That's why sometimes I don't put much effort into it and be sweating with no money to show for it.

While I was in the dressing room the girls were talking about how it be Wednesday night. They said that some big BIG girls have been showing up. Yeah, I need to go and piss a few people off. I don't care if I make money on stage. I just want to show off and laugh.

Now, remember when I was telling you about a customer who got mad at a girl for showing a boob to a chick for $1, but she ain't never showed him anything after he spent hundreds of dollars on her? Well guess what!

So, I was sitting down chilling by the door. This White guy was at the bar talking with one of the girls. I didn't see his face and wasn't tripping off him. But then when he started talking to security I heard his voice. I told myself, "Self. That sounds like that guy from that night with that girl bout them hundreds."

Myself said, "Yep! Dat's dat foo!" I had to laugh at seeing him there. I wondered if he was still dealing with the chick. And her huge gap. Ewe. And her bald sides. Ugh! Anyway, he was talking to the security guard about working at the club as security. (cough, cough)

Now, let me be honest. This guy is old. He's not someone that looks as if he would be able to stop a fight between some men if one broke out. He look like he would get broke off for trying to stop a fight. And why would he want to work at the club? He looks like he needs to be at home waiting for his social security money to come in. The security guard he was talking to felt that he was not the right guy to be working at the club. Not when he has something like that going on with one of the girls. That don't sound or look right. Hell no!

I spent most of the day sitting down, with my phone in my face after my customer left. One of the girls I'm cool with was having problems when the shift started. All I know is that while I was in the bathroom putting my contacts on my eyes, she busted in the bathroom crying. She wiped her face and stuff but I didn't say nothing. I don't want to get in peoples' business like that. So she had one of those days where she was ready to go home soon as it started.

Then when she was getting dressed, her phone rung, and after she answered it, she started getting into it with someone. She ran out of that place when she was dressed. Plus, she lives so far away. Like a two hour drive. Crazy stuff. I now she likes women and it's funny to see women have women problems.

January 16, 2013

A Good Thursday

Before I talk about what happened today, I have to talk about Wednesday night first. I went like I said I would. There were not too many girls on the day shift and the customer count was low. Even when the night shift started it was still slow. Some people thought I was doing a double after I got dressed. They know I mainly work the day shift. They were surprised to see me for the night shift.

Now this is funny in a way. One of the girls was dancing on stage. She's real cool. She came to the edge of the stage and steppe down onto the floor. She lifted up one of her legs onto the stage and started to shake her booty. I noticed something moving between her legs. Looking harder, I noticed she her tampon string was hanging! She was wearing a black thong so the string was showing. When I was going to tell her, one of the other girls who was watching from the bar went over to tell her. She sat on the stage as she was talking to her then looked between her legs. She covered her mouth and leaned back on the stage laughing. She asked the girl, "What should I do?" I don't know what the girl told her, but she stayed right there at the edge of the stage and put her string back inside her panties and kept dancing. That's why I cut my strings after insertion.

After an hour or two, I started talking with this one customer who I talked with from the last Wednesday night I worked months ago. He was happy to see me and had the nerves to tell me that I ended his relationship. He had came to the club with his girlfriend and I was dancing on stage. She got upset because he was telling her about my booty, then she had a chance to see it for herself. She felt that he had a crush on me and liked me. He explained to me that she was very insecure with herself because of being mistreated in past relationships. That sounds like she was the cause of their break up. Not I.

As time went on, more people started to show up. Even Hairy was there. When I was dancing on the last stage, these Hispanics walked in. The one that was looking at me, I was sticking my tongue out at him. When I got on the floor and was standing with some of the girls I'm cool with, he started throwing money around because me and one of the girls were dancing for him. So I picked the money up off the ground and put it in my purse. I had to go with the flow.

I told myself that when the amateur girls start arriving I was going to move my things to the dressing room in the back. I didn't want to be bothered with all of them girls when it came time to change. As I was moving my things, two girls started to get into it. I don't know exactly what was going on, but one girl was accusing another of not working at the club and didn't want her in the dressing room. It was the smaller dressing room next to the one I be in. It's the size of a bathroom.

When I walked up, one girl was telling the other to get out the room because she didn't believe that she worked there. One of the amateurs that had just got there stuck her nose in the mix and they were going back and forth. I didn't see it, but I think the girl took the other girl's purse and threw it out the room. Forcing her to leave. I felt that was very cruel but I wasn't bout to fight someone else battle that I don't know.

I had ordered some pizza because I was hungry. When I was sitting down eating one of the girls came over and had some of my food. We started talking about seeing the customers outside of the club. She was telling me how she sees some of them outside because they pay her hundreds of dollars to spend time with her. They even take her shopping and stuff. That's all fine but I don't want them getting attached and thinking sex will be next. She has a few that comes in handy for her when she needs them. I just don't want to be annoyed by them asking about when can they see me again.

As the girls got there, I saw that one funny looking Black girl that doesn't wear her make up right. She was dark skinned but her make up made her look five times lighter. Especially around her eyes. And her smile was horrible. Then her red weave. When you get a weave in your hair, isn't it suppose to be even at the bottom all the way around? Her stuff wasn't even cut right. She looked a mess. Boney little thing.

Then there was the big, short girl that was wasted. She was getting on my nerves because she got on the stage before the contest started. She was not suppose to be up there. Then after it started, she was trying to dance on stage with her friend. But she was so wasted, she couldn't really dance. It looked like she would fall over or slip. Security had to get her off stage and block her from getting back on.

One girl that was on stage didn't want to be there. She had that look on her face like, why am I here? There was a guy next to me who was talking to his friend. He was telling him that his homeboy made her come. I'm guessing she was a prostitute.

There were a few dudes trying to talk with me but wasn't tipping. These were the ones I didn't spend too much time talking to. I didn't come here to meet new people. I came here to watch and see what was going on.

People were really enjoying the contest. I was bumped up on the list because I had to leave early. I was happy to leave because things were crazy. When I got to work today I was told that the girls go into it again over changing in the dressing room. The girl that was kicked out, I think she went home. I don't remember hearing her name after the incident when it was time to dance. The girls didn't fight. They were just arguing again. I think the girl who kicked the other out was fired. I'm not sure. She looked like an ugly man anyway.

Now today. The parking lot was not full when I pulled up. I got dressed. Flat ironed my hair and put a little curl at the end. I was ready to go. There were a few people that showed up. They were getting some food. I decided to take my time today because I didn't get much sleep from the night before. I'm not going to say what I was doing, but I did enjoy myself. I danced to slow music so that I wouldn't be too tired. And of course there wasn't too many customers there.

Tips were nice through out the day. I have no complaints about that. I didn't spend too much time talking with security. I was either dancing on the stage or talking with a customer. There were like eight girls, and Ms. K was there. I know someone seen me when I called her a b!tch before I left.

I had changed my clothes and was standing at a table next to the DJ booth. I was getting my money together before I left. She was walking past me laughing and got too close to the point that she bumped me. The dam girl kept walking! So I looked back at her and said b!tch with my lips. I'm sure someone seen me and I don't care. She is rude.

I don't know what makes men think that as a woman, you will accept an open drink, that you did not see being made in front of you. This Mexican was trying to give me a beer with a lime sticking out the top of the bottle. I don't drink beer. And I was getting ready to leave. I'm not drinking scrap! He said he was walking around trying to give the beer to someone. I don't know what you put in that drink. One customer I was talking to yesterday told me that the last time I seen him, he was so juiced up because someone put something in his drink. Wow. And he's a man.

Well, tomorrow is Friday and I'm so excited. That means there will be money floating around and I can't wait! If things are really going good, I'm going to put the extra effort in to make as much as possible. I might do a double if the night is going real good. I have to wait and see. It would be nice if my construction manager would come in and share some of his money with me.

January 17, 2014
Such A Big Difference

Friday. The day I been waiting for since Sunday. This Friday was much slower for us dancers. And there were a lot of Mexicans there today. I mean, we were like, where did they all come from? The day started off slow then picked up. There wasn't too many people for me to talk to because I didn't want to worry about a language barrier. Or they were talking to other girls. I did talk with a few customers, and two of my regulars showed up.

One girl who usually dance on Fridays didn't today. I don't know what happened, but she stayed at the club for a few hours. I guess she was waiting on a ride. I didn't want to ask her about it. I just figured something serious happened that kept her from dancing.

Not too much happened. Things was pretty smooth. What I wished I could of seen was when Miss Stiffie was getting angry with the customers. It was probably about an hour or two left of the shift. I had just came out the dressing room and went to the DJ booth. She was asking me if I seen what Miss Stiffie was doing. I told her no, and she explained that she was pointing at the customers sitting at the tables to tip her. Thing is, none of them were paying her any attention.

See, that's why I tell people that I don't go around pulling the side of my panties out asking for a tip from customers. If they wanted to tip me, they would do it without me asking. And a lot of people want to tip a female they find attractive or who dancing they like. Some might not find her attractive or like her stiff dancing. And if they were not sitting at her stage, how can she point her finger at them to tip her? The DJ said she was drunk. As I watched her on the other stage, yeah. She looked drunk as she was walking off.

Okay. Someone did something today that was not called for. Someone told the security guard that I was showing my private area. I was on the last stage getting ready to dance by he door. He came over and told me that someone told him I was showing my bottom. I looked that man in his eyes and told him, no one has been tipping me for me to show my private area. I don't have any twenties or tens to justify me doing such a thing. He looked at me and laughed because he knew I was telling the truth. I told

96

him I should start showing it since I'm being accused of doing it, so then that person won't look like a liar. He laughed some more.

I'm not stupid. I'm cautious. After that happened, my next dance on the stage was cool. This one customer sat at the main stage and watched me dance. He tipped me some ones. I went to the second stage and danced, he came over and tipped me a twenty. I didn't show my private. No way. I kept it clean so that I wouldn't get caught in a set up. Even at the third stage, he tipped me another twenty and I still didn't show it. I hadn't been doing it all day, and I was doing just fine.

Now Ms. K got fussed at for climbing off the stage, onto the table, and wrapping her legs around a customer's neck. I don't know what made her think that was gonna fly. The DJ started talking on the mic that the tables are not for dancing, the stages are. When I first heard her say that, I was looking around to see what was going on. Then I heard what she did. She be pushing the limits. Can't stand her.

Tomorrow, I'm not even worried bout much. I'm gonna show up and try to just have fun being there. The big football game is Sunday, and I am eager to see who will win. Especially since Californians have been blocked for buying tickets to see the game in Washington. No Bay Area fans allowed there! So funny to me. I don't want to be dancing on stage while everyone is super focused on the game. I'd rather be watching it myself.

January 18, 2014
I Was Happy Today

Saturday. I felt today would have been a slow day for me. But it was actually a nice day. I showed up early, sat at the bar, ate my food, then got dressed. There was about eight girls that came today. I decided on my way there that I was going to dance to Reggae. Do something different while enjoying myself.

The first thing that annoyed me was coming out the bathroom and seeing that one Mexican customer who get on my nerves. It starts out cool talking to him, them he ets real grabby and keeps talking bout the same crap and asking my about stuff I don't want to talk about. He's also the same one who keeps asking me for a kiss and he knows I don't like to kiss. And what the Hell makes him think I want to kiss him? He's been drinking beer and I don't know him to be kissing him. I don't trust people who's all kissie kissie. You don't know where they like to put their lips.

I dealt with him as long as I could. He started to annoy me when he was asking me about the dude I mess with. And my book I wrote about my past relationships. Don't keep asking me questions when I already said that I don't remember everything I talked about. That was over a year ago when I wrote it. I had to keep walking away to the dressing room or other customers or the DJ booth. He was tipping but I was loosing my cool with him.

I got real happy when I saw the manager of the construction company. I couldn't wait to get away from dude and go sit with him. When I did, we had a great conversation. And you won't believe what he told me! He had came to he club one night and was at the stage tipping a girl. While she was dancing, Ms. K went on stage and licked her between the legs. The customer got up and left because he knows that we are not suppose to do stuff like that and he didn't want anyone to say anything to him. Like he paid to see something like that. I just made a face and shook my head. She does too much and I don't understand what her problem is. Some customers like that and some don't. She be looking crazy on stage. Like she's on crack.

Then when I was talking to the DJ, she told me how some of the customers were watching how Ms. K was acting, and they told her that she must be on drugs. It's bad when customers think you're on drugs. Even the customer I was talking to called her high strung. I'm so happy I'm much more relaxed.

Nope. No Sunday work. I'm going to the movies with my daughter after I get my much needed wax. Gotta keep myself smooth down there. Monday I might stay home because my kids are out of school. It would be nice to stay home and rest. Take my daughter to the park and relax while she runs her batteries low. I cold go to work, but staying home to rest sounds so much better right now.

January 23, 2014
Pretty Okay Day

What a slow day! I got there and the place was looking like a ghost town. After things got started a couple of customers showed up to get food at the restaurant. When I got on stage to dance for the first round, I noticed my clear bottom shoes were messed up at the bottom where the rubber is. I couldn't believe that the rubber was pulling back. I don't wear them shoes that much and when I do, I'm not a lot in them because of how high they are. I think they're eight or nine inches. Well, I'll be super gluing them for now on!

When I changed my outfit, I went and sat at the bar. One of the girls came over to me and told me to come sit with one of the customers that was with hers. It's these two men who comes often and spends money on the girls. One of them has two girls that he really like. Miss Stiffie is one and the second is the girl. This girl is now wearing a short Peter Pan hair cut.

The part that got me, is when I noticed Miss Stiffie was talking to different customers while her regular was there. While I was in the dressing room with Peter Pan, she told me that when she was by the front door, the guy came in. She was giving him a hug when Miss Stiffie seen him and yelled over to him, "Hey! I got our seats ready!" It was rude of her but that's how she is.

Then the customer had to tell her to go walk around and talk to other people, because when she's sitting with him, the other girls aren't comfortable being around her. She gives an attitude and mean looks. He told her that he is not her boyfriend and don't want her all stuck under him. He wants to be able to talk with the other girls. Like when I'm sitting with his friend, he'll come over and give a little touch or tickle my feet then tip me. He don't want no one keeping the other girls from him. Even if she's one of the main girls he spend money on.

Every time I went to the bathroom and saw the two of them sitting with him, I had to smile because Miss Stiffie had to share him. That man has enough money for the both of them. I believe he took them to Vegas last week. Funny. I just sat with my customer and danced to the music that played and received my tips from him.

And guess what! When day shift was about to end, guess who I saw high tailing it out the club? Miss Stiffie. She was NOT doing a double today. I don't know what was going on with her but she was dressed and making her way out the building. When I saw her buttoned up in her black jacket, I smiled and laughed at myself. That chick is always doing doubles. Even when she isn't making any money she still stays. Be sleeping in the dressing room. Just go home!

This was one of those days when you make more money on the floor spending time with the customers than dancing on stage. I did pretty good. I was happy when I left. I had to avoid one customer the last hour because he wanted to sit and talk but he wasn't tipping. At the same time, I didn't want to talk to him. Or hear what he had to say. I wasn't in the mood. I was tired from not getting a good night sleep.

Tomorrow is the birthday party for one of the girls who dance and bartends. I don't know how busy it will be but hopefully there will be enough people there with money to spend. A few girls are waiting for the customers to get their W2s and file their taxes. Don't mean they'll be giving it to us. They gotta take care of themselves first. But yes, it would be very nice to dance for tax money. ☒

I'm thinking about doing a double on Saturday. I'm hoping that I can have fantastic day shift so by the time night shift comes, it won't matter if I don't make as much money. But I can still have a little something coming in. I wonder how many girls will be working. Not a lot I hope. But Saturday nights are usually full of girls. Oh well.

January 24, 2014
I'm Not Feeling It

So here I am on this Friday. Sitting in the dressing room because I'm not liking the crowd outside. When the shift first started it was packed because someone came here for a birthday party. That was very short lived. Then we were left with the Hispanics who're were off of work and speak no English.

When I moved to the third stage on the first round of dancing, this one cute guy who was sitting next to the stage wanted me to sit with him when I was done. I sat with him and chatted for a while. There were two other girls at the table but I'm cool with them and he was paying me equal attention.

I had developed an attitude before I could sit at the table with the guy. Not an attitude with the girls, but with a customer. There were no more chairs at the table. One table close by had two Hispanics and two empty chairs. I looked at the guy to ask if I could take one of the chairs. Instead of this bastard letting me take the chair, and getting another from the other table, he looks at me as if to say, "Go over there and get a chair!" I just rolled my eyes at the jerk and pulled a chair behind me from the third stage. Screw him.

As I'm sitting at the table talking with the guys, one of them tells me that the girl on third stage next to us was moving stiff. I had never seen her before so I guess it was her first day or something else. Then I noticed that Miss Stiffie was on the second stage. I told the guy, "You think she's stiff, check her out." He watched her for a few seconds and looked back at me and said, "Hey you're right!" He hadn't seen stiff yet. And the girl was dancing fine to me. It was a slow song she had to dance to.

I haven't seen any of my regulars today. I think I might just spend some time back here till some customers come in that I can easily vibe with. One girl came back here hoping that no more Mexican music will be played for a while, and she's Latin herself. But she looks white. She feels the same way I do about the Hispanic construction workers. She said they come in her for free, there's no drink minimum so they get all these pitchers of beers, and watch us dance for free. And if they do tip, sometimes it's so crappy. I had two sitting at my stage and I know I was giving a great show. All I got from them was $2 each. The next song I dance to will be slow. I'm getting upset with them in here. Whatever they ass is building, I hope they hurry up and finish it and go somewhere else cause they ain't doing the majority of us no favors.

The shift is over and I'm at home. Us girls agreed that today sucked. When I was doing my last round of dancing, I wasn't putting much effort into it after the main stage. I just stood around on the second stage. I sat in front of the fan on the third stage. And I talked to one of the girls that was leaving on the fourth stage. When I was done I hurried up and got myself dressed to leave too. I didn't even count my money because it would of just made me feel like things are getting bad.

My attitude was so bad by the time the shift was over, I ignored a customer that was trying to get my attention. Like I said. When I got to the third stage I sat down in front of the fan and watched one of the TVs on the wall. The girl dancing n the main stage was dancing to a song I really don't car for. Every now and then I would look around and didn't see anyone sitting at the stage. So I kept sitting. I got my purse, walked down the stage, and walked by a table full of Hispanic men. One of them was calling for me to turn around and I didn't look back. Why you didn't get up and say something to me when I was sitting on the stage? I would have gladly danced for you after a tip. But that lazy stuff is what makes some of us dancers have an attitude.

And you know what tragedy I almost go into? It was my last round of dancing and the girl before me was dancing. I told the customer I was sitting with that I had to go to the bathroom. As I'm using the bathroom, I looked down at my white bottoms and saw a huge red spot right between my legs! Oh my God I freaked out and ran to the dressing room to put on a tampon. I had to put on a black thong under another pair of white thongs because I was wearing all white. I finished my half assed dancing, because at that point I didn't care to dance anymore, and rushed outta there. Oh boy how horrible that would have been to go up there, open my legs while laying on my back, and having someone see bright RED. Much different from a little white string hanging.

It looked like I had over $50. I'm just stuck on how full of money my purse was back in December. It's gonna take me a while to get over that. I'll be fine.

January 26, 2014

I Loved That Saturday Double

So yesterday, I went to work not knowing what to expect. I knew I had to take my time and pace myself. Not too many people were there so I sat by myself at the fourth satge with my face buried in my phone. I noticed when one of my regulars walked in. The Mexican who comes in every week and does work on peoples' houses. The same one who likes to bit on my neck. I didn't feel like being bit so I didn't go over to him.

When it was my turn to dance, I noticed that there were three tables with guys sitting at them. I had seen some Hispanics walk in, so I thought the tables were filled with them. As I danced I didn't look at the tables. I had a mean expression on my face. And I was in my own world. When I was done dancing and was walking to the next stage, I noticed it was Asians sitting at the tables. If I would of known that I might have showed a little more attention to them. They don't come in the club that often.

Tips were good for the day shift. Things went good. I ended up sitting with the bitter and getting some money from him. Thank goodness he didn't stay for long. I was using the towel and alcohol I bought before the shift started came in handy to clean the poles and have a better grip on them. Now I just need to take some more pole classes so that I can give a better show for the customers. Step my game up.

When the night shift was starting there still wasn't too many people there in the club. I wasn't sure how the shift would go but I knew it would be better to add to what I had already made. But things had started picking up after 9:00 pm.

I was shocked when I realized that I wasn't spending too much time sitting by myself like I thought I would. Then my regular who has the pony tail showed up and things were real fun after that. Before he left with his friends, I was dancing on stage. They tipped me a lot of money on their way out the door. Sitting with them and listening to the things they talk about is so entertaining.

Miss Stiffie was sleeping in the back with her blanket over her. I don't know why she just didn't go home. I don't think she made that much money on the night shift. I tried to watch her on stage to see if she was going to do anything funny. I was too busy talking with someone or dancing to watch her when she was on stage.

I spent some time with one female customer. I found out later that she likes women. At first, she was sitting with a Hispanic male at the bar. He called me over to tip and get a feel of my booty. I talked to her for a little bit about piercing then went to the dressing room. Later on she asked me if I'd like a drink and she bought me a few. She asked if I was straight and I told her yes.

Now, this woman was pretty in the face. Dressed nice. Owned her own business. And didn't look like she had too many worries. I told her she was pretty and she didn't take it so good. She brought up how if she was 200 pounds lighter. She wasn't that big and like I said, she was dressed nice. But that let me know how she feels about herself. Then some dude, who I don't think she knew, started talking to her. I mean he was all up in her face. I thought to myself, see. I told you you're pretty.

When people started showing up the fun began. The money was flowing. I felt liked, a little. I was entertaining. I enjoyed picking up a beer bottle and giving it a blow job in front of the customers sitting at my stage. They got a real kick out of that. The guy stood up and acted like he was going to throw his whole wallet at me. Yeah right.

Then of course there were the few who sat there and looked like they didn't want to see me dance. I just ignored them because I knew someone out there was enjoying it. Just like this other chick who came to the stage as I started dancing. It was very clear she liked girls. I had got on my knees on top of the table to shake my rump, and she put her face in it. Security had to come over and he had a crazy look on his face as if he was confused about what to do. Then when I went to the third stage to dance, I heard her telling someone, "I'd take care of her. I'd take care of her kids. Make sure she gets to work everyday on time." I almost busted out laughing if it wasn't for me being upside down concentrating on what I was doing. She wanted a hug from me when I got off the stage. She didn't ask for my number, thank you God.

I lost count of how many drinks I had once number four had arrived. But I wasn't drunk to where I couldn't function properly. I had a little buzz. I do remember when the night shift was getting ready to start and the girls were in the dressing room getting ready, this White girl I had never seen before was in there. Something was wrong with her face. The skin on her face. Her cheeks were red and she had a lot of bumps on her cheeks as well. I don't know if it was pimples are something else.

I didn't go home early. I stayed till everyone had left. The night was good and I loved it. I didn't have time to turn in my ones so I'll do that Monday before I leave work. I need to get my kids some shoes. I want to order another pair of black shoes because mine are starting to smell and the bottom keeps coming loose. Yeah, putting super glue on them when they need it is fine but the smell is there to stay.

JANUARY 27, 2014
Monday. . .

I am here at the club as I type. I brought my laptop with me incase it's a slow day and I can do some things in the dressing room to not be too bored. Anyway, I was sitting by the door talking with security when a customer walked in. Now I don't remember if I mentioned this customer before. He's an older White male who always come here to see that White girl who dances super slow. He only sees he and sometimes he gets on her nerves and she runs to the back to get a break from him. And when she's on stage, he watches her like a hawk. Even when she's sitting with other customers. He watches her like a hawk.

Now, he walked in and security turned around to see who was coming. He asked security if she was here today and he told him no. I can imagine the guy's face when he said that because he was like, "Something's wrong. Just like last night she wasn't here and she was suppose to be here." The guy pulls out his phone and starts talking about a text.

He was explaining how he sent her a text to ask if she was working today. Instead of him getting the response he wanted, she sent him some half text that he didn't understand. Security told me that maybe she was screwing her dude. Like what do dude think? Just because he's spending a lot of money on her and buying her gifts don't make him her man. And for him to act like it, he's crazy. I busted out laughing soon as he opened the door! He didn't look too happy. If he had another girl or took interest in the other girls here he would be a lot happier when he walks in and she's not here. Driving all the way over here for one person who's probably not here. Ah haa! Just what he gets.

That man was so concerned about that woman! I know she's super happy she didn't give him her number. And the funnier part was when security told me that he lives forty five minutes away, so he took a drive to come see her and she wasn't even here! Too funny! She has another job so she ain't worried about this place. And that man be smelling like an ash tray. He'll go smoke outside and walk back in like he was smoking in the car with all the windows rolled up. Who wants to sit with a man that smells like that? Ewe.

So far it is slow. I'm waiting for the second round to start. I'm the first girl on the list today since I came early to practice some tricks on the pole. I couldn't do some of the stuff I tried but I learned another move I didn't know I can do. And I also learned I need to stay on my sit ups so that I can pull myself up on the pole. Yes, time for more pole classes! One more week!

I'm at home right now and all I have to say is. $9. Really? This was a bad day for us. The number of customers did not increase as the day went on. I stayed in the dressing room working on another book. When I had to go out on stage for the last time, I did not put any effort into dancing because there was only eight customers and I knew they weren't going to tip. Then the song I danced to was only one minute and some seconds. I was happy when it stopped. The DJ was trying to get me to finish it because I guess her computer messed up. Hell naw I ain't dancing no more! I'm ready to bounce out this mofo. I went to the next stage and sat my ass down on the bar and watched these people play pool. Then I turned in my ones from the weekend and went home. Screw that mess.

The end of the month and first of the month is a killer. Oh boy! And we had a new girl start today. She's friends with the girl who's wearing the Peter Pan hair cut. She wasn't putting any effort into dancing either. I think she's Mexican but she looks white. Oh well.

January 31, 2014

Last Day Of January

I actually felt real good when I went to work today. Yesterday I ordered two pairs of dancing shoes. One pair is red and the other is black knee high boots. Looks like I'll be getting them on Monday, hopefully.

When I got to work there was no telling how busy it would be. Things started out okay the first round. I had a guy tip me some fives on the main stage. When I got to second I attracted a customer from last time who followed me all the way to the fourth stage. I sat with him and talked till he had to leave. Things were okay after that. People were showing up and enjoying themselves.

As usual the place had people but the tips were slacking. Girls in the dressing room were sharing their feelings so I didn't feel it was just me. I was happy that I made a solid $100 but knew I could of done better.

When one of my regulars showed up an hour before the end of the shift, I was just happy to have someone to sit and talk with. The table he normally sits at was packed with his friends. They put two tables together because it was such a large group.

I was irritated with a customer who kept putting his dam hands inside my panties. I told that fool don't put your hand inside, and he kept doing it! And he wasn't tipping me! I got up and walked away to go dance on stage. He tried to get me to come back where he was sitting when I was done, and I told him I wanted to stay where I was. Screw you man.

It is so funny to be in the dressing room listening to the other girls talk. They mainly talk about getting tans, the White girls, and the tan lines on some of them are crazy. They talk about looking pasty. Whatever that is. Must be difficult being a White female at times worrying about looking pale then going to a tanning salon to look darker than what you are. Hmmm. . .

Now I heard that it got crazy yesterday. One of the quiet girls did something she wasn't, or should I say, shouldn't have done. She got on top of the bar and I guess she put her finger in her private area. I think it was said that she let a customer touch her down there as well. One of the girls said she was drunk. I don't think I have seen her drunk before. Not that it probably hasn't happened before.

And the DJ was just upset over the whole thing. I feel she shouldn't have that much say so in what happens. She's the DJ, who used to be a dancer. She is not the manager. She just wants her two cents put into the twenty five cent machine. I feel that if the managers don't say nothing, YOU don't say nothing. Now, of course I feel that home girl did wrong. But for the DJ to come in the dressing room talking about she's gonna send people home if she catch them acting like that again, is too much. Sit yo a$$ down and play music. The male DJs don't trip. Why are you?

I kind of wanted to do a double today, but when I seen how many girls there were, I told myself I was good. Maybe tomorrow I will try to pull one but I don't know yet. The Super Bowl game is Sunday and I might work Sunday night just to see how things go after the game. I know that since it's slow I should be working more days to make up for the difference but sometimes I feel like I could of stayed home. Like Monday. Leaving with $9 because the place was empty. What kind of mess was that?

The new girl who started Monday worked today. She don't really do nothing. And she got the nerve to be shy and don't want no one to look at her. Huh? You want to be a dancer, but don't want no one to look at you? I don't get it. She said she worked at a different club before but I don't see it.

When I was getting ready to leave, one of the girls I'm cool with who works the night shift told me that someone stole her wallet Wednesday night. One of those amateur girls probably did it. I told her to get a locker so she can keep her important stuff locked up. She wasn't sure about doing that since there wasn't too many lockers available. I have a spare key for my locker, and all I keep inside is my shoes and girly items. I gave her a key to help her out. I can't stand the amateur night girls!

FEBRUARY 1, 2014
A Fun Saturday

It was a good day. Meaning that I enjoyed myself. This is how the day started off. I got there and went to the dressing room to get ready. The new girl was there flat ironing her hair and putting her hair pieces in. Wow. The female DJ came in and started fussing about something the new girl did the day before.

What happened was, the girl was at a table with some customers and I guess she stood up and was dancing for them while a girl was dancing on stage. The rule is, you can't dance for customers while a girl is on stage. It takes the attention away from her. She was told by security that she can't do that and has to sit down. She did, but the way the DJ was fussing, it seems like she stood up and did it again. They went back and forth for a few seconds before the girl dropped it and the DJ walked out. She told her that she should work nights since she don't want to listen to her. The girl told her, "Noo, I can't work nights." In a sarcastic manner. That woman gets too dam worked up about things.

As I was talking to security by the door, my regular came in that likes to bite me. Oh my gosh that man is really starting to get to me! And today, I felt him dragging his teeth on my skin. I couldn't believe it! I told myself, I would never EVER want to have sex with him because he would bite the Hell out of me. No thank you. When it was my turn to dance on the stage, I was so happy to get away from his teeth. And when I was done, I went to sit in the dressing room just to get away from him till he left.

Things didn't start picking up till around three. I had went to the fourth stage and there was a guy already sitting there with his back facing the stage as he faced the main stage. I did not notice him turn to look at me not once. One guy who was sitting at the bar came over to tip me. When I was done dancing security asked me if he had tipped me. I didn't think he had so I told him no. He asked if the money on the stage was from him and I told him no. When he told the guy that he has to tip while sitting at the stage, I was shocked when the guy said he tipped me $10. I went over to tell him thank you and give him a hug because I really thought he wasn't paying me any attention.

Tomorrow I'm going to work the night shift. Hopefully it will be a good day after the game. If the team that I want to see win have a good outcome, I will be happy no matter how my night turns out.

Before the shift started, we were told in the dressing room that stage fees and drink prices will be going up on the 10th. I have no idea how that will affect the girls and the customers. I know on the slow days during the week, the number of girls might drop real low. How you raise the stage fees on the slow days when girls will probably not make that money back? And you want to remodel. How do you raise the drink prices and stage fees before the remodel? At least give people a reason to pay more first. Things are going to start getting ugly. They're so worried about drink sales now. Them people are turning stupid.

I know what I will probably do is work some night shifts before the fee hike. I will be alright on the days I have to work for now. And when people start getting their taxes back, maybe it will get better.

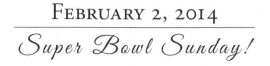

Sunday. Super Bowl Sunday. Night shift. It is currently 11:37 pm and there isn't too many people here. I'm sitting in the dressing room because I'm starting to feel tired. I have sat and talked with some customers and there's two that I could be sitting with right now, but I'd rather wait to go out there the next time I have to dance.

There are about twelve girls I think. Things are going smooth. The DJ, a male, told me the last dance I had on the main stage about my bottoms. He told me that I had pulled them down in the back too far. OMG. Did I really? I just be trying to do something else on stage so the customer don't get bored. And I haven't been told by the female DJ who works the mornings about me pulling the back of my panties down too far. She watches like a hawk and I pull them down the same length every time. Oh well. I just won't do it any more.

And I found out why the prices on things are going up. The club has new owners. I think what I want to do is go to one of the other clubs and see how things are over there. Because I'm starting to get tired of all these restrictions. I can't wait to go to Miami in April and enjoy being full nude! But until then, I have to deal.

There is a Russian customer here who has taken a liking to me. He doesn't speak much English but his friend translates for him. He likes me because there isn't too many Black girls in Russia and he thinks I'm exotic. I can dig it. He enjoyed my dancing and I spent some time with him while he played pool. He's good. I tried to knock off his concentration by leaning over the pool table so my boob would be in the way of the hole, and he still made it in. He's good.

When I was sitting at the bar earlier I over heard a conversation about a girl who got in trouble over the weekend because she was giving a lap dance. A serious lap dance. I heard that she was suspended but another girl told me she was fired. And someone else got in trouble too. This place might start loosing money. I need to go check out to clubs in the area and see how I do there. But I like this place so much! Dam! Dam! Dam!

When I came into the dressing room to sit and type on my lap top, some girls were in here talking about something that happened on the floor. I don't know who the girl was they were talking about but it sounded pretty serious. One girl thought she was spat on and got all bent out of shape and told one of the managers that she didn't want to talk about it now, she would come back later. I kind of think it was someone who work here but then again I don't know. Anyways, they went back and forth for a while before she said that to the manager. I didn't ask who they were talking about because I didn't want to seem nosey and the girl who was in the mix, I don't really talk to her. So I felt I had no place to ask about who she was talking about.

Maybe when I go back out there will be more people. But that still don't mean it will be better for me. I haven't had too many people coming to the main stage when I dance. Some will come when I'm at the other stages, and that's why I don't worry too much about main stage because I'll make money at the other stages. And plus I'm starting to feel tired and sleepy. I'm ready to go home! But no, I will stick it out till I know the manager will let me go home. Think I'll sleep all day tomorrow after I take my kids to school. Hopefully my friend don't try to come back with me because I really don't want to be bothered with him tonight. I want to go to sleep until I have to take them to school, then come back home and sleep.

And guess what. When I pulled up, that customer who came looking for that one girl who wasn't here that day was standing outside. I don't know if the girl was here for the day shift, but he was standing outside smoking. I had to smile and laugh to myself. He seemed mad that day and he's not even the boyfriend. His bad.

So, just as I was getting comfortable in the dressing room, my freaking name was called. I went outside and the club was looking like a ghost town. A lot of people went home and some of the girls did too. I just picked a song I liked from years ago that I haven't heard in years to dance to. An Asian guy came to the stage to watch me. He told me when I was done dancing that he was there with a friend. And his friend had his gay friend with them. He wasn't comfortable with that. The other two guys were White.

When I asked him where the gay guy was, he told me he was behind him at second stage. One of the girls were dancing there and he was watching. I told myself that I was going to pick on him and have some fun. When I got over there they were watching me dance but the gay guy was trying to cover his eyes.

After a while, I got in his face and asked him how he was doing. You know what he said to me? He told me, "Honey, you need to talk to him cause I'm gay." And said it with an attitude. I was hella shocked and moved away from him laughing. I went to the other side of the stage where a customer came up. I danced for him instead. When I was done, the White guy came over and asked me what did I do to his friend. I told him I asked him how he was doing. He said he ran over to the wall and stood over there. I didn't care. He's in the wrong place to have that kind of attitude.

When I got to the last stage I didn't care to dance anymore. I was even more sleepy and tired. I was doing little stuff while watching the TV next to the stage. I seen a dude move to the side with a drink in his hand, but I wasn't paying him any attention. I looked down at the stage and seen some money. I looked at the dude and it was the dark skinned dude from New York.

When I seen him I smiled. I was happy to see him. I got off the stage and went to sit with him at the bar. He got off work early and came to see me. We have been getting close since I stopped talking to my high school crush. I like him.

The night was okay at the end. I made my minimum mark and was happy with that. Sunday night went good. Made me wonder how other Sunday nights would be. This one turned out better than the day shift. Might have to try it again. I stayed till closing because the manager wouldn't let me leave early since I wasn't doing a double. I didn't have a problem with it.

Miss Stiffie was there. Yes. She was sleeping in the dressing room most of the time. I don't know if she was drunk but I'm waiting to see if she gets in trouble again for being drunk and messing up with witnessing and dancing on stage.

I'm excited about going back to work Thursday with my new shoes. I hope I can dance in them. I'm really excited about the red ones. Oh boy!

February 6, 2014

Drunk and Drunker

What a day today! The first thing I want to say is, that guy with the girlfriend came back! Oh my goodness! So when I got dressed and ready, I sat down by security. There wasn't too many people there so I was chilling. I think I was walking to the bathroom and he said something to me. I hadn't noticed him because he had on some black frame glasses. He told me he was the one with the girlfriend who came in acting up. He wanted me to sit with him so I did.

Now homie was doing good. We were talking, he was tipping, we were laughing, and having fun. Then the chick that the bald headed customer started liking came over. I thought she was just saying hi, but her ass kept standing there like she was waiting for something. So he invited her to sit down with us. Hell no. That's not how I roll. She pulled up a chair next to me. I got up to leave after a few minutes. I don't work with other girls and it's one customer.

I went to talk with other customers. He kept trying to get me to come back and sit with him. I waited till she wasn't sitting with him anymore. Then when his beer kicked in, he was real touchie touchie. Even tried to get me to kiss him on the lips. Ewe. That fool was trippin. I did not want to get felt up on by a drunk. I went to the dressing room to hide from him.

I am so glad I did. I heard a bunch of girls rushing into the dressing room looking for me. See what had happened was, he was sitting at the stage watching that girl dance. His girlfriend stormed in, snatched the money he had on the table for the girl, and started going off on him.

Now, if I would have been sitting with him still, and she took some money that was for me, that I earned, we would have gotten into it. I will not have the same person messing with my money. No way!

That man told me today that he told her where he was the last time. He also told her he likes to come to the club once a month. So why she with him and can't deal with something he is not gonna stop doing for her? That is some funny stuff. I do not want to talk to him again. His girl got it coming. The ones who saw it happen were all excited and saying what they would have done if it were them. The girl didn't do nothing. She just kept dancing with a smile and the men who seen it gave her money because they knew she had took money from her. Smh.

The day went good. There was a second guy, who I normally don't talk to, but we're starting to talk to each other. He was drunk out his mind too. I don't know why White men like to tell women, "I want to be inside you." I have heard that so many times at the club from White men. There's no problem with it but I guess it's something they say.

I had one customer tip me $20. It was my last round of dancing. He looked like an older White or maybe something else. Not sure. Then he tipped me again when I went to the next stage. I made sure I hugged him when I got off stage. When I finished dancing I went back to him to talk for a few more minutes before leaving. That's when he handed over a twenty. He said he normally comes on Thursdays, so I'll be looking for him next week.

There has been a lot of talk about the higher stage fees taking effect next week. No one is excited about it. I wanna see how it affects people. I don't work Mondays and Tuesdays anymore because of how slow they are. So I guess the number of girls will drop. I might start working Mondays again depending on what the fee will be and if the number of girls drop. To me, it will mean the customers that do show up will have to tip who's there to dance and talk to or just keep their money for another time. We'll see what happens.

And I danced in my red heels today. I love them! Seven inches are not bad. Tomorrow I'll try out the boots. Those are going to have me worried because the bottom don't look like they will have the grip I need to keep from slipping. I'll just take my time while wearing them to make sure they're good to wear. But I so love dem red ones!

FEBRUARY 8, 2014

Friday. . . What happened?

Yesterday, Friday, was not good. The shift started out ok. This one dude who likes to come in and talk to me showed up. I was sitting with a customer when he walked in. I was happy because the one I was talking to was starting to get on my nerves. I enjoyed sitting and talking with him.

Before he showed up, I was at the bar by myself. I noticed some guys sitting on the other side with a drink. I decided to go try to talk to them and see what happens. The first guy was White. I went over and said hi, then asked if he wanted some company. He said no he was good. I walked to the Mexican behind him and said the same to him. He said the same to me. So I walked away to the bathroom. The very reason why I don't just go up to customers anymore. I'd rather them show me some interest first.

I didn't make too much money yesterday. There wasn't too much tipping going on for me. Plus with me spending the time I spent with the three people I talked to, dancing on stage is where most of my money came from. A lot of girls were talking to customers so they were occupied. But in the end the day was good. Nothing bad happened. The girls looked like they were enjoying themselves.

One girl had an issue with one of the songs I danced to. Turns out, the song was by a group of rappers from the Bay Area. One of them is her baby daddy. I still don't know which one is hers and I don't care. That's her problem. She shouldn't have had a baby by a rapper. I'm not gonna stop dancing to music by him, which ever one it was. That's her problem. Not mine. She's a stripper. Strip clubs play rap. Her baby daddy is a rapper. What the Hell was she thinking? And I know it really had her vexed because a customer came to the DJ booth when she was crying about her baby daddy and gave me some money for dancing to a song from the Bay. Oh well!

I didn't notice that new girl who started like a week ago. I guess she decided not to work here anymore or it was because she got into it with the DJ that one time. We'll see if she comes today. It's Saturday. Her friend that works here hasn't said anything about her not working here anymore as far as I know. Oh well. I might not be working here anymore depending on how things go! I'm so curious to see who's not gonna be here after the change! And the night shift. I can only imagine.

So my Saturday day shift was okay. It started out interesting. While we were still in the dressing room getting dressed, the DJ came inside and asked who wanted to do a birthday party. I asked her what race were the men. She said they were White and Mexican. When I asked her who they wanted, she said anybody. I shook my head and told her I'd pass. Then I told her the story about yesterday when I was trying to chat with a White and Mexican man who rejected me. I didn't want to do a birthday party if I wasn't asked for.

Miss Stiffie ended up doing the party. And she said she doesn't like the partied because she doesn't do much as it is. She feels embarrassed. I watched her dance for the birthday guy and she did good. He was trying to push his head into her butt every time she bent over. He looked like he was enjoying himself. She did good. The men were trying to take pictures of the dance but were stopped by security. I think in the end, she had fun.

I wore my glasses today. I was not feeling it. I did good wearing them. Since they are new, I didn't have to worry about them falling off or moving around a lot. They stayed in place. All I had to do was move my hair when it got on my lip gloss.

So. . . My construction manager came in today. I was happy to see him because I enjoy talking him. He always have good stories to tell. We talked about the Bahamas and what it's like. That's where he's from. It was funny because he told me about his middle life crisis he had a few years ago. He was pissed at his wife. One of the guys at his job pissed him off. He said "F#ck this country!" and bought a huge SUV, drove to Florida, bought a boat, had the SUV shipped to the Bahamas, and took the boat there. He had a house built and lived there for about ten months. That's when his daughter started crying for her daddy. YES! He left his wife and daughter behind! He was serious about that anger! Too funny!

I had a few people who were actually trying to talk to me but I was with a customer. And one dude was with a chick. I don't know who she was but I couldn't talk to him because my little boo thang showed up and it's his birthday today. So I had to spend time with him. I thought he would have asked for a dance but he was worried about getting up there and having a "hard" time getting things down. If you know what I mean. Lol!

This morning when I was on my way to work, I turned on my pre paid phone and a text message popped up. It was from a customer I met

Thursday. This jerk was trying to get me to meet up with him after work that day and I told him I already had plans to go home. I have kids to care for. So the message from him this morning said,

"Hey, I have the house to myself for a while. Would you like to come through or should I delete your number?"

Can you guess what I told the jerk?

"Hey dude! I'm on my way to work now, so if deleting my number makes you feel good go ahead. I don't jump when a person tells me to jump."

Then I turned off the phone and continued on to work. The nerve of that jerk! This is why I don't like to give out my number because they piss me off. And how can he say something like that after two days? What the Hell was he thinking?

Tomorrow I'm going to work the night shift and I don't know what to expect but I won't be disappointed.

What A Bummer

Yesterday was Sunday. I went in to see how the night shift would be. I expected for things to be slow. And it was. So slow I wish would have brought my laptop with me so that I could have been doing something constructive.

There wasn't too many people there. When the shift started there was a group of about five Indian guys who were there for quite a while. They kept moving around but wasn't tipping. My little boo thang was trying to get me to dance to some Indian music to get them to tip. Nope. I don't think so. If they really wanted to tip, they would have tipped when I was dancing for them on the edge of the stage.

The night was pretty cool. I was talking with one of the girls and she asked me if I was cool with the girl that has a huge gap and her sides are missing on the side of her head. I told her I don't talk to her but I say a few things to her every now and then. She told me that the girl gets jealous of other girls. I never noticed it before. But she looks like she could be the type.

I also noticed that after I gave my little boo thang a lap dance for his birthday, the same girl was getting kind of touchie with him. His co worker had showed up and we went to the pool table so they could play. I seen the gap chick standing close to him with her arm wrapped around his waist. I didn't trip because he's not my man. But I did see how she was looking at me. Nope! You will NOT get a reaction out of me! Please try again!

Now, I have taken a customer to the ATM to get some money before. He was really drunk and need help working the machine. I did not touch his card or punch any of the buttons. I did not want him to come back blaming me for something after he sober up. But from what she told me about the girl, she has seen her handling the guys cards at the machine and punching in the numbers. She thinks the girl is hustling the guys. She also told me that she's aggressive with them when it comes to the money. Called her money hungry. Some people need the money more than others.

At the end of the night, I did okay. I made my minimum mark for a slow night. Yes! Wish I could of did better but I was still happy. The same girl I was talking to also told me that one girl, who spent most of the shift in the dressing room, was upset because she didn't make any money. Well, I made some because I didn't spend the whole shift in the back. I gave people a chance to at least see me and have a chance to tip me. Oh well. Can't worry about everyone else.

And the White girls who worked and was in the same dressing room as me sure think highly of themselves. They weren't doing much dancing but was talking but mess like the female customers were jealous of them being on stage. I don't think so. You didn't bring enough to the table for someone, even a heavy set female, to be jealous of. Even for my last dance, I was more entertaining than them with the things I was doing. I can do more stuff on the pole than them and I wasn't talking mess afterwards. But like one girl said. She's dancing for her self confidence. Maybe they are too.

February 12, 2014
What A Wednesday!

I decided to go to work today to see how much money I could scrape up. I have been thinking about maybe adding Wednesday to my schedule, depending on how it goes. And today went good.

I got there on time for review. I was feeling good because I told myself, "Self. Let's not be bothered by what happens today, and by what doesn't happen today." Even when the shift first started there was no one in the club. I did stretches and moved around a little. The second round there was more people there to entertain and that went good.

The thing I really liked about today was sitting with a customer who was tipping me $20s. I think what he was trying to do after a while was get rid of me. Which I totally had no problem with. The three he gave me was enough to not be greedy with.

I didn't have anyone annoy me. I talked with some new customers. They were fun. And I was really into how I was dancing after more people showed up. We had like twelve girls and I hope it be that many on Mondays and Tuesdays when it's slow.

Now. Remember that guy I told you about who came to see a certain girl that day, and she wasn't at the club, and he was all like, "Something's wrong." Well he came today and she was there. Security told me that the girl had to check him. He must have been getting out of control and really bothering her. I noticed that she wasn't sitting with him like she normally does. And he wasn't watching the stage like a mother protecting her young.

What I saw was him talking to another girl that I never saw him talk to before. I was shocked! And I saw him doing her, like he was doing the other one. This is going to be a great show. I wonder if he's going to give her presents and stuff too.

Since Valentine's Day is Friday, not too many girls have plans with anyone. They most likely will be at work. I will be too, since my boo thang has to work. We'll go out Sunday night for seafood. I was being told by one girl who worked at the club last year that not too many people showed up on Valentine's Day, and night shift was dead. So maybe there won't be too many girls working, but I got a feeling there will be.

I stayed a little later instead of leaving at six. I was waiting for the traffic to die down since I could stay as long as I wanted to for Wednesday. When I left at eight, I had made some more money and traffic was non existent. Straight shot home. Yes!

Turned Out Okay

The shift for today almost started out like yesterday. No one was there when we started dancing. I was happy and feeling good. There was a customer sitting at the stage tipping all the girls dancing for the first round. I had danced my two stages and did not go to the third stage because there wasn't too many customers there that looked interested in me.

So I sat at the bar with my face in my phone. This White guy came and sat a seat down from me, since I had my legs in the chair next to me. He asked me why I didn't go to the last stage. I told him because there wasn't too many people there and I didn't want to work up a sweat for nothing. He tells me that he wanted to see me dance again. I looked at him like, where the Hell did you come from?

I talked with him till he left. He tipped me good and was enjoying the view of my booty when I stood up and shook it for him. He was nice to talk to. Lunch break from work. Likes women of color.

My second round of dancing was not productive. That's cool. Shift not over with yet. It reached a point that I seen all the Mexicans sitting at the tables. No wonder. While I was in the dressing room some of the girls were talking about how they don't like Black girls. I believe half of that. I have had a few Mexicans come for me, but some, like the real Mexicans don't make for good customers. The younger, thug ones are better. And cuter.

When I decided I wasn't going to put much effort into dancing, I sat at the bar watching other girls dance. Me and another were cracking up at this one girl on stage. It's the same new girl who got into it with the DJ that time. She finally came back. This chick was dancing as if she was scared. Like she wasn't sure how to move. And she did this one move when she swung around the pole, and kind of let herself fly across the stage by letting go of the pole. It looked so uncoordinated! Even security was laughing. She claims she has danced before but it sure Hell don't look like it.

Then I noticed a dark skinned dude in a suit who was running to the stage to tip the White girls. It's always the dark men showing attention to White women. Whatever floats their boat.

One girl tried to encourage me to come talk with this dude who was playing pool. Handsome, older Black guy. When we walked over to where he was, I just stood against the wall. She was talking to him and I really just wanted to sit down. I didn't want to talk to anyone. Just dance. I ended up walking away and sitting back down.

My next time dancing, I didn't do much at the third stage. The same guy came over and stood by the stage. I didn't know he was watching me. I was busy playing around and watching myself in the mirror. He asked me about my snake tattoo. I didn't care to talk to him so I went and sat down by the door.

Next thing I knew, he had walked over and started talking to me. We had a very interesting conversation. He used to be in the service and been to a lot of places. And he told me that ever since he was younger, he always had a thing for Asian women. Had a son by one too while he was overseas. Then one day he seen how White men were passing up beautiful Black women and he felt he wanted to support his own race. I should not have taken that to happen for him to want to support his own.

While I was talking to him, my little boo thang walked in. He went outside after a while and came back in holding a glass vase with red roses in it and a little purple teddy bear holding onto the vase. I was not expecting it! Such a surprise.

The day went okay. I made my minimum and I can't be happier since the day was crappy. Yesterday was much better. Tomorrow is expected to be slow. With few girls and customers. I hope it really turns out like that so the ones who do show up can benefit. Like on New Years day. That was sweet.

Some more girls were having a heart attack about the fee increase. Boy, those new owners have no idea what they are doing to people and how much they are hurting them. Some really do depend on making this extra money. And because the fees are low, it makes it better as a dancer.

And guess what interesting news I heard. So I was in the DJ booth talking with the DJ and Miss Stiffie came in to see who she was after. She thought she was after one of the other girls but she read the list wrong. She doesn't want to be behind one of the Black girls because, as I was told, she's pretty and the customers will follow the girl to the other stages to watch her dance. Well, maybe if your stiff behind would loosen up and put more effort into your dancing, you wouldn't have to worry about that.

My only concern when dancing after someone, is if I can dance to what they're dancing too. I'm not worried about looks. That would make me insecure about myself. And I'm not. I also don't see someone as a threat. Someone will always like me. Maybe not that many, but I will be liked by someone.

February 14, 2014
Valentine's Day. Dog Crap

When I got here this morning, to tried to sike myself out by saying that I was going to be happy no matter what and that today was going to be a good day. But all that went out the window when this place became busy and no one was making the money they should have.

There is over twenty girls here. There are a lot of customers. A few of the girls have said that tips are almost non existent. I've heard a few times that there isn't anyone to talk to. I do see girls talking to customers, but I guess they aren't tipping. Even the customers I talked to didn't tip. But I know it's not like this for everyone. I tried to have a positive attitude.

I even went out there and danced to a nice song and was putting effort into it. I broke a sweat. Not one dollar. So this next time I go up, I'm not doing much of anything. All these people here and I can't make money dancing, but they wanna stare me down when I'm walking by. Take in my jiggling booty as I'm moving past them. But not tip? No.

There were two birthday partied today. The second one was with a girl. When it was her time to give the dancer a lap dance, she really gave her a lap dance. Put her head between her legs. Put her boobs all in her face. She was moving like she's done it before. Then she went to the pole and knew how to work it. She's danced before. It was funny.

Right now, I'm sitting in the dressing room. By myself. Working on a book. I don't even wan to go out there unless it's to dance, pee, or my little boo thang is here. It don't make sense for this place to be this busy and to not be making money. I'm fine where I'm at cause I'm still being productive in my mind.

So. The shift ended like this. I stayed in the back till my name was called. I had put my shirt on that I wore into the club. I had on a black thong. I walked out to the floor like, screw everybody. When I got to the DJ booth, standing there was a dude I know from the motorcycle set. He's an a-hole. I couldn't stand him after a while. I wasn't bothered by him being there. I just told her what I wanted to dance to then went on stage and danced with the meanest face. There was a lot of people out there and a few at the stage. They sat and watched me. They tipped. Some were throwing balled up money at me when I was done. Guess it was money I left behind. After all the stages were done I hurried up to get dressed so that I could leave.

My dinner date for the night showed up and I was so happy. I ran out of there. The thing that really messed up my attitude was the amount of girls that was there. The customers had too many distractions to pay much attention to anyone else. I did make an okay amount. Better than I thought I had made. There is always tomorrow!

FEBRUARY 15, 2014
A Better Day Than Yesterday

I enjoyed today because there were less girls and the customers were generous. I didn't spend too much time talking to security today. I spoke with new people I never talked with before. Like this one White guy who wears glasses that comes in often. He came and told me that the guy he was sitting with "was going ooddles" over me. He was a tall, dark skinned guy that was watching me dance. I wasn't paying him much attention. He seen when I did my trick with a beer bottle. I slid my mouth down the top of the bottle as far as I could. I went all the way down till the bottle got wide. It was pretty far since it was a tall bottle.

It wasn't all that busy for the day shift. So we only had to dance on one stage to two songs. I went to three stages so that I could maximize my money making. It worked out great. I was very pleased.

One of my regulars came today. I think he was a little upset because while I was talking to him at the bar, one of the girls heard me talking about spiders and she started talking to me about them because she has a few tarantulas at home. I was happy she was talking so that I could avoid my customer's breath. It kills me. When I went to dance, he left by the time I was done. Yeeesss.

On my last round of dancing, a guy came to the stage to watch me. I was on the first song when he sat down. So the second song, I noticed he was sitting at a table next to the DJ booth behind the stage. I went over and did a little dance for him on the poles. I held onto them and flipped my feet up so that they would touch the ceiling. He wanted me to sit and talk with him. I did.

He told me that he has about a month before he goes to jail. Did some things that got him in trouble. He was cute too. Poor dude.

You what? I am so mad at myself that I forgot to mention this before. Now I don't remember what day it was that I was told. It was a few days ago. So. One of the girls that I'm cool with who works the night shift was telling me how Wednesday, after I left, that the new White girls that were working started talking smack.

They were saying in the dressing room that they were going to take over. I guess they were really feeling themselves and got ahead of themselves. Now from what I saw, they cannot dance all that good. Some don't look that attractive. And I don't care of you can out your leg behind your head, can you make it look sexy and graceful? Because that's what dudes wanna see when they come to such a place.

The girl who heard them say that was shocked. Another Black girl came in and started going off on them. Man do I wish I was there to hear it! I would have been laughing at them goofy girls and expressing my feelings as well. How dare you say something like that? That's how problems get started between dancers. People speaking out like they better than others. Just keep it to yourself.

February 17, 2014
Awesome Sunday!

Yesterday turned out to be a good day for me. Mostly because I enjoyed myself and secondly, I made money. The only thing I didn't like was when I hurt my left arm at the beginning of the shift during review. I was doing a simple pole trick that never bothered me before. Pulling myself up on the pole and pushing my legs out. Oh boy did it hurt me all night.

Hairy was there last night. He was sitting at the bar when I was hurrying to the bathroom before review. I was being nice by waving at him as I ran by. He sat there as if he didn't want to wave. No problem.

After the review, I seen one of my regulars walk in with another guy. I was going to sit with him but they wanted to get their drinks first. So I sat at a table with one of the girls. She was called to dance on stage and I kept sitting at the table. The people behind me wanted to talk to me and I heard them debating about asking me to sit with them.

Just as Hairy was walking over to sit with me, thank God the guy tapped my chair and got my attention first. Yes, I went to sit with them in stead. They were cool people. Two women and one guy. He was clearly gay from how he was talking and it was a ball. He had a great personality. Then I was called to the stage to dance.

This is when I got in trouble. When I got to the last stage, the girl on the main stage picked a dumb song to dance to. Some kind of combination of house and Mexican music. I turned the fan on, kicked my leg up on the bar, and laid down. When I was getting off stage, the DJ called me to the booth and told me I can't just lay there and not do anything. I have to entertain and move something. If nobody is sitting at my stage, what's the problem? And if it's my stage, what's the problem? Whatever. . .

After that, I sat down with a customer who comes in often with one my regulars. Him and I had an interesting convo. Since Miss Stiffie was on the stage in front of us, he told me a story of when he used to like her. How they went sour is when he invited her to the table with him and some guys he was working with. They were tipping her good and things were going good. When they were at the end of the visit, her patted her on the butt and I think he told her good job, or something like that, and she asked him where his money was.

That's why I don't ask customers for money. If they want to give it to me, they will. I have to be doing my part to make them want to give it to me. He brought her to the table to make money from them men, and she had the nerve to ask him about his money. He cut her off after that. Guess that's why he said that time, that he would pee on the stage while she was dancing on it! Still funny!

He also told me about another girl he used to be cool with but she was pocket watching him. He was getting ready to leave and he was walking by her. She pulled on her top like she was asking about money. He told her he didn't have any more money, so she replied, "Yes you do. I just saw you put some money in your pocket."

Okay. What makes you think he don't need that money for gas? Or to buy some food on the way home? How about this. What if that was the last little bit of money he has to last him through the week?

While I was talking to him, he told me that he was just laid off from his job. He's okay and excited about having the time off to go places for the next few months. Then he'll go back to work in April. I'm happy for him. I want to do more traveling myself. Some girls just don't know that they mess up a good thing by asking for more. Be happy with what was given to you sometimes.

While talking to him, another girl came over to say "hi." I got up and left because the other customer that came in and wanted to have a drink first was waiting for me. So I went over to him and spent some time. He had his brother with him from Africa and they were tippin nice. We had a cool conversation about things. They stayed for a while then left.

One of the girls was in the dressing room talking about how she thought the guy had his private outside his pants while she was talking with him. She had looked down and seen that his pants were unzipped. I told her that I was sitting with him and I didn't feel any skin to skin. I did feel when he shifted himself but nothing else. Not too many girls liked sitting with them. I know his brother was getting on my nerves when I was trying to leave to go to the bathroom or dance on stage. He had wrapped his arm around my body and didn't want to let me walk away. I had to pull and push away from him. His brother was even telling him to let me go. I can't stand that.

One of the things I was told by my regular was, "God made me after lunch." When I asked him to explain what that meant, he said that he took his time when he made me. Some people he rushed to finish them before lunch time, and that's why they have no ass or they are lacking a nice body. With me, he took his time and made me right. Especially when it came to my booty. I thought it was hilarious.

The night was pretty good. Even when the fight broke out between the Hispanics. Two of them started fighting when I was done dancing on fourth stage. It was weird because they were both drunk and too close together to really make good contact with the punches. Kind of funny to watch. I was happy when it broke out. I had some customers who were getting on my nerves at the time. I hurried up to the dressing room and got dressed. I was ready to go.

I have to say this. Lately I have been having good talks with Miss Stiffie. She was getting ready to leave at midnight because she did a double, and she opened up to me about how she feels embarrassed dancing on stage for the night shift. The people laugh and make fun of her because her body looks nice but her age shows in her face.

I feel like this. Don't stay if that's how you feel. Go home so you don't have to feel that way. She said lately she hasn't been doing too many doubles. She's cut back. That was nice to hear. She needs to spend more time out of the club and create a healthier life for herself.

I did good at the end of the night. The club was busy all night and I enjoyed myself. There wasn't any issues between the girls, as far as I know. We got ready to go home when it was time and had to wait for these customers to leave the bar. For whatever reason, they didn't want to leave. It was crazy.

Then, we get outside and that one short guy who be doing drugs and kept asking me if he could get inside me, got into it with another customer in the parking lot. While my car was warming up, he was threatening to kick the customer in the face because he said something disrespectful to his brother. Which was probably bull crap. He made such a big scene and didn't do not a damn thing. The customer's taxi showed up and he left. Party was over.

February 17, 2014
Good Monday

Monday. Today is a good day. Money has been good and I don't have a bad attitude. One of my regulars came in and took car of me. Biting on my back and crap. My arm still hurts from yesterday. I'm wondering if I should take the next few days off and go back to work Saturday. But what I want to do is work Wednesday then have the next few days off. I'll see how I feel in the next days coming up.

I been trying to take it easy. I'm wearing my glasses so my eyes can get a break from the contacts and breath. It's nine girls here. The stage fees have gone up and when I got here, the DJ had everyone signing a paper saying they are aware and agree to the hikes. Bastards. The other girls who would normally be here aren't. One was suppose to be on her way. She's not here so maybe she changed her mind. I'm happy with this Monday.

I'm still sleepy from last night so I'm thinking about leaving early so I can go home and relax. Tomorrow I have things to do so no work. I also need to buy my plane ticket for Miami! Can't wait!

The thing that shocked me was seeing the guy I know from the motorcycle set come in for the second time. The first time was seeing him Friday. I really didn't care to see him then. I don't know why he was here but I hope he don't start coming. He don't tip nobody. Just sit there drinking beer watching with his big'ol belly. I did not look at him not once. He got on my nerves when I used to talk to him.

I did good. I made my mark and a little extra. I hope the rest of this week can be like today. Or close to it.

Not Like Last Wednesday

Today I actually went to work thinking it was going to be an awesome day like last week. (deep breath) It was nothing like it. The customer population was low all day. No one was tipping for the first five hours. That's what it seemed like. It got to the point that I didn't dance. I just did things to pass under the radar.

I was hanging out by the door when the customer from Florida walked in with his friend. I knew it was going to be a good day then. They are awesome to hang with. I had got Bacardi 151 with pineapple when I was asked if I wanted a drink. That had me feeling a lot happier! We were laughing, joking around, and I stopped trippin off what wasn't happening. I was like, screw these non tipping customers! I'm gonna have fun!

Now, I didn't leave at 6:00 pm. I stayed a little later to make a little more money. And to spend some time with my boo thang. He was off today so he came by to see me. When I was sitting at the bar with him, Hairy walked in. I didn't speak to him because I'm done with that.

As we watched one of the girls begin her next round of dancing, the first thing I noticed was how loaded she looked when she was walking out onto the stage. She almost didn't make it to the pole. It was funny. I watched her walk off stage and over to the bar. She was loaded for sure! Later on, I looked to my right and seen that someone was on the floor. Like they fell. It was her. Two men were standing around her. Looking. I was the only girl who walked over and carried her to the dressing room. She was hurt and wasted. White girl wasted at that. I thought she had some friends that should have came over and helped her, but nope. Just me. I carried her in the back and told one of the girls to move the bag that was on the chair. Sat her down. Her ankle was messed up I think. I'm sure she didn't know it was me helping her. Man. That was crazy.

There wasn't too many girls on the list for the Wet T Shirt contest tonight. I was shocked. But I know a few girls will be happy about that. Them chicks that be coming for that are a pain. I used to be one, but I didn't act or talk like I was better than others.

After I went to the back to put my clothes on then came out to the front, there was a Black dude dressed in a red, feather, pimp outfit. I mean, the long coat to his ankles with the huge hat. I had to stop walking and turn my body so that my back faced him. I couldn't believe there was someone in there dressed like that. And to top it off, the DJ was playing the pimp songs! So dam funny!

Now, I heard something that I didn't know was going on with one of the girls. She was in the dressing room telling one of the girls that she has to be moved out the place she's staying now, because her suppose to be friend don't want her living with her anymore. The friend, which happens to be the same skinny chick that the customer was talking about her holey stockings, claims she don't approve of her lesbian lifestyle. When really she don't like the person she's with.

Now, these two have been friends for years. Over six years. And now you can't support her being with women? I did kind of notice how they weren't talking as much as they did but didn't pay no mind. The friend had her move from Utah to Cali. So she don't have anyone out here. How mad crazy is that?

And to top it off, she's telling the stuff to the customers! How messy is that? Straight hatin. They have to see each other when they come to work at the club and thank God they don't share the same dressing room. I can only imagine. I don't like that she's doing her like that. Putting her out because she's dating a woman, but from what I heard, she wanted to sleep with a female co worker herself. People need to spend more time worrying about their money than other people's business.

I am happy to not be going to work till Saturday. I don't think Thursday and Friday would turn out good for me. I feel there would still be a lot of girls showing up paying that $20 stage fee. I'll stick with the slow days for a while. That way I won't have too many girls causing distractions with the customers.

FEBRUARY 24, 2014
Catching Up On Days

Today is Monday. I have to fill you in on Saturday and Sunday. So here I go.

February 22, 2014

Today was a slow day for the day shift. There was a cool number of girls present. I was doing alright. By the time the day shift was over, I had a solid $60. I told my mom already that I might do a double. My plan was to wait and see how many girls there would be for the night shift. When it came time for it to start, I checked the dressing rooms and didn't see too many girls. So I decided to stay.

The thing that made this night so different, was my little boo thang showing up before the day shift ended. He was trying to see me before I left but when he found out that I was staying for a double, he felt that we could kick it. And we did.

There was a cool number of customers that was there. But no one was really showing interest. Sure, a few might have said something to me while I was walking by, but I wasn't getting too much "love", as they like to call it. I wasn't tripping because I was still making money at the other stages, and my boo thang was tipping me as well.

Things was going pretty good for the night shift. There were a few birthday parties. The night was fairly simple. I think I discussed one guy because he was sitting at the stage with his friends. He had a Corona bottle sitting in front of him. As I was dancing, no one seemed entertained. So I took his beer bottle and took it as far in my mouth as I could. I pushed it back to him and kept dancing. His friends started laughing and I heard someone say, "That's not right." When I was done dancing he told me I could have the beer and he pushed it over to me on the table. I pushed it back and told him I don't drink beer. Then I walked off. I didn't care how he felt.

Now, I did have some extra fun when the shift was over. My boo thang was so worked up from kicking it with me and being teased, that he wanted to have sex. I wasn't chipping in for a room because I really wanted and needed to go home. I couldn't stay out all night. He said it would be okay to go to his dad's place before he get home from the club. I was cool with it.

I think the thing that messed up our time was him getting another drink after I told him I was going to get dressed so we could leave. Why he thought that was a good idea, do not know. While he was finishing his drink I was warming up my car. When he did come out we went to his dad's around the corner. We were able to get to it but right when he was at the big finish, his dad was coming through the front door.

Did I mention his dad has a studio with the bed RIGHT by the front door? Soon as I heard that key in the door, I pushed off that bed and ran for the bathroom. His dad caught him with his pants down and asked him if he was drunk. I know he seen me running for the bathroom but I didn't want him to see me naked from the bottom down.

The part that made it bad was his girlfriend was with him. And she already has issues thinking he's messing around. When I got my pants and stuff on, we went outside to leave and they were standing right outside. I looked at his dad in case he had something he wanted to say to me. He was angry at my boo. I kept walking because I didn't want to hear them talk. He told his dad he would talk to him later. He feels that since he pays rent there, he should be able to have company. I think he was mad about us being on top of his bed.

We left and I dropped him off then went home. I felt bad. I didn't think his dad would come home so soon. But he wasn't tripping too much about being fussed at. He got what he wanted. And so did I.

FEBRUARY 23, 2014

Sunday. I came in for the night shift and was shocked when I found out that it was only four girls for the day shift. I couldn't believe it. I know the girls did hella good. One of them had all her money stuffed in her little purse. She couldn't fit no more inside. And she had me laughing before she left. The girl who she used to be cool with went sour on her.

They used to be roomies but she didn't like her girlfriend, so she asked her to move out. That girl was dancing to this old song. The one she asked to move out was after her. She danced to the same song! I had to laugh. She did that on purpose to piss her off. I liked it.

Things were pretty good. It was still slow. The thing that made me happy, was sitting with a customer early in the shift who was tipping me nicely. It didn't matter that I wasn't getting much tips on stage. I was still making money. And the convo was great.

Now, the thing that was annoying me were the two customers who kept trying to get me to sit with them, but would never come to the stage to tip me. This is my thinking on that situation. How can you expect me to come sit with you, when you're not tipping me on stage? And I know they didn't know this, but I was making good money sitting with who I was sitting with. So why would I jeopardize myself and sit with you, and you haven't showed me any money? No. I will pass.

When it got to midnight, I was starting to get cold. I was already sleepy and hungry. It was still slow. Not anything exciting going on. It reached a point where I told the DJ that I didn't want to dance anymore. I wasn't leaving. I was tired and didn't want to do it anymore.

He must have ran it by the manager that wears button up shirts that exposes his hairy chest. Like, where the Hell are you from? Who is still doing that besides you? Anyway, the DJ ended up calling my name. I came out with my clothes on to tell him I was done dancing. He called me to the booth and told me the manager said not to skip any girls. So I told him to let me go change. I left my long sleeve shirt on, took my pants off, and put my dancing shoes on. Told the DJ to put on something slow. Got on stage.

There was a guy sitting at the stage. I just knew that he would have gotten up and walked away once I started dancing. But he looked like he wanted to watch. So went over to him and danced. He enjoyed himself. When I go off stage the DJ called me back to him to talk. He told me basically, the manager wasn't happy that I hadn't been tipping him when I work on his shift. So he wasn't letting me have my way. He wanted me to dance.

Screw that man. I only been working on his shift for three Sundays. I don't even deal with him. I tell him "hi" and that's it. He get's paid as a manager, gets tips as a bartender, AND gets tipped from the other girls. Every girl who works on his shift do not have to tip him. There was a good twelve girls working and he's so worried about me. He's one of thoses greedy managers and I don't like him. I'm not working Sunday nights no more. I'll do nights when the other manager is working. I'm not dealing with that crap.

I went to the next stages and when I got to the last one, I got a surprise. I thought I was gonna play around on stage cause the place was still dead. Next thing I know, two people had pulled up a seat and sat down. So I started dancing. When I seen the money they had threw on stage, I took that long sleeve shirt off and danced in my bra and panties. I got off stage and flew to the back to put my clothes on. I was tired.

FEBRUARY 24, 2014

Monday. I got to work about ten minutes late. I had a few things to do and ran out of time. It didn't look like there was going to be too many girls working. But of course some showed up late. My little boo was there hanging out for a little. I wore my glasses and was taking it easy. Things got pretty interesting as time went on. It was slow but fun. Eight girls were there. I was the only black girl.

The customers that were there was chill. A group was there that was enjoying the third stage. They were nice. One of them was drunk. I seen him at the bar with one of the Mexican girls. She was sitting on his lap. The other Mexican girl was drunk. To the point that some customers took her wig off and was wearing it. Even when she was dancing I thought she was gonna fall. She didn't look right in what she was wearing. Ewe. Even in the dressing room the girls asked her what she was wearing. Nasty looking.

I did good for a Monday. Wednesday is my next working day. I might work Friday depending on if certain customers bring their friend in for his birthday. That will be fun. I heard last Friday day shift was dead. Oh well. Gotta try to make the best of it. And one of the girl's is being given a birthday party on Friday too. I thought it was last Friday, so it will be nice to be there for her party. I might even go on stage when they take pictures. It would be even better if that one girl I can't stand didn't show up that day. But I know that's not gonna happen.

FEBRUARY 26, 2014
Just The Wednesday I Needed!

When I got to work today for the day shift, I thought the place was going to be dead. The rain moved in so I wasn't too confident about there being a nice number of customers. I knew if anything there would be a few construction workers there because the rain stopped them from working.

One of the girls told me that our customers for the day shift was going to be messed up since they closed the resturant down. I guess they're starting the renovation there first. No one has really told me anything about it. But I guess the people who came to eat decided to stay when they found the joint was closed. We did good for the day shift.

I had got kind of happy when one of the girls was talking about a customer who was sitting at the stage. He was talking to his friend next to him about how the club was suppse to be a strip joint, and the girls weren't showing much of anything. The Mexican girl had on a haulter top with a thong. The Black girl had on a leotard, then the other Mexican girl had a little top on with a thong. While they were dancing, they wasn't showing or trying to show anything.

I knew he'd like my dancing. I be showing! I got on stage and walked over to them licking my lips. I bounced my booty in front of them then turned around and pulled out my pireced nipple and licked it with my pierced tounge. They got a kick out of that. Then I pulled my bikini bottom up so that the front was thin and it looked like they were going to see my private but didn't. Another guy pulled up a seat and sat down. I put my leg up on the table and shook my booty for him. I got the money and gave them a little more of what they wanted to see.

When I went to the next stages, the same guy followed me over and enjoyed my dancing. He was a cute White man. I think I can remember him if he don't cut his beard. And the table of Mexicans! Oh boy!

Right by stage four, were four Mexicans. They were tipping nice but were doing too much. Trying to stick their finger up my butt and trying to lick my nipples. And yes, they were only tipping dollars. They added up, but a dollar at a time for what they were trying to do. They should have been tipping more. It's a shame that the ones who are not trying to feel up on you, will give you more money, than th ones who are tying to violate you. One of them pulled the back of my bottoms down like I was going to the bathroom. I don't know what hey be thinking.

Then my regular came in that likes to bite. He stayed for a cool minute. It wasn't so bad this time with him. He came in around the same time as Hairy. I haven't been seeing him as much lately. Guess he's been busy. I wish he'd stay busy. He didn't say nothing to me and I didn't say nothing to him. I sat at the bar with my biter and he sat a few seats away with another girl. He didn't stay that long. He left like after fifteen or twenty minutes.

And that girl who was wasted and fell last week showed up. I wanted to ask her if she was cool but decided not to. She didn't say nothing to me. I wondered if she remembered that it was me who helped carry her to the dressing room. It didn't really matter. I think she only danced two rounds before she left. I seen her name crossed out on the list and she was gone. Oh well.

When it got closer for the night shift to start, things slowed up. I was going to leave because of the slowing. After talking to one of the girls, I stayed for two hours till traffic went down. I made my stage fee back and a little extra. I had a customer come over to my stage and tip me. Then he asked me to come sit with him at the bar. He was a handsome older man. I liked his hair because it was almost styled like a Mohawk.

While I was sitting with him, my boo thang's boss was sitting next to him. It was funny because, he had called his boss and he told me. I answered the phone and was playing around with him. He didn't know it was me. He thought it was some chick that his boss was with. He didn't show up today because it was raining and he didn't want to get rained on. Get an umbrella fool!

The night shift was slow for the first few hours but I know it will pick up for the girls. I was ready to home. I think I'll come back Friday depending on how I feel. I know it's gonna be a boat load of girls and I'm not in the mood for that. Plus the first of the month is Saturday. It will probably be slow after people take care of their rent and bills.

March 1, 2014

Starting to Get Tired of Friday

Yesterday was Friday and it was okay. The only thing that got was the, no I'm not gonna talk about it.

Anyway, I was sitting at the bar looking at my phone. There were a lot of customers at the club since the resturant was closed. He looked like he was Indian. He came and sat next to me. I saw that he kept looking at me but I didn't turn to face him. My attitude was messed up so I didn't show him attention.

He hd me shocked when he pulled out some money and asked if he could tip me. I stood up so he could put it on me. Then I hugged him and started rubbing on his back to make him feel good. He was the first person I made some money from. I was happy after that.

I wasn't really dancing on the stage. I didn't have that much excitement in me. As I moved to the other stages I didn't dance much. Starting to get tired of dancing for people to watch but for no tips. There was one time I had got to the third stage and was ready to just stand there and watch TV. But I noticed this Black dude behind me waiting for me to start dancing. So I danced for him.

My day didn't get fun till I had some Bacardi 151 with pineapple. That made me happy. It was funny because everyone knows when I've been drinking because I come to life. The DJ was even calling me by my stage name with "151" at the end. I was cool with that.

Then when it was time for the birthday girl to blow out her candles, I was on stage to help shower her with money and take pictures with everyone on stage. It was fun since I like the girl who's birthday it was. And that Ms K chick was not there. I couldn't have been more happier. It was great to not see or hear her.

The day went good. My little boo thang was there. I sat with him for a while. Nothing much happened so it was good. I was feeling good when it was time to leave.

And when I was talking to one of the girls, she told me something hella funny. That Mexican girl that don't dance good was at the bar. She has cheetha print tattoos on her body. I also noticed some on the right side of her forehead. Not the girl I was talking to told me that she used eyeliner to make the prints on the side of her forehead. I busted out laughing. So when she sweats, do she forget and wipe her head and smear the eyeliner? Wow. I just enjoyed it all.

Saturday

So today, is the first of March. Let's see how today goes. So far I got some tips from being on stage. I really thought I wasn't going to so I didn't dance much. Not too many people in here. And I don't feel like talking to anyone. I'm sitting in the dressing room. I might go out there and watch he other girls dance. I feel like I'm loosing my drive with these people. I need to just say, "Screw them all!" and just do my thing. But sometimes it does get to you. And you start to think about how they see and think about you.

The shift is over and I'm at home. The day went really good. We were dancing to two songs one stage. I had people coming up to the stage to watch me dance. I couldn't believe it. They must be getting their tax money back. I wonder how tomorrow will be when I work the day shift. And I bet it's gonna be hella girls working too just because I'm coming back.

One of the sexy customers came in. I was sitting by the door when he walked in and the first thing I saw was his big chest muscles! I had to squeeze them cause they looked so good. I took him by the hand and walked him over to a table to sit and talk. It was fun talking to him. He was there with a co worker.

I stayed in the same outfit the whole shift. I was busy talking to the customer that I wasn't tripping off changing. Tomorrow I want to go early so I can practice a few things on the pole. I saw some tricks online that I want to try. Gotta keep practicing so I can give a good show.

MARCH 2, 2014
A Good Sunday With Tricks

I got to the club early to practice some tricks. There were a few customers there already. Like three. I couldn't let them keep me from my chance at practicing. I went and changed in the back then came out and started trying the moves I had been seeing online. I had the pole to my back. I was holding the pole above my head. Then I kicked my legs back and grabbed the pole with them. I went into a hand stand and moved around a little before climbing down. I can also do the same thing while sitting on the floor. I'm learning how to hold onto the pole with my legs and feet while upside down. I need to build those muscles.

When I got there, Miss Stiffie was on the phone. I think it was with her car insurance people because she told me her car was hit last night. Now if I'm correct, I saw her and one of the managers getting into a customer's car when I was leaving. So I think it happened when she came back. The camera caught what happened but it couldn't show the plates. She was highly upset that she had to pay the deductible from her own pocket. She said her car has been hit five times while it's been parked at the club. Wow. It was the passenger side by the door that was hit. She parks in the back. I be parking in the front. Screw that!

We had nine girls that showed up. There was a nice amount of people that came today. I had charged my MP3 player so I could dance to the music I wanted. The DJ who plays a lot of oldies was there. I did not miss him not one bit.

I didn't talk to too many people today. I did meet a new customer when one of the girls came over and told me he wanted to meet me. Only thing was, she asked me to talk with an accent as if I was from South America. Sure, no problem. Played it off real good for that Black man. I guess he likes that kind of thing, or she wanted him to think I was from there. Hell, I was about to go home soon anyway.

I felt real good today after I knew I could do those few tricks. I now need to do push ups and get my arms stronger, so when I'm upside down, I can do push ups. That will look really cool.

MARCH 3, 2014
Oh Boy What A Monday!

Today was awesome! Like I would have not expected today to be so fun when it was hella dead! There was ten girls that showed up. I was number two on the list for dancing. It started out with I think four or five customers. So I danced to a song from the 80s. Didn't want to work up a sweat anytime soon.

When I was done dancing for the first round, I noticed a guy who was sitting at my stage that had moved to the side by the wall. When the girl he was watching had finished dancing, I decided to go over and sit with him. We talked for a good while.

When the Russian woman got on stage, we were already talking about fake boobs. He asked me if hers were real and I said no. He wanted to go sit and watch her dance because I told him she can make them move up and down by flexing her muscles. He asked me if I would mind if he went over to watch her, I told him "no". Go and enjoy yourself. Have fun. He pushed me some money that he had on the table and told me I was awesome. I wasn't tripping. He want to go watch someone else, go ahead. I am not a warden.

A little earlier when I was sitting at the bar, a Black dude walked in. He went and sat at one of the tables. I didn't think nothing of him. But while I was sitting down chatting with security, he told me it looked like the guy was looking at me, because he's sure he wasn't looking at him. I decided to go see if he would talk with me.

I sprayed on some perfume and went over to him. I had a big smile on my face because I was laughing on the way over. I told the security that I hope he's not one of those Black men that like White women. And here I am going over to talk to him. But things went good. He was welcoming and we had good conversation. He said he used to come often but haven't been to the club in a while. Some of the girls knew him.

When some of the girls were dancing on stage, he'd give me some money to tip them with. It was funny because he asked me if I knew Miss Stiffie. I told him "yes". I also mentioned that she has her good days and bad days. Then he tells me he's friends with her on Facebook. Wow.

There was one time I went to the bathroom and came back to him, she was giving him a mild lap dance. I wasn't trippin. I just sat down in the chair. She tried to have me sit on his lap but I told her to go ahead and have fun. I wasn't worried about that. He had bought me a few drinks and I was happy sitting down drinking them. Then that's when one of the girls I'm cool with came over to talk.

She was having problems with her girlfriend and was taking it pretty hard. She was confiding in her about some things from her past and her girlfriend judged her and made hurtful comments. She was crying and very emotional because she really loved her. I told her that she let her know she is not the one. The guy I was talking with was buying drinks. So yeah. She got drunk. FAST! I was drunk too, but you know I can hold and deal with my liquor.

She know I don't like chicks. But he was talking about how she would do me. I told her I would go with her to a gay bar or club just to comfort her and give her a chance to meet some new people. Then I explained to her not to get crazy with me because I'm in there with her. She said that she might try to kiss me. The guy got excited and bought her another drink. Actually he was buying her shots. He didn't know at first that she was talking about a girl. So when I told him she was talking about a girl she was having relational problems with, he kind of got excited.

Now when she went to dance after all those shots, she couldn't properly do the upside move she normally does. She still did it just not how she always do it. She was real upset. I hated to see her like that. The guy was just taking it all in. Trying to comfort her. How nice of him.

Then my little boo thang showed up. It was funny because he was at the bar where the guy was sitting. The guy was getting ready to leave and wanted my number, but I didn't want my boo thang to see me giving him my number. Plus he had one of the girls sitting on his lap. So I didn't feel bad. I was just laughing as I talked with my customer.

When I was at my last round of dancing, this Indian guy was trying to talk me into having sex with him. I turned him down. I'm not there for that. I was tired and ready to go home. I did not want to have sex with him. No way.

Then Hairy showed up. He was actually trying to chat with me today. He was in th DJ booth when I was giving her the song I want to dance to. He thinks I'm mad at him. I told him I wasn't mad the last time. When I went to the next stage, he came over. I was shocked. Still didn't talk to him.

It was a good day for me. I was irritated when the Indian guy followed me outside and was still trying to talk me into sex while I was in my car. I didn't even let it warm up. I drove off just to get away from him. My boo had already left so he wasn't around. Tomorrow I'm working the night shift and I'm kind of not looking forward to it. I might not go depending on how I feel.

MARCH 5, 2014
It Went Down Last Night!

I went to work Tuesday night and it was awesome. I get there and it was a lot of people inside. Not a whole lot but it was looking good. One of the security guards told me it was Fat Tuesday, and we were allowed to flash the customers and not get in trouble. Great. Awesome. I like that. The customers were walking around with bead for the girls. Some had beads.

I got dressed and was wearing my blue and black dress with the black fish net stockings. I looked so good. A lot of the customers loved it. When I walked out I saw a customer I had talked to a while ago. He was sitting by the second stage watching the show. I talked to him for while.

Then I seen another customer I talked with before. I was having a good conversation with him. I was having a few drinks and enjoying myself. A great time. There were a few dudes that was in the back throwing money around. They looked white, maybe Mexican. And the only girls they had sitting with them were the White girls.

Of course I didn't bother to go over to them. Some of the other black girls went over and tried to make some money but it didn't, look like they were making it rain on them like they were with the White chicks. So that was a waste of their time. They looked stupid standing near the wall watching the dudes throw money at the White chicks while they danced on stage. They looked kind of lonely, and sad.

Now, remember the Black girl I told you who has a gap and her sides make her look like she bald? And she's the same one who showed her boob to the heavy set girl when she wasn't showing anything to the guy who was spending hundreds on her? Okay. I was sitting at the bar waiting for my name to be called for the last dance of the night. This White guy came and sat next to me and started talking. He tipped me then asked if I knew a such an such. I told him yes. He asked me to give her $5 because he knew she was in the back and he was getting ready to leave. I took the money and went to her dressing room to give it to her.

She was talking on the phone when I walked in. I handed the money to her and whispered, "A customer wanted me to give this to you." She had a dirty look on her face and didn't want to take it. I told her which customer it was and she got mad. "He told me he was going outside for a smoke and he comes back in to give me $5? Oh Hell no!"

I was shocked that she felt that way. I would be VERY happy with a $5 tip from a customer that did not have to tip me. He could of easily walked outside, smoked, then said "F#ck that b*tch", and left. She finally took the money then told me, "Next time someone give you some money to give to me and it's not a $20, put that sh&t in your pocket." She is a terrible person. Whatever I get that is more than $1 will be appreciated and added to the pot. She trippin.

When it was my last dance, I got on stage and danced. There was a couple there that liked my dancing so they were sitting at the table watching. I was very proud of myself because I did my shoulder hold while standing up, and I left my feet come back down to the floor slowly and gracefully. I was happy I did it like that. Makes me want to practice more to get better.

One of the new girls got chewed out in the dressing room because she said something that offened one of the other girls who been working at the club. Before my last dance, they called all of us girls to the stage to dance together. We made a lot of money. The one girl went to the dressing room with another girl to count the money. Everyone was trying to be in the room and it was getting hot. I was in my dressing room cause I knew it was going to get hot.

The girl made a statement that everyone does not have to be in the room because it's two people counting the money and the room will be getting hot. One of the new girls took it hard and left out talking smack. The waitress, who was off that night but showed up to have some fun, heard her and came back to find out what had happened. When the other girl had a chance to confront her about what she said, she did it in the dressing room while we were getting dressed. They exchanged words and left it alone. I was like wow.

I went out to my car to warm it up. While I'm sitting there, I see one of the girls I'm cool with come outside without her things. She was followed by her friend. They were looking for that one White girl who be talking bad about other girls and be disrespecting them. She has a problem with that. She got choked out by one Black girl because she kept saying "Nigga nigga nigga." Stop being disrespectful when a person tells you they don't like you saying that.

The girl had walked over to the other side of the parking lot looking for the disrespectful chick. One of the new girls had just got into a car that had pulled up. I drove around to the other side of the parking lot watching the other girl because she was pissed about what the other chick said about her.

Oh. My. Gosh. When she seen that little White girl in the front seat of the car that the other girl had just got into, she ran up to it to keep the guy from driving off. She hurried to the other side to open th passenger door, and she grabbed her by BOTH sides of her hair and snatched her out that car. Funny part was, she still had the seat belt on her. She was screaming when her hair got pulled with such force.

What I don't understand is, if you just got done talking mess about that person, how do you ask them, "What did I do to you?" when they kicking your a$$? Then she yelled to the driver, "I told your dumb as# to keep driving!" So you knew it was about to go down. Trying to play the victim.

Two security guards were there trying to get her to let go of her hair. That did not happen for a good two minutes almost. It was fun to watch. I finally got to see an incident happen! When she did let go of her hair she jumped back in that car so fast. Don't write a check your as* can't cash. I wonder if she will be back to work? Because the other girl will be waiting to see her again. I don't know what she said about her, but I heard she was talking about and laughing at her. She had no reason to do that because the girl she was talking about don't both or talk about people.

Looks like I won't be back to work till Saturday. I want to rest and do a few things. And I don't want to see all those girls on Thursday and Friday. I kind of want to work Friday but I think I might pass. Take a little break. I need to work on my stretches.

March 8, 2014
Saturday of Weird

This Saturday was different. As I get into detail you know why. The day started off good. There were a few customers there and they were tipping. We dance to two songs, one stage. Not enough customers there to dance on two stages.

The DJ had some Chinese food brought to the club. I don't eat none of the noodles or spare ribs. I stick with what I know, and it was the fried rice. Then later one of the regulars came in and he brought more Chinese food in. I had some of the beef and broccoli and more rice. Didn't want any of that other stuff he had either.

Now this is the customer I said Miss Stiffie be trying to keep to herself and has attitudes when other girls come around him. Well guess what happened today? Today when he came the other girl he likes was there talking to him. They both were standing next to him. He offered to buy me a drink and I accepted. I wanted to hang around but didn't want to look at Miss Stiffie's face. She has this fake a$$ smile she wears that screams, "I hate you!"

I took the drink he got me and stepped away a little so that she wouldn't get too offended. He looked like he was trying to talk to me, but his two girls were standing with him. They were talking and enjoying his company the best they could. Miss Stiffie was walking away every now and then to talk to other customers. I know she hated that.

The day went pretty good. I had a nice time and wasn't bothered by anyone. I made my money and was happy. I was in the dressing room counting my money when the other girl for that one customer came in and told me that Miss Stiffie is going to be cut off by that customer. She done messed around and told that man that she loves him and don't want no other girls around him because she wants to be the only one getting his money. I was shocked! Didn't she learn from the last time he told her he is single, and likes to talk to the other girls? So now that she's cut off what is she going to do? And that man was taking her places. She messed it up!

Now it was the last round of dancing. My little boo thang was there playing pool with one of his friends. He wanted to see my new trick so I waited till I was at the next stage to do it. Miss Stiffie was dancing on the main stage. I had one customer sitting at my stage. I did my trick when I pull up on the pole with my shoulder against it and wrap my legs around the top. After I did it, I didn't have people running up to the stage. They kept sitting down. I wasn't even paying attention to the customers. I was busy dancing.

Before the song was over, it just stopped. I looked up because I was laying on my back with my legs in the air. I got up, collected my money, and left the stage. I was going to go to the other stage but didn't feel like it. It was an option. When I got to the dressing room I sat in the chair by the door to count my money before getting dressed. I didn't know Miss Stiffie was in there till she started talking to me. She told me she was sorry but she can't dance after me.

When she first said it I didn't get it and didn't care. Then she said, "With the things that you do, I can't dance after you. I love you, but I can't dance after you." I told her okay, I understand. Went back to counting my money. So from my understanding, she felt people were watching me dance more than they were watching her. So now she has an issue because she's not gonna want to be after me on the list, just like she don't want to be after that other girl. I don't know how the DJ is going to do the list now, but I'm not stopping or changing my sh*t for NO ONE. I'm working on stepping my game up for a reason. And I like it.

I think she was having a bad day after that one customer had a talk with her. You have to learn to share. That man is not coming there to be cuffed by her old ass. He likes the young girls. He was being nice to her and she messed it up.

Then a few minutes later, she starts telling me about a lady she was dealing with over Ebay. She was arguing with her about an item she had sold to her and the lady decided she wanted to return the item. She went as far as saying her famous line: "I hope you die, b!tch." I don't understand why she's like that. I don't be feeling like that with people. That is way too serious! God forgive her soul if she ever gets sick. Something is seriously wrong

Tomorrow, I'm going to work Sunday day shift. I have no idea how that's going to go. I just hope it's a busy day and I make my $100 or more. And I also hope there isn't a lot of girls there. And that dam oldies playing DJ. Oh boy I hope tomorrow goes by fast!

MARCH 9, 2014
Go By Fast Sunday Shift

I'm here at the club. Early. Not too many girls here yet but there's still time. When I walked into the dressing room, Miss Stiffie was talking with one of the other girls who's older like her. (I guess then that would make her a woman instead) They were talking about the remodeling of the club.

Stiffie was saying how they were going to close down certain sections of the dressing rooms to remodel. The other woman mentioned the possibility of them making one big dressing room. Hell no! There are certain chicks I do not want to be bothered looking at. I don't want to be around. And the same with the other girls. They feel the same way. I'll really start looking for another place to work. And when they shut the place down to remodel, I might just wait it out depending on how long the shut down will be. I might go somewhere else and not want to come back! Who knows.

The DJ is here playing oldies. Last week one of his CDs he was using started skipping. Then another one was skipping. With the same girl. This man announces over the mic, "Hold on everybody, let me clean the CD." I know the customers were looking around like, "What the Hell did he just say?" Yeah this old head is funny.

The day went good. I didn't hit my mark but that's okay. I did my trick a few times today. I even tried to pull and push myself up the pole while I was upside down. Yeah. I need to work on it more and build arm muscle. Guess I'll start hitting them push ups.

There was one time while I was sitting with a customer who comes to the club with Miss Stiffie's favorite customer, the older Black guy who's getting ready to cut her loose, and she was getting ready to walk away from him. She leaned over to give him a kiss on the cheek and I heard him tell her, "Now what I told you about that? Don't be kissing and hugging on me. You don't have to do all that." I started laughing to myself. She really trying to put some work on that man. I don't know if he told her yet but I don't care anymore.

I was the last girl to dance for the day shift. When I went to the dressing room, there were a lot of girls getting ready to work for night shift. We only had nine girls for day. I'm glad about that. I'm happy I left and if felt good to walk out of there and know the manager I don't like anymore was watching. Yeah, I'm not working your night shift anymore you greedy bastard.

Hairy came by. He came the past two days now that I think about it. I saw him talking to the new Mexican girl that started Saturday. I know he was probably trying to work his way into her pants. I just waved at him and kept going. I don't care to talk to him anymore. Someone else can be bothered with him.

Now tomorrow, Monday, let's see how that day goes. I'm going to take it easy. I will enjoy laughing at that one girl who can't dance to save her life. And I really be cracking up when she starts to fan herself. You hot? But you wasn't doing nothing! Omg!

March 10, 2014
Slow Monday

Today is real slow. A lot of the girls have been talking about how the changes are hurting business. The restaurant has been closed for three weeks. The lunch people got the hint that it's going to be closed for a while. No work for remodeling has started in the kitchen. No news of a new cook being hired either. So exactly what are they doing?

Whatever stupid person or people that's in charge don't know what the Hell they are doing. They are loosing more business trying to remodel than they will probably get after everything is done. This place is starting to get on my nerves with the new owners.

I hurt my right arm doing my half trick. Maybe I need to stretch my arms before I start dancing. See if that will help. It hurts between my elbow and shoulder. That part. It hurts after I pull up on the pole to do a trick. Maybe I'm doing it wrong. I hate when I hurt it cause then I can't do my tricks no more because of the pain.

I'm sitting in the dressing room because there isn't too many customers to talk to. A few Mexicans. Then the other girls are talking with customers. I'm just ready to go to sleep. I'm sleepy.

MARCH 11, 2014

Slow Tuesday

Tuesday. Night shift. Very slow. Not happy. Only Black girl on shift. Not an advantage tonight.

When I got here, I was told that the day was slow. Not too many customers were in the club. I don't know how many girls were on day shift. One girl that I'm cool with told me she only made $20. Dam. And stage fee is $10 for day shift. I got dressed and went to hang outside on the floor. There were two Hispanics that I spend time with when they come. They're cool. I talked with them for a little while.

When I got on stage I got no love. All the White girls were getting tipped by the White customers. Me. Nothing. I realized fast how this night was going to go. Yep. Hella dead and slow. I did have one customer that I met last week that came in and spent time with me. Then there was a cute Mexican who came to my stage twice. I think I'm doing better than most of the girls working tonight. One girl said she has $60 and I know I have over $80. There's still a good hour left before closing. Who knows.

Then, I was having a stroke because when I came to the dressing room to change into a red outfit, I couldn't find my shoes in my bag. I was panicking. I left them from the last time I worked. Probably Sunday cause I didn't remember seeing them Monday. Long story short, I was in the dressing room and felt like I was being watched from the corner. When I gave in, I reached over, moved the clothes that were bunched in the corner, and seen the bright red shoes! I could of cried. I'm the only person with these shoes. I was so ready to buy new ones online. No joke.

That White girl who got them hands put on her for talking about that one girl last week showed up. I was shocked when I heard her name called. She looked real quiet. And the funny thing was, she is after the girl who almost made her bald! And to add, my first dance, I dedicated my song to the girl who snatched her out the car. She was in the dressing room laughing. It was that 2Pac song, "Hit'em up". Yeah I did it.

Well, this is how the night went. It ended good. I made my minimum back. And the cute Mexican stayed till his friends made him leave. He was really enjoying my company. But this fool was talking crazy. He wants to have his own strip club and have about ten or twelve girls working for him. And he want them to give him some of the money they earned from tips so that he can put it away, so in ten years, they will have their own house.

Now I know he was drunk, but that is still a form of pimping. And if he thinks that I would ever "work" for him, he can go choke on something. He thinks it's a good idea and yeah, it will work for him because there are dumb females out there that will fall for that talk.

I was talking with the customer who came to see me and he almost go cussed out. I don't like when people ask me what do I like to do. I do not want to go down the list. I tell them I'm out going and that should settle it. He asked me what do I like sexually and I didn't want to talk and it. The fact that my period is about to start made we want to avoid all sexual conversations.

He asked me about kissing and I told him I don't like to kiss. That fool told me, "That's a turn off." So. I don't like the feeling of someone's tongue in my mouth. Especially if they have stinky breath. I don't even like them to kiss me on my lips. Some people turn me off with all that kissing. Then when their dam breath dries up, you can smell it on your lips. Ewe.

When we closed there was no fights. Now, one of the White girls fell off the stage and I missed it! She was drunk and that's why she fell. I don't know where I was but I heard about it when we were all waiting to leave. I think what happened was she fell after she was done dancing. Right down the stairs. Man I wish I could of seen it.

A few girls had a bad night. One told me that she took day classes and changed her schedule so that she can work at night. And things have not been going good for her. I told her, I miss when I could walk out of the club with two or $300. It's just March but DAM! She has rent and bills. She's been stressing and worrying. I feel what she feels.

MARCH 12, 2014
Shaking My Head. . . .

I don't know what it is. I got my hair done Tuesday. My nails are done. I smell good. Look good. I don't think I look hella mean when I'm dancing or walking around on the floor. Today is like yesterday. I get on the stage on no tips. So it got to the point where I don't put any effort into dancing because it's not worth it.

At the beginning of the shift, my regular, the Biter, showed up. I was happy to see him till I remembered he bites. But I was happy to see him. I sat with him for a while and talked. He came looking for me yesterday and I told him I don't do the day shift on Tuesdays. It was funny because I walked away to change my clothes and another girl was sitting with him when I came out the dressing room. So I went and sat by the front door and played a pool game on my phone. He came and sat in the area to let me know he was free and wanted me to come over. Feels nice to be wanted.

There hasn't been too many customers in here. I been spending more time in the dressing room. Miss Stiffie was telling me that she's been hearing that the owners plan on firing her because of her age. Well dam. How old are you? She said that anyone over forty was getting let go. Wow. We need to have that variety for the different customers that come in here.

About two hours before the end of the shift a few more customers came in. It was still slow. I had sat by the front door for a little and got scared when this ugly chick walked in. She looked like Freddy Krueger in the face. Dark spots all over her face. Nasty looking. Her hair was messed up like it been time to take her braids down. And she looked pregnant. She walked in upset and security stopped her from walking in.

She said she was looking for her baby daddy. Since she didn't have her ID, he couldn't let her in to look around for him. So he went to look for him and didn't see him. She looked even more upset that he wasn't in there. When she walked out, I told security, "I see why he would be in here!" She was hurt in a very bad way. Fell off the ugly tree hard.

After my last dance I got dressed and went home. I was tired and ready to relax. I told the DJ I would be back Saturday. She looked at me like, "Saturday?" YES! I been working since last Saturday. I need a break to do some things. Maybe next week I'll work Thursday and Friday and see if things will be better for me. I'll do that.

Middle of the Month

Well, I'm here at the club for the day shift. That one Mexican who gets on my nerves when he drinks is sitting at the bar. I seen him when I went out to get a napkin to wipe my lips and put on my lip gloss. I acted like I didn't see him. But when I was walking to the bathroom to brush my teeth, I had to look at him as I walked by. I am not messin with him today. And he already has half his pitcher drunk up. I hope another customer I know comes in so I can sit with them instead.

That Mexican girl I told you that can't dance for sh&t probably didn't like what I said about her but I had to grab the bull by the horns. Her friend was telling me about something that happened with another girl. Then she got to talking about how the Mexican girl can't dance. She looked at her like what she said wasn't true. I threw my hand in the air and said, "I second that." Yes you cannot dance. And since she said it first I'm saying it second. And it was to your face so you had your chance to say something to me about it if you didn't like it. No, she didn't.

So. Luckily I wasn't bothered by dude. I walked out and sat with security. Shortly later I had to get on stage to dance and he came up to sit and watch me dance. When I was done with main stage I went to the next stage just to not have to deal with him. There was another girl he liked and he was talking to her. Thank you God.

People started coming in around two, three o'clock. I was shocked. This one dude came and sat at my last stage. I went and sat with him and was completely discussed. This man kept digging in his nose the whole time I was talking to him. I wanted to just get up, walk away, and never come back to him. I mean, if you really had a problem inside your nose, why not go to the bathroom and dig that sucker out to be rid of it? He kept digging then touching my leg warmers and legs.

When I couldn't take it anymore, I told him I had to go tell security something. I went to the bathroom and wiped my body with my alcohol towel where he had been touching me. I felt so much better. I decided to go back and sit with him till I couldn't take anymore because he was tipping me good. By the time I went back to him, He had stopped digging in his nose. I was happy. Maybe he had finally got it out.

Then my little boo thang showed up and sat at the table right next to me and the Booger Man. When the guy started talking to his friend, I moved over and sat with my boo.

The day been going good so far. I'm doing night shift now. A double for the day. It's 10:38 pm. I was sitting at a table with a bunch of Hispanic males for a while. They tipped me better when I was sitting with them, than when I was on stage. It was about six of them. They were tipping all the other girls when they came to the stage next to the table, but when it was my turn by the table, only two came over and only one tipped me $3. What the Hell? When I was done dancing, I didn't go back over to them. But that's how they do.

Then Hairy was here. Looking at me. I just ignored him because I wasn't in the mood to play nice. He had been watching me while I was sitting with a Mexican who had tipped me nice and was kept kissing me on the side of my cheek. Then he was trying to stick his finger in my butt and I think he even smelled it. Weird.

And you know what? That dam Ms. K is working tonight! She is a waitress! Why is she here? If she is working Saturday nights now, OMG. She hasn't been getting on my nerves tonight. But just to see or hear her. Ugh.

I am soo tired and sleepy right now. I don't want to go back out to the floor unless I have to dance. I'm ready to go to sleep. I asked the manager if I could leave at midnight. I can't make it past midnight. I didn't sleep good last night because my nephew was leaving in the middle of the night to go out of town, and he kept making so much noise. I kind of thought he was doing it on purpose because it didn't make sense for him to make that much noise. Hell, I might not come in tomorrow for the day shift. I might stay home and sleep the morning away then twist my son's dreads.

MARCH 16, 2014
No Expectations Sunday

Last night felt terrible. Mainly because I was so tired. I didn't even do as good as I used to do when I do a double on Saturdays. Made me feel like I don't want to work a double till the summer hits. Get past all this tax crap.

The manager let me leave at midnight. I was very happy and relieved. I didn't even tip the DJ. It seems like since I stopped working Sunday nights his attitude has changed. It had nothing to do with him so I don't know why he would act funny. Oh well. Next!

I still didn't sleep good when I got home. I guess when I get home tonight I'll pass out. I will try to put some effort into working today but I know I'll be more annoyed than anything. Then the old DJ will be playing 80s all dam day. It would be sweet if he didn't show up for work today and we had someone else. I won't hold my breath for that.

And my period has started. Now I have to work and worry about that. Why couldn't it start at the end of my working days? Why start at the beginning? Oh well. As long as I don't have to deal with it while in Miami. Hopefully I won't.

Today was good. It was slow as Hell but I was shocked by the attention I received. I arrived late because I had a hard time waking up. Then I had to got my nails done. I got there, got ready, did my little dance, and was making a little money.

One guy came over and talked to me at the bar. He remember me from the last time he came and I was wearing my purple outfit with the white boots. We talked for a while. He was cool.

Then we were laughing at the dam DJ. This one girl was dancing to a song she was playing through her phone. He stopped the music, or should I say, he cut it off before the song was over. She got pissed. Then there was another time a girl was dancing on stage to some old crap, and the fool said over the mic that the song was his favorite. Then it cut off like something was wrong. Dam shame. Always cutting the music off early.

Security explained to me how it works in the customer's mind when they tip you more while sitting with them, versus when you get on stage. I had never thought about it the way he explained. When you're sitting with them they tip you to keep you sittin with them. I mean, I been got that part. But they feel they tipped you enough by the time you gt on stage, and they're trying to plot out their money for other girls. The way them fools were talking, they had thousands of dollars in their pockets!

I wore my glasses today. I didn't feel like putting on my contacts. I really didn't feel like doing anything, but I made it through the day. The day seemed to go by fast too. And the greedy DJ from last had the nerve to tell me about leaving early and not telling him, then mentioned the fact that I didn't tip him. Jackass. I tell you about some people. All the girls that worked last night, over fifteen, you would think he'd be satisfied with their tips.

March 17, 2014
St Patty Day!

Monday. I was expecting it to be a slow day. I went to work with my glasses on and wearing a large, white t-shirt with jeans. I took my time getting dressed since I was early. I was trying to watch the news to find out what happened to that plane that went missing. When it was time to start the show there were only a few customers there.

I was happy today and feeling good. Maybe it was me finally having a good night sleep. It sure wasn't the fact that I was on my period. Or it was the motivational speech I gave myself. Yeah, it was that.

After taking the time to think about this past weekend and some of the other past weekends, I felt that I should have done better and I should have put forth a lot more effort. I told myself, when someone asks you if you like what you do, you don't tell them yes. You tell them you love it. So act like it. Even if things aren't going good. Act like it is and still put on a show. Don't get on stage and look like it's the end of the world.

I wore my black boots to start off. I had on a green necklace that I tied up so it would be on my neck like a choker and not fly around and slap me as I'm dancing. It looked cute. I danced like the good mood I was in and enjoyed myself. I didn't worry about nothing but dancing and getting ready for Miami. Might as well practice and get up on my skills.

I had took a seat at one of the tables because I was going to play pool on my phone till it was time for me to dance again. The bald headed, white guy who's a lawyer that I had stopped talking to came and asked me to come sit with him. I got back up and went to the bar with him. We talked till I had to go to dance. It was nice talking to him again.

I had a situation as I was walking to the stage. My tampon was soaked and leaking. I told the DJ I need her to call the other girl so I could fix myself up. I had to change tampons and wash my bottom. Yes, I still wanted to wear it. I hand washed it in the bathroom and put it on. Just the middle part was wet and it felt so good!

When I had finished dancing I want and sat with my Mexican regular. He had came in while I was sitting with the other guy. I tried a new vodka today that I never had before. It was cherry flavored and awesome. That was drink three for me. I felt good.

Then before I had to go on stage again, the girl who's having problems with her girlfriend wanted to talk to me. She decided to go to Miami because the girl told her to not be considerate about her feelings. She should just go to Miami and think about herself. I see that as a nice way of her saying, "You don't know this, but things are about to change between us." She wants to get her ticket to go.

Now this is what I don't get. If you know that you have stuff to do or want to do, why would you not be productive and go to work to make that money? She didn't show up to work Saturday or Sunday. That is two days she could have been making money. Money to save or put towards something. Now that fool tells her that and is still dealing with her exes. What is she thinking? I would have been coming to work everyday and doing doubles to get my money up to get my stuff together, and leave her. That doesn't sound like a good idea?

Anyway, Things got funny when I had walked away from the old guy I was talking to to use the bathroom. As I was on my way back to him, I met eyes with a light skinned guy at the bar. He was staring into my eyes as I was walking then stuck his arm out to lead me into him. I sat down and talked to him till I had to dance. When I was done with the second stage and was moving to the last, I decided to leave my drink with him so I didn't have to carry it around with me.

When I walked over to him to sit the drink down, I noticed that Miss Stiffie was on the other side of him. He had his back to her but it looked like she was talking to him still. I sat it down and told him I'm leaving it there. Then I walked away to the last stage. When I came back he told me that he was happy I did what I did. When she seen me put my drink down, she told him, "I guess you're busy." He told her he was and she walked away. I just didn't want to carry my drink around anymore!

A while ago when she was having car problems, she asked him to help her out and give her a ride home. He stayed and waited for her over an hour. When it was around the time she said she would be ready to leave, he called her on the phone. When she answered the phone, she told him she was almost home. That man was pissed. And she never said she was sorry.

He went on to tell me that she slept with a lot of guys who were on some football team. One guy she slept with, she went back to the club and told everybody. They guy stopped messin with her after that. He even said that she is clingy. I wanted to tell him so bad about that one customer who's about to cut her off but I felt it would be best to not talk about it. He was doing enough himself.

March 18, 2014

Looks Slow To Us

Yes, this Tuesday night will be slow. It was slow when I walked in at 5:40 pm. Dead. I was lucky to make my $20 stage fee back on my first dance. This White guy came to the stage to watch me and tipped me over $20. I was shocked. I could tell that he wanted to talk to me when I first went out to the floor and sat at the bar.

I tried to talk to some customers. Two of them. One was a White guy that was sitting at the bar by himself. I asked him if he would like some company and he said yes. But then he acted like he didn't want to talk to me when one of the girls walked up trying to get a shot from the bartender. He had his back turned to me so I walked off. I know what that shit means. He was waiting for her to talk to him.

I went over to this guy who just came in. He had his beer and was sitting on the other side of the bar. I walked over and asked him if he wanted some company and he shook his head no. So I told him to enjoy his night and he asked me my name in Spanish. Yeah, I walked away. If he's speaking to me in Spanish when I spoke to him in English, it was not even gonna work. I walked around for a little bit then went in the dressing room.

Some more customers have come in but it doesn't look like it will be that exciting till maybe later. I still feel good but might sink back into my "I don't care about dancing" attitude. I know not to expect too much from tonight.

Then that Indian guy came in and one of the girls almost broke her ankles running over to him. She danced to some Indian music and he put money on the stage. Then two more girls did the same thing. I don't think so. I don't mind some Indian music but I'm not dancing to it.

Now. This is what I can't stand. A group of Black dudes came in. When it was time for me to dance, not one freaking dollar was thrown. Them assholes came to recruit girls for prostitution. That was so annoying. When I was done dancing, my little boo thang showed up. I played pool with him at the table and that's when the bastards wanted to look at me.

Them one of the jerks came over and wanted to talk to me. He really thought that I would be interested in going to Vegas so that "we" could make better money. I hate it to Hell when dudes say that. I'm happy with the money I'm making on my own, by myself, without you. Get out my face!

The night ended good and I was happy. I was tired and ready to go home. Boo thang wanted to get a room but I was not feeling it. I'm on my monthly and don't want to be bothered. Plus I have to keep some distance between us because I don't want any attachment. And that's what he's getting.

March 19, 2014
Terrible Wednesday

I got to work ready to see how the day was going to go. I was the first girl on the list to dance. There were three customers there. Eleven girls. It didn't get any better. I made a little money but the customers were not feeling me. There was not anyone that I wanted to talk to. I spent most of the time in the dressing room.

And you know what happened? There were two older Hispanics sitting at the table watching girls dance. I don't know how much they were tipping everybody else. When it was my time to dance, they were talking to each other so much they didn't pay me any attention. I just danced on the other side of the stage away from them. When I was done dancing it looked like they had put a dollar each on the table. I walked off the stage not picking up the money. I didn't like how they sat there talking to each other then tipped me a dollar. How rude. Then they looked at me as if to say, "You're forgetting your money." Keep that crap punks.

I hope that Saturday is much better. I can't wait for the summer. Maybe things will be better then.

MARCH 22, 2014

Two Bulls. One Pen.

When I got to work today I was a little late. I had clothes to wash and food to get for my kids before going to work. I was about ten minutes late but I got ready quick. There was a nice number of people in the club when we started. Around eight. I was sitting by the door talking with security till it was my turn to dance.

I was feeling good today so I got out there and danced like I was in a good mood. The first thing I noticed was when this short, Black dude came to sit at my stage. I was shocked. I seen when he came in but didn't expect him to sit down and tip. I went and talked to him after a while. He was sitting at the bar with his Mexican friend. I think he was on something because of how he was acting. And I know he was upsetting the girls because he would whistle, hollar, and stand at the stage watching them dance, but he wasn't tipping.

I think it was my third round dancing, I went over to the Black dude who had moved to the pool table. I played a game with him, just for amusement. While I was playing him, my boo thang came in with a friend. They came and played pool at the table next to us. It didn't bother me at all.

Now, what DID bother me was when the short dude, who is from Atlanta, wanted to get my phone number before he had to leave. I didn't want to exchange numbers in front of the boo thang. I told the guy that I'd rather get to know him first. Even though he said he's out here for eight months because of his job, I don't want to get too comfortable with him.

It got to the point were I was talking to short dude at the bar, and boo thang came over to talk and cuddle on me. I wanted to push his behind to the floor! Why are you over here?! Go play pool or talk to yo boy. Short dude was just sitting there like, "Dam. I was talking to her." I had got up and walked away because he was really starting to annoy me. He followed behind as I walked away.

We were standing by the DJ booth when short dude came over and asked him if he could have a minute with me. Why did boo thang push him back with his arm, to block him from me, then told him, "No, you gonna have to give me a minute. Unless you tipping her you can wait!"

He was putting money in my bottoms when dude walked up. I was just hoping that things didn't turn into a fight. OMG.

When he was done puttin the money on me, he said a few things to me then walked away. Short dude really wanted to talk to me more. And he was tippin me when I was on stage. And he bought me a drink. I was happy with him. He was cool and I enjoyed our conversation.

When I came out the dressing room to go home, I went to the bar to turn in my ones. I was talking to one of my favorite customers. Boo thang ran up behind me trying to take my bag so he could carry it to the car. I wanted him to wait because I knew he was putting on a show for the short dude.

I had to talk to him outside about something he told me inside. I couldn't really talk to him because one of the girls that was just getting there called him over to help he carry something in. While he was doing that, short dude came outside and was talking to me. I hoped that boo thang didn't come over talking mess. He didn't. He carried what looked like a pet carrier inside for her.

Another one of the girls was leaving. Two dudes were with her. Short dude seen how she was getting inside of a Cadillac truck. He told me that he wasn't tipping her anymore because she has money. I looked and felt like, if she ain't driving it, it ain't hers. But he still felt like he wasn't gonna tip her anymore.

After he left boo thang came back and I told him what I had on my mind. While we were still inside, h told me that he was gonna be spending more time in my city to be closer to me. I didn't like hearing that. I'm not trying to spend time with that man like that. And when I'm at home, that's time for me to be with my kids. Not time to be with him. I had to explain to him that I don't want him doing that and to leave the door open in case he takes a liking to someone else. Cause if I find someone I like more, it's curtains for him.

At the beginning of the shift, one of the girls who I haven't seen in weeks was there. She went to working on Thursdays and Fridays. I asked her where she been and she said she got a job that starts at the end of the month. She cleaned out her trunk because soon she won't be working any at the club any more. I guess some of the other girls will be getting jobs as well. We shall see.

I was disappointed because the girl who needs money hasn't been coming to work. She didn't show up today and I wonder if she will show up Sunday. People like that, you can't help them unless they want to help themselves. And she's too worried about her troubled relationship with that chick.

March 24, 2014
Sunday Sunday

Yesterday was pretty cool. It was slow but it didn't feel like it. There were two guys that I sat and talked with for a while that made a difference. It was funny talking to them. One of them had ordered more beer then asked me if we were aloud to drink while working. I told him yes and the other guy was like, "Yeah cause that one girl with the big tits looks wasted." He was talking about Miss Stiffie. I just turned my head to the side and said, "I wanna change the subject."

I wasn't paying attention to her all day while she danced on stage. I don't think she had been drinking myself. I think they were talking about how she was dancing. I just didn't want to talk about her like that. I have noticed that a few customers talk bad about her, and I don't even be starting the conversation off like that. That's why I try to stay good with customers so they don't talk bad about me like that with other people.

One girl came to work with ten inch heels. I couldn't wait to see how she dance in them. She did real good. There was one point when she was walking to the pole and her right ankle twisted to the side and she almost went down, but she was close enough to the pole to grab it in time. I don't want heels that high. Seven is high enough for me. I move around too fast to be in anything higher than seven.

I think it was my last round of dancing, boo thang showed up. I was on the main stage dancing when he walked in. I was happy it was towards the end. He's always there even when I'm not there. One of the girls I'm cool with told me that he came in Friday, then the next day he was still wearing the same clothes. I don't like mess like that. That's why I don't like his situation. How does that make me look for being with someone like that? Stuff like that bothers me. No thank you.

I asked the manager if I could leave early since I was done dancing on stage for the day. He said yes. The girl I'm cool with called me over to her. She was with Hairy. She wanted to know if boo thang had said anything to me about what I told him the day before. I told her he didn't say anything about it.

Then Hairy's dumb self said, "This one right here hates me!" I looked that man in his eyes because I wanted to throw something at his face. I told him before that I don't hate him. I just can't deal with him anymore. So. Before I walked away, I told him, "I don't hate you. I just don't f#ck with you anymore." Dude, I'm not tripping off you!

I didn't have a drink for the whole shift. It felt good. Sunday is only for four hours during the day. No need to drink. When I was in the dressing room getting dressed, one of the new girls came in the dressing room. I really didn't want to be in there with her. She be talking crap that don't make sense sometimes. Plus she was drunk so that made it worse. OMG.

First, she's Mexican. And she was talking crazy about shaking it on stage for a dollar. She don't have much to shake for starters, and why do that for a dollar? See what I'm saying? Then she was trying to dance and almost tripped over the chair behind her. I couldn't get dressed fast enough. She was trying to get dressed too to leave. How was she going to drive and she messed up? I don't know about some people.

March 25, 2014
What An Awesome Night!

Yes, Tuesday night was awesome. Mainly because the shift was not slow all the way through till the end. It started off great. I got there and got ready. Put my blue dress on. Had my hair down and straight. No curls. I had already seen Hairy's behind walk in when I got there. So when I went to the bathroom he was sitting in the corner at the bar.

When I came out I sat at the bar and pulled out my phone. I didn't see anyone I wanted to try talking to. The manager came over and told me that someone wanted to buy me a drink. I knew it was Hairy. I accepted the drink then went over to talk to him. Can't be too rude by taking a drink and not talking to the person, right?

I went over and had a nice conversation with him. He really misses my company and wants to take me out to eat. He thought I was mad at him over a purse. No way buddy. I could care less about you buying me a purse. After we got that cleared up, he told me that I was his favorite because I never asked for money. The other girls that he took out always asked him.

The times that I went out to eat with him, I already had it in my head that he would give me money for going out with him. Which he did. And I was happy with the $200. I never asked for more because I didn't want to mess up a good thing. If I wanted money, I'd just go out with him. He was trying to go out to eat once a week! Only thing was he wanted to eat at funny places. Sushi and Vietnamese places. Ugh! Don't like it.

There is one place he took me too that I really liked. I do want to go back there again. I'll let him take me there again just to enjoy the food at his expense. I sat and talked with him till I had to go up on stage. When I was done dancing he had left. No problem. I had started talking with other customers who were there and wanted a conversation.

We had over twelve girls. Things was good at the beginning of the shift. Then it got slow around 10:00 pm. But it was okay because the shift had a good start. There was one point when I went to the bathroom to finally take care of some business, and one of the girls I'm cool with came in there upset.

She was talking to a customer, well, she was venting to a customer because one of the girls tried to talk bad about her. She was asked if her black, curly hair was her own. Ever since the first day I saw her, she has been wearing her hair like that. It never gets longer or shorter, like some girls. She was really upset that the girl, whoever it was, said that to her. I told her some people like to pick at the ones they feel are competition. Just scratch the side of your face with your middle finger the next time you're around that person.

Now check this out. I said I was in the bathroom taking care of some business. I was still in the stall trying to finish wiping myself as I was talking to her. One of the other girls, who I'm cool with, walked in and heard a small piece of the conversation. I had the door open with my bottoms down, but I was holding the door with my head poking out.

The girl who walked in thought I was talking about the other girl, who she's cool with. This child pulled the door open, got in my face asking me, "Why are you talking about her?" I almost pushed her out my face but the other girl grabbed her and corrected her. Looked at her hella crazy! She started laughing when she heard the whole story. We was about to have a misunderstanding up in there! She wouldn't tell me who said the mean thing to her, so I didn't worry about it. She didn't want no drama to come from it. Which I can understand.

As the rest of the night moved on, it became dead around 11:30 pm. I was ready to stay in the back but my boo thang brought his little peanut head there. I was winding down and here he was wanting to see some energy. I was so annoyed with him. I told him I wanted to go back to laying down. I was tired.

I had my beach blanket laid down in the dressing room. One of the girls was sitting in a chair hunched over. She was done. Like high as a kite done. Even when she was dancing on stage she was making out with her home girl as she sat watching her dance. Then when it was her turn to dance, she went to her stage and made out with her again. It was funny.

Anyway. When she seen that I was laying down, she wanted to cuddle with me, as she called it. I had turned onto my left side so that she could have enough space on the blanket. This woman was serious about cuddling. She grabbed my arm and put it around her. I'm like, please just lay there and don't do nothing else. I know you hella high right now, but I'm not in to this!

I laid there for a while because she was falling asleep and wasn't doing nothing else. But soon as it was getting close for me to dance again, I got up and went to the DJ booth. Walking outside to the floor, there was only three customers still in the club. Wow. I was ready to go home.

The night was good. Fun. I was happy with what I left with. Now let's see how the rest of the week will go.

MARCH 27, 2014
I Was Not Expecting This

Thursday. I got to work half sleep and started the process of styling my hair and getting my outfit ready. When the DJ came into the dressing room to see who would go first for her, I told her I would. Since I haven't worked a Thursday in a while, I would go first.

There wasn't too many customers in the club when we started. Then there was a new girl who started. A few people customers knew her from another club she worked at and said that she had been trying her hardest to get in here. She's a Black girl with glasses and short hair. She danced okay. Didn't really do much.

The shift went pretty good. I talked to a few customers. There was a bout fifteen girls working. A lot better than twenty. One time I went to the dressing room to wait for more people to show up, and I was talking to the girl who's coming with me to Miami. We were talking about the other girl who wanted to come, but we think she's letting her bogus girlfriend keep her from going. I told her I'm not trippin off her going anymore because once I seen that she had bought some new ten inch shoes, that was a sign to me that she was not trying to go anywhere.

Then she starts telling me that some of the other girls were planning on going to Miami to party. She told them she was going to dance, and now they want to go with us. I don't want to be out there with a bunch of girls, but they aren't gonna stop me from making my money and doing what I want to do.

Now. There was one point when I was talking to a customer and had to go to the bathroom. On my way there, Ms K was talking to the girl who's coming with me to Miami. The girl called me over to tell me something and then Ms K got in my face and said, "We're going with ya'll!" I looked at the girl with a confused look on my face then asked her, "Where are we going?"

The girl pointed her finger at me and said, "Don't start!" Ms K stepped back and said, "It's okay. I know you don't like me." So I took the moment to make the situation clear. I looked her in the face and told her that I didn't like her because of what she did while I was talking to a customer.

I felt that it was a rude action and I don't like rude people. She explained that the customer had told her to come over earlier so that's why she came over the way she did. She apologized for it because she made me think she was rude.

I felt a lot better telling her to her face how I felt about her. She knew I didn't like her and seen the face I gave her that time she said "hi" to me. A lot of people were standing around watching and listening. I guess they thought we might start fighting but it wasn't that serious. We cleared something up and she was happy about it. She gave me a hug and shouted, "Now we can have sex! I been waiting to feel on this booty!" Oh my God that woman is CRAZY!

I was sitting with my two favorite, crazy customers! The guy from Florida and his friend who was in the army with him. While I was sitting with them, I noticed that little boo thang had came in and was at the pool table. I was happy he was busy so that I could enjoy myself with someone else.

I had walked around a little because they started talking to the security, then started arguing with each other about something. Boo thang came over and had to talk to me. He asked when we were going to hang out again. I told him I don't know. I'm sure that I want to hang out with him again. I want to tell him I'm going to pull back from him to get some space in between us because I feel he likes me too much.

One of the girls told me that he came in the club last night with a girl. That put a smile on my face. I was happy. I don't care who she was or why they showed up. I was just happy he was with another girl. If the new guy I like a lot more comes to watch me dance Saturday, I don't want any issues when we start to hugging and stuff.

When I had sat back down with the two guys, oe asked me to come hang with them. They were going out to eat. I was hungry and did want to hang out, so I told them sure. I just had to get dressed, get my things together, and get to my car without boo thang seeing. I got dressed, got my things together, and I went to sit them at the table with them so I could turn my ones in for bigger bills. As I was going to my car to put my bags up to wait for the other guy to finish flirting with one of the girls. The guy carried one of my bags to the car with me. Tell me why, when we got outside, boo thang was standing outside smoking a black?

I was irritated with him. I bet he seen me getting ready to leave and how I had my stuff around the dude's table, and took his silly a$$ outside to see if I would leave with them. I put my things in the trunk and went back inside. He followed behind me trying to talk and be noisy. Other dude was still flirting so I went to the bathroom then went back outside to warm my car up. His black a$$ followed me outside! I was like DAM man! What the hell yo butt want? After my car warmed up I remembered that I needed to get gas. I just left and called the guy to tell him I was going to the gas station. He said that boo thang was still standing outside when they came out.

This is the crap that pisses me off about people like him. Stop acting like I'm your woman. Stop trying to keep an eye on everything I do. I went out to eat with them anyway. It was awesome. They are great guys and gentlemen to be around.

MARCH 29, 2014

Awesome Saturday

Yes, I had an awesome Saturday. It wasn't all slow like I thought it was going to be. It was pouring down raining when we got the show started. People was still coming in. I was happy to dance on the stage. I was going to sit down and chill for the shift, but I had went to the fourth stage because I didn't want to sit around.

At the last stage there was a guy sitting there. He had a beer and was watching the TV by the stage. I didn't think he would pay me any attention so I was dancing with my back to him. I felt something hit my leg and looked down to see some money on the stage. So of course, I turned around, looked at him, and started dancing. (I had to make sure that it was him who threw the money) As I was looking at him, I could see his front shirt pocket with money in it. The first bills he had showing were twenties. So when I was done dancing, I went and sat down for a while to make sure that no one else came to dance at the stage.

When no one showed up, I took my time going over to him. I asked if he would like some company. He said yes, but told me he was going outside for a smoke. When he came back in, I waited a while before I went over and sat down with him. Long story short, I spent the rest of the shift sitting and talking with him. Then when his friend came, I was sitting with them getting tipped. Two of the other girls I'm cool with came over to sit and talk. It was nice. I even danced to a song for one of them.

Then when I was on my last round of dancing, I seen that one customer who tips twenty dollar bills. It's been months since I've seen him. He came to my stage. When I was done dancing, I went over to sit and talk with him. He always have great conversation.

When it was time to leave, I had all my bags together and was making way to my car. When I got outside, guess who was standing outside? Yes he was. It is now okay to change his name from "boo thang" to "old thang". He was waiting for me to leave so that he could take my parking spot. He was driving someone's car. Figures. I was going to stay a little to talk with one of my home girls, but decided to go home. He didn't really say much to me and I was happy about that.

MARCH 30, 2014

So Slooooooowwwww

Today is bad. And slow. The only money I made was from Hairy. He came and stayed for a while. He tipped me while I sat and talked to him. Then he tipped me again while I was on stage. He left shortly after. There really isn't anyone here!

I had talked with one of the girls in the dressing room and she told me that old thang was here with a old, white woman. I'm still happy. When she told me that, I felt that like someone had asked me to baby sit their baby, then they called me back later and said, "It's okay. I found someone else to baby sit him!" Thank God!

I don't know what was worse. The shift having five to eight customers throughout the day, or hearing at the end of the shift that the owners are going to ban rap and sexual music. THAT right there pissed me off so freaking much. You have a bikini bar that sells sex, and you're taking the sex appeal away. I don't know what's wrong with these dumb people. Then, come to find out, they tried the same crap some years ago twice and it failed. So why would you do it again? I am so ready to work at another club. These people are loosing their minds.

MARCH 31, 2014
A Much Better Day

When I got to work today, Miss Stiffie was talking to one of the girls about the car accident she had last night after she left. She was hit from behind because a SUV jumped back in front of her after trying to get off the freeway. Another truck smashed into her from behind. She was okay, but she has more work that needs to be done to her car now.

When I thought about it, I had to laugh at myself because the other day, one of the girls was talking about how negative she is. Maybe that's why some of the bad things that happen to her be happening. She kills me when she gets mad at someone and says, "I hope they die." That's just evil. It makes me wonder what kind of things she's been through to be like that. Dam shame. I already know that she was wishing death on the guy who caused the accident.

It was funny because when I did my first round of dancing, I noticed a Black guy dressed in a Red Skins hat and jacket sitting at the bar. He was on his phone when I looked at him, but I didn't pay too much attention to him. When I moved to the next stage he came over to sit and watch me dance. It was the construction manager!

I was happy to see him. He looked good dressed down and smelled so good. I couldn't wait to go talk to him. I was already sitting with my Mexican regular but I wanted to catch up with the Red Skins. Get it? Things have been going good for him since the last time I saw him. He's on paid leave from work. I think he called it a rest down, or something. His job is paying him to stay home for a while. Can you believe it? He's not sick, injured, or being punished. He's being rewarded. Life is good.

It was kind of funny because he went to lean over to put some money in my bottoms, and he fell over. He was wearing the thick construction boots and one of them got stuck in between the rail and the bar. I thought he might of hurt his leg the way it was twisted. The bartender thought he was drunk and fell out the chair. Oh boy!

Later on, this Black dude came in. The first thing I noticed was his black Gucci bad he came in with. His Murse. (man purse) Security told me that he pulled up in a Bentley. So? I know he probably has money, but don't mean he's gonna give me any. Even when I was dancing on stage, he didn't come to tip me. The only Black chick working the shift. He just sat at the table having a drink. I went back to me regular to finish collecting.

My day went good. We were busy and I didn't have any issues with any customers. I really didn't spent too much time in the dressing room. It was my last round of dancing and these two Hispanic men came and sat at the stage. They couldn't speak any English because I was smiling at them while I was dancing. One acted like he was shy about watching me. I told him it was okay for him to look at me and he still tried not to make eye contact. I mean, you came to sit at my stage, look at me dammit!

Before I left Hairy came in. I sat with him for a little and talked. He seems much happier to be talking to me again. Guess I'll let him take me out to eat, maybe this week.

April 3, 2014
Catching Up On The Days Past

April 1, 2014 Tuesday. The night shift went a lot like this. I showed up and there wasn't too many people there. I got dressed and walked out on the floor. I was trying to have some time with the day time security before he left. But I was approached by a customer before I could get comfortable.

It was an Indian guy with glasses. He walked up to me and asked if I was free. I told him yes and went to sit down at a table with him. We had a nice conversation and he kept buying me drinks. I didn't get nothing too strong so that I could enjoy a few of them and not feel wasted.

He stayed for a few hours. Enjoying my company. He stayed till about 10:00 pm. The thing that was cool about him being there, was the fact that I made most if not all of my money from him. For the first three rounds of dancing, no one was tipping me on the stages. And I was dancing my ass off! I mean, I was putting some serious effort into my dancing and got nothing. So when I was done on the stages, I always went back to him and got money from him.

And yes, old thang showed up. I tell ya, that man has nothing better to do with his life but stay in the club drinking as many drinks as he possibly can. He was playing pool with someone while I was with my customer. And yes, he had to let me know he was there by putting a dollar in my bottoms while I was hugging the customer. SMH. . .

After he left, I went to the dressing room to lay down. I didn't have a nap before I went in so I was winding down. I went to lay down. The old thang wanted me to hang out with him on the floor.

This is what pissed me off. You started hanging out again with the older woman you tried to have a baby with. You're driving her car, hanging out with her in the club, and God knows what else. Why are you trying to come hang out with me? Don't get back with someone from your past then still try to mess with me. That is not a smart move.

A perfect example of what I'm talking about. He decided to ask me to get a room with him. Just when I felt that he was leaving me alone and starting something with someone new, here he comes with the "Let's get a room" gig. I told him no because I was tired and sleepy. I don't want to be bothered by him trying to get some while I'm trying to sleep. Hell no. This fool tells me some crap, "I'll wake you up then put you to sleep." That is not what a sleepy, tired person wants to hear. I still told him no.

After a while he told me he was leaving. I was happy because I could go back in the dressing room to lay down. The few customers who were there did not pay me any attention. At all. They were wrapped up with the other girls. I'm guessing they already knew them. I didn't care. I was too tired to care. Even after my Indian customer left, I stopped putting my all into it. I danced to slow songs and at the other stages I didn't dance at all.

When I left, guess who was standing in the dam parking lot? Old thang. Like, is this what you call leaving? This fool asked me, "If I call me sis, can I ride with you?" He wanted to ride back to my city to go to his play sister's house. But she wasn't answering the phone. This dummy STILL got in my car to ride out there with me. Then when we got close to the exit, she finally answered the phone and told him she wasn't at home. Smart move sport.

I took him to ge a room, and this fool was still trying to get me to come spend the night with him. Go get some booty from the older, White woman fool. I dropped him off and went home to my kids.

April 2, 2014. Wednesday. This day was much better. Mainly from one customer. I was sitting at the bar on my phone when he walked in. It was the Hispanic guy who was sitting at the stage with all his money sticking out from his shirt pocket. He showed up and was waiting for some other people.

After he got his drink I went to sit with him at a table. Then his people showed up. We all sat at the table talking and drinking. It was cool. A few other girls came over but not too many. It was cool. I enjoyed it.

I don't remember any issues. I did walk away when I was talking to security, and that White girl who's been rubbing people the wrong way came over to talk. I just picked up my purse and left. I want to avoid her as much as possible to hopefully keep us from having issues. I'm doing good with not getting into it with anyone. I want to keep that record up.

Oh, you know what? That's right! The regular DJ for the day shift wasn't there. She went into surgery. So the grouchie night DJ who don't like rap was there. He was soo annoying. Even when I was sitting with the group, they had asked me to dance to a song for them. A rap song. He acted like he didn't want to play it. He was about to get cussed out. Play the dam song since you're always looking for a f*cking tip at the end of the shift! Man I can't stand him! Bastard.

He even came to the dressing room to ask me if I was tipping out. I only gave him $4 because I knew he wanted more. Next time he work during the day shift, he's getting $3 since he has a problem with the music I like to dance to.

These past few days, I have not seen that one girl at work who wanted to go with me to Miami. I don't know what's going on with her, but she ain't gonna make it too far at this route she's going. And the chick she messin with obviously ain't no good to her. Shame.

One of the girls was tripping big time when her ex that she was in love with showed up at the club. He was tipping other girls and trying to make her jealous. The fool who wanted to come to Miami to make money for butt shots but can't dance was sitting with him getting all close and stuff.

I tell you, when that woman flew into the dressing room to tell her friend to get that chick, I thought they might fight after the way she was talking to her. She told the chick that was her ex she was in love with, and he is a convicted rapist of four under aged girls. That's why they broke up because she found out. And the fact that she had been drinking didn't help the situation at all. But things turned out good and peaceful. They had a talk and the chick didn't sit with him anymore. But the dude stayed. Waiting for her to get off. Claiming he wanted to take her home since she had been drinking. She didn't want him to because she knew she was going to end up screwing him. I don't know how things ended. I left.

A Nice Return

So this past weekend I went to my cousin's wedding in Southern California. It was beautiful. I was so happy to be there. I was happy to come back home so that I could go to work and make money for Miami!

So when I started the shift there wasn't too many girls there. I thought one annoying girl was going to work today because her car was in the parking lot. But she never came in. Guess she left her car there and came back to get it later.

There wasn't too many customers but it got busy as time went on. The construction manager showed up. I was shocked to see him. He was there with some guy, maybe someone he work with. I watched as they played pool. When I had to get on stage they left. He told me that when he came Saturday, there was only four girls at the club. I had to laugh because it would have been nice to be there. But then again it was nice to be gone.

I spoke with the DJ and she told me something that upset me. That one DJ who don't like rap went to the owner and told him that we be playing gangsta rap, and he basically cried and pissed himself like a sissy little boy. I really don't like him any more. He if he don't like that kind of music, then maybe he should go to a different club that plays country music all day.

Then she was laughing at me because when I went to the booth, I started clapping my booty. At first, she didn't know what was making the sound. She looked down then busted out laughing. She said, "Do it again!" I made it clap again and she started laughing again. I been practicing and I'm very happy with what I can do.

Today went pretty good. No incidents. No drama. I was sitting with that one customer who don't like Miss Stiffie because he waited for her to get off work, and she had already got a ride home from someone else. Well, I saw him on my way to the bathroom. I sat down to talk with him, and Miss Stiffie came over to talk to him. I really didn't care. I thought it was funny. He was annoyed with her.

Then in the dressing room, she was trying to explain to me that she's known him for while and they dated before. Umm, I'm sure if I told that man what she said to me about them, he would blow up! But no, I don't care about "them". No, I wasn't bothered by her being over talking to him. He tipped me, and she made it clear that he never tips her. Nothing for me to worry about. Boom.

Tomorrow I'm getting my hair done for Miami. A long sew in weave so that I don't have to worry about my hair out there. I can just brush and go! Plus they like it long out there. The men. And it looks awesome when you're dancing and swinging around the pole.

APRIL 7, 2014
I Am Shocked At This Change!

Tuesday. I went to work with my hair done and ready for Miami. I have a sew in with long black and blonde hair. The blonde highlights look great and the girls didn't recognize me. The hair goes down my back almost touching my booty.

I went and got dressed. I made sure I ordered some tacos because I was starving! When I was dressed and ready, I went out to the floor to wait for my tacos. I seen old thang standing in the open by the door. He was wearing a basketball jersey and shorts. He looked at me and I gave a little wave, but he had a stupid smile on his face and he looked away. I kept walking to the security to tell him about my food but the lady had already walked in. I went and caught her then took the food to the back.

I was eating in the dressing room then went to the bar to get some water to drink. There was a Black dude sitting at the bar. He seen me walk up to get the water and said to me, "Why don't you just get a drink?" I looked at him and said, "Are you offering to buy me a drink?" He said yes. So I told the bartender to change the water to a Barcardi and pineapple.

I went to get my tacos from the back and I came and sat with him at the bar. We had a nice conversation. When it came time for me to dance, it felt a little strange dancing with all the new hair. But it felt good. Besides the fact that the night DJ who don't like rap was working. Oh boy!

I felt that more people liked me with the long hair. Or they didn't know it was me. The guy I had met when the girl was crying and getting drunk at the bar because of girlfriend problems came to see me. He liked the hair. I sat with him till he had to leave. He couldn't stay long.

The night went good with no incident. I sat and talked with a few customers till things got slow. There was even a tall white guy who kept coming to my stages while I was dancing. He was actually cute. Did I mention he was tall? I forgot how tall he said he was but he was almost seven feet. I sat down and talked with him too. He was cool.

He told me that earlier he had a slight incident with that one crazy customer, who threaten to kick another customer in the face after the club had closed. I think he's on drugs. Well, the tall guy told me that the druggie customer came up behind him while he was standing at the bar trying to get a drink. The guy is short, so the fact that he grabbed the tall guy by the arm and moved him to the side so he could stand where he was, amazed me. He let the incident slide for a while but the dude came back up to him later and apologized after a little talk they had. Short guy bought him a beer and things were cool.

The funny thing that happened was when the short dude got in an argument with the female bartender. It looked like security was going to put him out if he didn't calm down. The tall guy went over and stood by the short guy. In case he tried to act up, tall guy was going to knock him out! When I saw him walking over to the short guy that was the first thing I thought about. I had to laugh. I would have loved to see that.

When it was about midnight, I was tired and things was slowing down for me. The manager wouldn't let me leave early so I went to the back to sleep. No problem. My night went good and I had no complaints. I was shocked at how some of the customers received me. Did my long hair really make a difference?

There was a White, older man who really took a liking to me. He came to all me stages because he said that I had him hooked. Talking with him, he likes French food. He wants to take me out to eat one day and I would like to go to a French restaurant. I explained to him that I would have to get to know him better before going out with him. Those are the rules.

April 9, 2014
Nice Day For A Wednesday

I wasn't sure what to expect for today but whatever comes I'll take it. The day started off fine. Just like any other day. My regular came in and I spent some time with him. He was in LA while I was in Riverside for my cousin's wedding. He said he's going to Texas soon. I forgot if it was for business. I think it's just to get away.

I noticed that when I went on stage to dance, I couldn't stop smiling and singing to whatever song I was dancing to. I was just happy that I was going to be leaving for Miami the next day! Also noticed that when I did my shoulder lift trick, I didn't get a ball on my shoulder blade like I normally do. Maybe I'm getting it used to the move. Well, we'll see what happens in Miami. Because I sure will do the trick!

APRIL 12, 2014
MIAMI

Today is Saturday afternoon and I'm still kind of tired from last night. We went to King of Diamonds to dance. It was so exciting! But before I get into that, let's start from the beginning.

Thursday morning I had a feeling there was gonna be something I didn't get to do before leaving. It was getting my nail painted over with the design. It had cracked the other day and I got it fixed at a nail shop I knew was still open after I got off work. I was still trying to do last minute things and ran out of time. I packed my things in two bags. The main bag had my clothes and shoes/dance shoes and stuff. The carry on bag had my dance outfits. When it was close to twelve noon, I was ready to go.

I caught the BART train to the airport and made it on time. Only problem I had, when I got my ticket online, I misspelled my last name. After they got it changed, I was ready to get on the plane. The girl I came out here with, she'll be known as Rainbow Bright, was jumping every time the plane hit a speed bump in the air. It was funny to see her get so scared. We made it here in five hours at night time. The weather was warm and it didn't look like it had rained.

We went to get the rental. She had a few cars to pick from. I didn't care what kind of car we got because I was ready to get to the room, shower, and get to the club to get started on dancing. She just wanted a car that had Bluetooth. All of them did. With Bluetooth, she could connect her phone to the car and when someone calls, she didn't have to be on her actual phone. It also allowed her to play music that was on her phone.

We headed to the room and that's when I seen how much of a crazy speed demon she was. She felt everyone else was driving too slow. The last time I drove in Miami, I wasn't doing dam near over seventy MPH. I was taking my time and watching the cars around me because some would merge into your lane. This child was driving like a maniac!

When we got to the motel, she felt that it was a hood motel. I had already explained to her weeks ago that I stay at a cheap motel when I go out there, so that I'm making money instead of spending it. It was cool when we went inside. We took showers and got dressed.

The club was okay as far as the amount of customers inside. The manager working didn't charge us the full tip out price to dance because the club wasn't all that busy. So nice of him. When we hit the floor I seen some familiar customers. One of the dudes didn't waste much time calling me over for a dance when he seen it was me.

The thing that irritated me the most was the older Haitian guy from last time. He would come to the club everyday and stay for hours. Sometimes he would leave and come back. Be there all dam day. He kept asking for dances, kept trying to pull his penis out while I'm dancing with him, kept trying to take me to the private room. I didn't like/want to do any of those things. Ewe!

I refused to go dance for him. I didn't want to do it. Rainbow Bright gave him a dance. She didn't like it because she was standing up dancing for him while he sat behind her. And he pulled his penis out so he could feel her skin rubbing against her. When she noticed he had it out she went off on him. He was also trying to get her to take off her panties while he had it out and that really upset her. She said that the dude caught and attitude when she didn't want to dance for him with his thing out. He tried one last time to get me to dance for him by having a girl tell me he wanted me to come over. I shook my head "no" at her. I was serious about not dancing for his old behind.

We stayed for a few hours and left when they started cleaning the stages. I did okay for them few hours. We were ready to go back to our room and eat the food we left. Before leaving the club, Rainbow Bright seen a roach crawling around on the counter. It creeped her out. We get to the room and turn the lights on, little roaches were crawling around on the floor and the table where our food was.

I almost fell out. We did not see one roach when we first got there. Now that we have food in the room and we come back tired and sleepy, they wanna come out and creep us out? I went to the front desk to tell the lady about it. She said she couldn't give me a refund for that night because ten minutes had went by already. But she refunded me for the next day I had paid for. She offered to give me a different room but I knew Rainbow Bright wanted to leave the motel altogether. I was very disappointed with that motel experience. That was really bad.

We found a different motel with higher standards. Only thing was, it was out the way. We were so happy to get inside the clean, bug-less room and get under the fresh covers. It was a ruff first night for us. Having to change rooms like that while tired and hungry.

April 14, 2014

Back At Home

To continue on with the story, the next morning we slept till we weren't tired anymore. Rainbow Bright wanted to try out at the King of Diamonds. I told her that was fine we could do that. The club didn't open up later at six. So since it was Friday we decided to hang out. I wanted to get some new shoes from the dance store out there because my old black shoes are about done.

We got dressed and went to the store. I looked around at the different styles and colors. I saw a yellow pair I liked but found a cute black pair. After I tried them on, I was looking around for outfits. There were some other women who walked in to look around at stuff. It was super funny because this one woman was talking to the sales man, and out of no where she said, "You know I'm a stripper", in this deep, very unattractive, man like voice. I had to stop and look at her. She looked to be like six feet and something. And like she had plastic surgery done to her face. She was not a nice look. I wonder in what country is she a stripper? That mess was super funny!

When we left we drove across the street to get some food. We went inside to order so that we could sit and eat outside. I was wearing a blue dress with no panties. It was warm inside. They must not of had the air conditioner on. Standing in line, I felt a little silly so I made my booty clap a little. I started laughing and so did Rainbow Bright. When she turned around to look at me, she laughed even harder. There was a White lady behind me that looked at me hella crazy! I don't think she knew what I was doing. She might have thought I passed gas. When I did notice the lady, she had let a Black woman go in front of her! She didn't want to be behind me anymore. I busted out laughing even more! I really didn't care, it was too funny.

Rainbow Bright wanted to go look for something at Target. So we found one and went to it. It was in a nice area. After we went to the store, we sat outside at a restaurant to eat and have a drink. That's when she noticed she didn't have her ID. It wasn't in her purse or in the car. When she came back from checking the car it wasn't in there either. After a while of thinking, she remembered that she didn't get it back from the club. Great.

We had to go back to get her ID. She was the driver and we can't get into King of Diamonds without it. I'm just glad she was trying to order a drink at the table and the guy asked for her ID. She's not a drinker so it was perfect timing for her to try to get one.

We went to the club and it was busy for a Friday afternoon. The manager who was working was trying to get us to stay and work, but she really wanted to go to King of Diamonds to try to dance there. I wanted to try to see if we could get in and have the experience.

We got there a little after six pm and there was nobody there. We went inside just to ask a few questions to see if we could dance and how much it would be. Soon as we walked in, there were two chicks at the front counter talking. It was very clear that we had waked in the building but these two rude ass b-words kept looking at each other talking. We just stood there staring at them like, "I know you see us." Then after a while, the one who works the counter says to us, "Give me a minute ladies." Oh now you wanna act like you have some manners? Them h*es made us stand there while they finished their conversation. She was talking to another dancer who had nothing better to do.

When she finally stared talking to us, she explained how things will go and said that the manager was on his way. We went back outside to wait for him and get our bags. He pulled up shortly in a truck. We went in and spent the next hour listening to him run his mouth about peoples' life storied who work in the club. He even told us that he held a big meeting with all the girls, asked them who live in the area, and when they all raised their hands, he told them they were fired. He did it because they were the ones bullying the out of town girls. That was not acceptable. He'd rather have the out of town girls come and dance.

When he was done talking, he told us to get dressed because things would be starting soon. I was first to get ready because Rainbow Bright takes her sweet time with hair and make up. I was told by one of the dudes who work there to go to make up. I hated it! And I had to pay for it out of my dam pocket. But when she was finished with my face, I loved it. Except for the eye brows. I hated them. It felt like weights were on my eye lids. But she didn't put a lot on me.

Now this is the big part. Inside the club it is big. That night there wasn't too many people there. Even the girls and managers were saying the same thing. As the people stared to come in, we realized the customers were mainly women. We were trying to wait for the men to come in so we could dance and talk to them instead. But it became clear that the women had as much money as any of the men!

Rainbow Bright had an issue with walking up to the customers to ask for a dance. I didn't. I was trying to pump her head up so that we could walk over together and ask a group of them together, but she was really nervous about doing that. So I finally picked a table and went over where these two dudes and two females were sitting. I asked one guy and he said to dance for his cousin, who was a girl. No problem! It was her birthday and she wanted a dance!

I started dancing for her and they started throwing the money. I noticed Rainbow Bright had came over and was dancing for the other girl. She made some money. One of the security men came over and started putting my money in a little plastic bucket. I felt good. When things slowed down with the money being thrown, I left. They had three hundred in ones on the table bt of course that was for other girls.

How it works is, when you have a bucket of money, you have to take it to the cash room where a lady counts it and keeps it for you. They add it up through the night so they can take their ten percent. Nice. And when you leave at the end, they give you what you made.

The night went pretty good. They were a few people who I asked if they wanted a dance and they told me no or come back later. I did not come back later because that to me, was another way of saying no. It's either a yes or no answer. Not, "Come back later." What dancer do you know wants to hear that?

Some time had went by and it became clear that her and I was not gonna get called onto the stage to dance. Talking to one of the dudes who work there, he sent the DJ a message to call our names. The night was almost over so we might as well get up there and do the dam thang. Rainbow Bright was nervous and didn't want to do it, but I told the guy I wanted to. Boy was I happy when my name was called!

I was smiling my ass off! I did what pole tricks I could do and some floor work. I was whipping my long weave around and smiling at nothing. I didn't care if no one threw any money on stage. I was too happy! One guy I was talking to before I got on stage came over and threw me some money and stood there to watch me. He made me smile even more! That did it! I was happy! Nothing else mattered. I don't care! One person was good enough for me!

After that we were ready to leave. I was having a hard time breathing for some reason and I didn't have my inhaler. Maybe it was the thrill of everything. I didn't make that much money on stage and I was still happy with that. I left out with a little over $100 after tipping some of the other people. I felt that if I would have asked more people if they wanted a dance, I would have made more.

The thing that kind of ticked me off was when the football players came. I waited for them to get settled in. Even to the point when two other girls had went over and started making money from them. I went to the other side where there wasn't any girls and asked one guy if he wanted a dance and he said to come back later, he's trying to get his drink down first. N#gga I bet you wouldn't be worried about a drink if you were about to get some p*ssy! Oh well. I walked away and stayed away from them. I forgot how much of an a$$hole them people can be.

I had got a few more dances before the night was over with. I knew I wasn't gonna make a few hundred dollars that night. But being that it was my first time there I was happy with what I made. I did put in some effort and wish I would have put in more effort. I just didn't want to leave Rainbow Bright behind. I understand that she was shy about approaching men, but sometimes that's exactly what you have to do in this business. Next time hopefully I'm by myself so all I have to worry about is myself. I'm not complaining. I'm just saying.

We went back to the room and I was so happy to wash all that make up off my face with hot water and soap. Pulling off those eye lashes was the best part. I felt like I could finally open my eyes all the way. I laid down and went to sleep feeling good. I danced at one of the famous strip clubs in Miami.

Saturday morning we took our time getting out of bed. Our feet hurt a little. Laying in the bed was nice. We decided to dance at the other smaller club. Make more money from there. We didn't go straight there. I wanted to change my piercing between my legs. We had to find a tattoo place. Rainbow Bright suggested going to Miami Ink since the first place we went to was still closed after one pm. We went just to be in another place that's been on TV before. It was located by the beach.

We had a difficult time finding a place to park. There were so many people there in the area of the beach and valet parking was $20 off top.

We just wanted to park for an hour. There was one street that only allowed parking for the residents. One car was in the process of being towed because it didn't have a sticker showing the parking was allowed by a resident living on that street. We went back by the beach and lucked up on a spot.

We went into the tattoo shop and left just as fast. They charge a minimum of $200. And they didn't deal with piercings. The guy told me about another place across the street that could help me. Going there, I was told that the jewelry I was trying to have put in was not good. There was also a price to change the jewelry as well. $30. I just passed on it. Never mind.

When we got to the club it was cool. People were really feeling Rainbow Bright. They were coming to get her and one dude wanted her to dance for his cousin. Who was a girl. She was trying to have sex with her but Rainbow Bright don't like girls. It was funny to me because I would look every now and them at her dancing for the girl, and she was rubbing all over her. Rainbow Bright was making all kinds of funny faces! Like she wanted to push her hands off her. I laughed at myself.

Later on she brought me into the Boss Room with her and the same people. She didn't want to be in there by herself. She got mad because there was this one drunk, little dancer who was dancing all over her. I mean, she was dancing all over her like she was a customer. Had her on the couch and was on top of her going crazy while the man was throwing money on them.

Now since they both were dancers, they were suppose to split the money. She followed the chick to the dressing room so they could split it and she said she wasn't splitting it with her. I would have went to talk to one of the managers about that. It's suppose to be both of you getting the money. Not just one. She let it go because she didn't want to trip off of it. The girl was drunk and you know how drunk people get when they get upset. All angry and violent.

I finds out later that the same little thing was also having sex with customers and probably wasn't using condoms. What kind of mess is that? She had did this one dude right on the couch in front of Rainbow Bright and his friend. When they were done, his friend asked him if he used a condom. That's bad when your friend ask you something like that. She was a drunk little thing too. She probably did do him raw.

Later on that night, there were a few performances by local rappers. I had asked one if they wanted a dance and then realized afterwards it was a chick! She looked like a dude wearing guy clothes, dreads pulled back under a hat, and her chest was flat. But her voice was girl. I felt silly. I went and sat at the bar till they were done.

We left when they were cleaning up for closing. I knew my feet were going to be hurting in the morning. Before we went to sleep we decided that the beach would be the main thing we wanted to do in the morning. When we got up, yup. Our feet were screaming bloody murder! The hot shower made them feel a little better. The drive to the beach was nice. We drove by the Port of Miami and seen the cruise ships lined up to sail off. Two of them were Disney.

There was a huge problem getting to the beach. Roads were blocked. Then we started seeing men wearing tiny shorts. And women holding each other's hands. Then we seen the rainbow stuff. Gay Pride. Dammit.

We paid $20 for parking and walked to the restaurant I had been telling her about that's great to eat at on he edge of the beach. We sat outside up stairs and looked down at everybody walking by. It was awesome to see how they were dressing and the laughs were non stop. The food was nice. There were so many good looking men we were hoping weren't gay. But it was still nice to look at them. I liked this one chocolate dude but he looked like he'd just got done taking it in the butt. He walked funny. They a few tables down from us was a table full of black dudes. All gay. Wow!

We went to the beach and laid down to enjoy the sun. Well, what sun there was. There was some serious cloud cover that really sucked. Just when we want the hot sun covering our bodies, it's playing hide and seek behind the clouds. But it felt so nice out there, we fell asleep. I don't know how long we were there but it was so relaxing. There was a cute light skinned dude walking around telling people he had something for sell. Rainbow Bright was shocked he was doing that on the beach. It happens everywhere girl!

When we had enough of the beach we walked around and saw more people enjoying themselves. We went to another restaurant and ate some more. The gay show was getting better and better. One gay couple walked in wearing black hats with penises sticking out from the top.

We left and headed for the club. Sunday was not expected to be too busy. But making that little bit of money before we left the next morning at 5 am was what we'd rather do. It was slow moving when I sat at the bar. One of the bartenders came over to me and asked me to stand up. She looked at my booty and pulled me to the Boss Room. There was a dude inside pouring himself a drink and getting ready to watch a fight on TV. She asked him if this is good, then turned me around. He smiled and shook his head. When she walked out the room I started dancing for him.

I seen the money he had sitting on the couch. I just danced to entertain him till he was really to start tipping me. Then some of his friends came in and another girl too. She danced for them while I danced for him. It was nice. When the fight came on, I picked my money off the floor and went to count it. There were dudes trying to have sex but my period had started and I wasn't feeling it.

Things had changed since the last time I was there. Now, dudes would rather not tip you, and hold on to their money to pay you for sex instead. I made more money giving dances last time. Now, they want the whole thing. It made me feel like I need to dance somewhere else. Try another state and maybe it'll be different.

When it was time for us to leave to get ready for our flight, the manager tried to act like we couldn't leave because it was too early in the shift. I told that man, we have to get ready for our flight. And cut. There was gonna be a problem anyway if he tried to tell us that we had to pay $20 after 1:00 am. Hell, we were leaving at one to get ourselves together.

The manager I'm cool with out there wanted to see me before I left. He came to the restaurant we were eating at. The thing that pissed me off was when he started talking to Rainbow Bright. They were talking about clubs. The differences between ours and the ones out in Miami. I felt that some of the stuff she was saying, she was putting a ten on a two. It was exaggerated. But I didn't say anything. I just felt that he should have been talking more to me about things instead of her. After a while, I just pulled out my phone and got on a social network.

The flight home was nice till I got home and found out that the airline put my bag on the wrong flight. I didn't get it back till about 8:00 pm. Boy, never had that happen before.

Back To Work

Tuesday night shift. I was not all that excited about going back to work. Back to all the restrictions and BS. But hey, it has to be done! The first disappointing thing I seen when I parked in the parking lot was the old thang. His sorry a$$ had just walked into the parking lot. Why was he the first person I had to see when I came back?

Getting in the dressing room some of the girls were still getting dressed and asked me how the trip was. I really didn't feel like talking. I wasn't in the mood. I was surprised at how people were tipping me when I was dancing on stage. I thought the night was going to be slow for me but it wasn't.

And you know something? Remember that chick I told you who copied my lip stick and my French braids? When I walked out onto the floor and was walking past her, you now what that female cow said to me? In front of two customers she was sitting with? "I like that weave!" I just smiled and said, "It's 22 inches" then started talking to a different girl. The nerve of her to say it like! I should dance to another one of her baby daddy's song's. That will really get under her skin.

Even when I was in the back just chilling, one of the girls came over to me and told me a customer was asking for me at the bar. I kind of thought it was the White guy I had talked to the week before but wasn't sure. As I'm waking outside to where I was told he was sitting, it was him. I saw old thang sittin at the bar as well. Just sittin there watching everything. I guess he's not working anymore.

I sat and talked with the guy for a while. It was cool. Then dummy had to walk past to get some quarters like he was going to play pool. I don't get that. How can a person walk by to be seen like that? It would really bother me to do that to a person I like. I see them talking to someone and I'm hanging out right there. What goes on in a person's head? How does it make them feel to walk past the person they like while that person is having a conversation with someone else? I don't think it feels that good if they're a jealous person. I can say that much.

After a while, I went to sleep in the back. I wasn't all that busy for me. I was tired. I woke up when I had to dance. There was a football player here and I really didn't care. Didn't mean he was gonna tip me anything. I did my last dance then got dressed. I was ready to leave. And I was cold too.

April 16, 2014
Yesterday Was Way Better

Today became one of those days when I stayed in the dressing room because things were not going good for me on stage and on the floor. I'd get on the main stage and get nothing. And there wasn't anyone for me to talk to on the floor. So I been in the back on my lap top.

I did get called to the floor because one customer was looking for me. I sat with her for a while because she couldn't stay for long. She got me a drink and we talked about a few things then she left. I went back to the back. Then when I went to dance on the stage, I had a customer come to the last stage to tip and talk to me. When I was done dancing I went to sit with him and spent time till he had to leave. Then I went back to the dressing room.

The day was pretty slow. Some of the girls in my dressing room kept coming in and out because it was slow. I was just done for the day. Plus I was sleepy. Didn't sleep as much as I wanted to from the night before. When it was my last dance, I was wearing my shirt I wore to work. Made it faster to get dressed when I was done. I tore out of that place so fast!

April 19, 2014
Good Day For A Saturday

Today started off slow. There wasn't too many girls so I thought it was going to be slow. But they just showed up late. I was happy to finally be off my period. One less thing to worry about. There was talk about the NBA Playoffs. The security hoped it would bring people in to watch. I don't like it because no one watches the stage.

When I first started dancing there were four guys sitting at the bar wearing orange shirts. I was surprised when one came over to watch me. Then his boys came over when the song was ending. The day was going pretty good. I didn't talk to too many customers. My regular Hispanic showed up and I spent the next few hours with him.

You know what he did? I was telling him that I wanted to get some yellow shoes to dance in. The lady who comes in the club to sell outfits came in. I asked her if she had some yellow clothes and she said she do. I was telling him what I was talking to her about, and he gave me $100 to help get my shoes. I was shocked! He said one of his jobs gave him a $600 bonus and he wanted to share it with me. I told him thank you and gave him a kiss on the cheek and a big hug. Now I need to go online and see what styles I can find.

Dancing on stage today was fun. I have to keep telling myself to not worry about the customers tipping. Just dance and enjoy my work day. Enjoy listening to the songs that are playing while you command the stage. Like in Miami at KOD. Once I put myself back in that "happy place" I was smiling and dancing. Nothing mattered. Just my dancing.

I didn't spend too much time in the dressing room. I seen the new girl got a long weave in her hair now. It's not as long as mine but it's longer than hers. Then one of the other girls is moving to the Southern part of the state. It's her last day. Things went pretty good. I stayed in the same outfit all day because it didn't get that busy. I didn't care about changing.

APRIL 21, 2014

Today Was Good

Pulling into the parking lot there was only two cars. I was thinking that this was going to be a dead Monday. I wondered how yesterday went. Easter Sunday. I want to come to work but after I got out the movies with my kids it was too late to go. So I stayed home with them and chilled.

There were a few girls getting ready in the dressing room. One was talking about some girl getting rehired after she was fired last year. I didn't know she had got fired till months later when some girls were talking about how happy they were she was gone. I don't even know what she did to get fired.

After I got dressed and went to the floor, I saw this White girl with real short blonde hair. I figured out who they were talking about. She was cool when I did work with her. I guess she rubbed a few girls the wrong way. I heard she would get drunk and do crazy things. Last time I saw her was the day before Thanksgiving. The reason why she came back was to have some more girls for the day shift. They really be tripping bout having girls and it don't be that many customers in there.

The first thing that shocked me was when I was dancing for the first round and this customer put a $20 bill on the table. I wasn't expecting no one to be sitting at my stage because it was slow. And he was White. But I gave him a show and he enjoyed it.

The manager introduced me to one of his friends at the bar. Older Black man. He was nice. After a while he asked me about being my Sugar Daddy. I told him we could work on it. He kept talking about spoiling me and giving me whatever I wanted. Yeah, we'll see.

I sat with one customer I've talked to before. Older White man who loves Black women. I think he's the same one Rainbow Bright was telling me about one day. She was hiding from him in the dressing room because he wasn't feeling him. I thought it was funny. He was tipping me fives while we talked. His convo didn't bother me.

I had to dance one last time before I left. I went to the third stage to dance and I seen there was some money under me while I was dancing that someone had threw on the stage, but when I was moving to the next,

I forgot it was there and left it. Someone told me I was leaving money behind so I ran back to get it but it wasn't there anymore. Guess they took it back! I laughed at the thought.

I didn't see old thang today and it was nice. I didn't feel as if big brother was watching me. I felt that I could talk to a customer without him letting me know he's there. I hope it stays like that!

I'm still trying to get comfortable in my new eight inch black heels. I just need to dance in them more. I be feeling like I'll fall over because they are taller than my usual six inches. But one more inch shouldn't make that much of a difference. To me it do!

I Need To Take A Deep Breath!

So the parking lot was dead when I pulled up. A sign that things were slow for the day shift. Walking in, there were only about five to eight customers. And not that many girls either. Going into the dressing room, I heard that it was dead all day and even slower Monday night. Wow. What's going on?

It didn't bother me. I already expected things to be slow because it's a Tuesday night. It don't really be going on like some would like. Well I got dressed and hit the floor. I went and sat at the bar so that I could get a feel of things. I seen old thang in the back playing pool. When I noticed him there I didn't give the back area any attention.

I planned on sitting at the bar on my phone. Nope. There was a white guy that had just came back from the bathroom and sat down a seat from me. I had my phone in my hand and I looked at him when he sat down. He looked at me and I smiled at him. That started it.

He started talking to me about how dead it was and he hope he's not the only man in here. I started laughing and told him it might work out in his favor. We talked for a little bit before he picked up his beer and sat right next to me. He had a good convo for me about his last relationship. Interesting in how the woman he was with left him for an illegal immigrant who she married in less than a year.

Things were going good. Surprisingly I was getting tipped on the stages. There was one dude who came with some friends for his birthday. They were great to talk to. I noticed how the girl who be copying my style was sitting with them and was trying to get a birthday party from the birthday boy. I knew she hella wanted to give him a lap dance on stage for his birthday. I could see it in her eyes. She even dedicated a song to him. But his attention was on me because I was the main one he was talking to till he left.

I almost went off on this Indian guy. He was sitting at my stage when I started dancing. I was trying to get him to smile and entertain him. There was an older white guy sitting a chair away from him. He really wasn't interested in watching me dance but when I was done he tipped me a dollar. After that he looked over at the Indian guy. He was sitting there holding his beer in his left hand with his black hair combed back. I told him, if you sit at my stage you have to tip me.

Can you guess what this bastard did? He turned his head to the right and shooed me off with his right hand. Like I was a peasant begging for money. I put my hands on my hips and said, "Oh like that? Really?" I walked off, went to security, and told them what he did. They said if he sat at another stage while a girl was dancing and don't tip her, they were gonna throw him out. That was out right disrespectful and uncalled for. I was pissed. Mainly at how he did it. Not the fact that he didn't pay me. It was the way he told me no.

When I was finished dancing on all the stages, I was standing by the front door waiting for one of the security guys to come back so I could ask him to get my black boots from my car. I felt someone pulling my panties back on the side and slip something under them. When I looked to see who it was, the Indian guy said to me, "I was just playing with you." I gave that man the dirtiest look a human being could give another human being. I wanted to cuss him the hell out but all the words were running into each other like a hundred people trying to run out of a small doorway at once.

He just looked at me with a smile. There was no way I was smiling back. I was even more pissed off and insulted. He really thought what he was doing was okay and I would feel better. No. I didn't. When I looked to see what he put in my panties, it was a tn dollar bill. Why do someone like that? Who do he think he is? Who do he want to be?

While I was sitting in the dressing room resting my body and mind, one of the White girls came in. We started talking about our night and come to find out, the same guy came to sit at her stage and didn't tip her either. He was doing that to a few of the girls. Wow. If I ever see him again, and he's sitting at the stage before I go up, I'm gonna tell security that I want him removed from the stage before I go up. I don't even want him sitting there while I'm dancing. Don't want to look at him.

The night got real interesting later on. More people came in for birthdays and a wedding party full of women. It was on! And old thang brought his dumbass in with some friends. So that was like his third time coming in I think. SMH.

It was my last time dancing for the night. I figured since I was already tired, finish it up! I had a slow paced song and a crowd that might receive me. I started dancing and a Black dude came from the back pool table area to sit down. Then the wedding party came to the stage. They were really amped up.

The one thing that made me wanna take my shoe off and throw it was when old thang made that loud, stupid noise I hate for him to make. He does that when he wants me to know he's there. I kept dancing and entertaining. Money was on the stage and floor. When I was done, I got a surprise.

I got all my money and went to my purse at the end of the stage. I was getting ready to walk down the stairs when the DJ told me not to leave, stay up there. Security had already put two chairs on the stage when I was getting my money. I didn't know someone wanted me for a birthday party. I hadn't done one in a while. I was honored.

There were two Mexican men, who already had a few dances from the other girls. Me and another one took turns dancing for them. It was fun. Then when that was over I went to the next stage and this older White guy came over to watch. At the end he told me he wanted me to come sit with him at the bar. I told him sure. I went to the last stage and the Mexicans from the birthday party were there.

The guys were throwing the dollar bills one at a time. The White guy from the other stage got fed up and walked over to throw a bunch of ones at me while I was holding my panties open like a basketball hoop. I just smiled and tried not to act super excited. But it was funny how he did it. They were playing.

As I got off the stage and made my way to the White guy, old thang came up to me and was trying to talk. I was not in the mood. I was trying to get to the customer! He told me he has a new job as a cook. That's nice. Now get out of the way. Even as I was standing next to the customer and put my purse on the arm of the chair, that fool was still talking. I think he was there earlier with his sugar momma. You don't have to talk to me thinking it's gonna make me feel good. I'm straight.

Now remember the girl I told you about who was trying to get a birthday dance from the guy I was talking to? When it was time to close the club, she came over to the White guy before I had walked away from him to tell him bye. I guess she was talking to him earlier or already knew him from another encounter. I walked away to go in the dressing room to get dressed.

At the end of the night, I had made a lot of money. Even more the last few hours after the party people showed up. I enjoyed this Tuesday night. It was fun and things went good. Now the next thing was to have a good Wednesday.

APRIL 23, 2014
Because I'm Happy

I got to work late and it wasn't like I was missing anything. It was not too many people there but they were coming in slowly. The regular female DJ was not there. The sub DJ was so things were gonna be fun.

I was sitting with the security by the door when Rainbow Bright came over to vent about the argument she just had with Miss Stiffie. I don't remember if I mentioned this before, but Stiffie is the type to butt nto your conversation or make opinions that she should really keep to herself. She has that habit real bad.

So Rainbow Bright was talking with a girl in the dressing room. She was talking to the girl about the finger foods the club was starting to sell to have something for the customers to eat. I've seen the food myself and they even had a little sign up for people to see.

Miss Stiffie came out of no where about how they don't have the finger foods anymore, and she said it with an attitude. Now, all Rainbow Bright was saying, was that it was good to have the finger foods. She didn't know they had stopped making them, if that is true. Then the argument started.

This is what I think. Stiffie is mad jealous that Rainbow Bright is the second favorite girl of that one customer she was telling she love with the money. Boom. That's what I think the problem is. Rainbow Bright was telling us that for the past week, Stiffie has been getting bad with her. Boy, when she sees that the customer is out of town and Rainbow Bright isn't at work, I wonder if she will put the pieces together that they went to Hawaii for vacation. ☒

Since things were going slow, me and some of the girls were sitting at a table talking. This light skinned dude dressed real nice from work came walking over. He felt our table was the place for him to be. I didn't think anyone was paying us any attention since we were sitting in the back.

As he was walking up, Rainbow Bright was on him like a fat kids walking past a bakery. He sat down and started talking to us. I already knew Rainbow was on him. So I told the other girl he was all hers. Then I said it out loud because he asked me what I was whispering. When I told him that he was all hers because she likes the light skinned men, she got

216

up so fast and walked away! We laughed so hard! When she came walking back to go to the dressing room, I made her sit down and talk to him one on one so they could get to know each other.

The day was alright. I wanted it to be over so I could go to my sister's house and have her take the weave out for me. I know some customers are going to be upset that the twenty two inches have been removed from my head. But it was starting to itch and needed to be washed! Oh boy!

April 26, 2014
A Nice Saturday

Today was a good day. I walked into the dressing room feeling okay and ready for the work day. I got dressed and when I took my scarf off, everyone was surprised about my hair change. I have it all braided to one side and my hair is straight. It's cute and I'm glad I have this style.

When things got started it was real slow. Then more people showed up later. My Hispanic customer came in so I was happy. Things been going good with him.

There really weren't any problems today. Things went smooth and that was awesome. Tips were good. I remember dancing on the last stage at one point, and there were two Black dude just standing at the stage watching me. They tipped me some money but because they never sat down I didn't think they would have watched me for the whole song. When the song was over, they walked out the door.

I feel like I need to get back on my sit ups and I need to start doing push ups. Get my strength up. I have no idea how many girls will show up tomorrow. I'll come and just be ready for whatever. I want to show up early to practice some things on the pole. I noticed that I'm getting better at holding myself up on the pole with this one move I've been doing. Yeeessss!!

April 27, 2014
Sunday, Honey Day

I got to the job early so that I could practice some things. No one was there. Perfect. I changed into some comfortable clothes, ordered some chicken tacos, and tried some things out. I can now do the caterpillar on the pole! I can push myself up, but I'm still having a hard time pushing my whole body back up the pole. That's where the push ups come in handy.

So, there were only three girls that showed up today. Miss Stiffie, the new Mexican girl, and me. So we had the three most common flavors. Get the joke? I wasn't trippin because I just knew some more girls were gonna show up. Nope. Not a single girl walked in late! The manager was pissed. But there wasn't that many customers anyway.

I sat at the bar and waited for the show to get started. The Mexican girl was first, me second, Stiffie third. I was chillin at the bar when two White dudes walked in. They sat next to me an one asked if I wanted a drink. I had to think for a second if I wanted a drink after eating the tacos, and then what drink I wanted. He joked with me about how I took too long to answer. I wasn't even expecting him to say anything to me let alone offer me a drink.

I went ahead and ordered a Silverback. I really like that drink. Yeah, it has 151 in it. I decided that I was gonna be the one to dance to rap. Worked like a charm. We had two songs, one stage. Perfect. With the other two, I was the perfect balance because I dance fast. The customers who were there enjoyed my dancing as well as the other girls. I was happy that I had gotten my pole tricks down packed. It felt good to be the only one doing things.

Those two guys, I spent most of my time there with them. The main one I was talking to really liked me. He asked me why I was working at a club that didn't have a lap dance area, and I have all this booty. I told him because I'm comfortable here and I make good money too. He understood and started talking about something else.

Now after the drink had settled in my system, I decided to have some fun. I danced to a nice slow song. Sexy. Then I put on some fast paced Reggae, took my shows off, and went wild on stage! The customers were shocked and entertained! I loved it and so did they. It was the unexpected.

I was tired. I had to tell the security to get my pump from my car because I was having a hard time breathing. That's how much work I put in. It was worth it. I made a good impression on them for such a bad day.

Then the one Black dude I had talked to a while ago that has a child with an Asian woman was there. He seen me sitting at the bar and came up to speak to me. He was under the impression that I was mad at him. That day I told you I had left some money on third stage, and when I went back to get it, it was gone. He had tipped me that money and thought I was mad at him and didn't take it. I don't think I knew who it came from.

So we sat and talked and I told him I wasn't mad. He felt better after hearing that. He told me that he couldn't even play pool the way he wanted because he was worried about how I felt about him. Then the lady who sells the bikinis came by and told me she has a yellow outfit for me. I wasn't trying to buy anything from her at the moment because I'm trying to build my money back up. The guy I was sitting with offered to buy it for me. I called her back over and told her I'd take it. It was a yellow bikini with the Warriors basketball team on it. Yes!

He wanted to take me out to eat when I got off. I didn't mind. I told my mom a customer wanted to take me out to eat and she said to bring her back some baby sitting money. No problem. We went to get something small to eat, sat and talked some more, then I went home. Nice day.

Today I kind of felt like a little star. I felt it was my show. I had earned all the bruises that were on my legs. Plus my arms hurt. Even though I did stretch when I got there, I still felt the pain.

April 28, 2014
Laid Back

Monday. I knew I was gonna take it slow today. I was still sore from my high powered performance. Driving to work was fun. This White guy in a big, Cheve pick up truck was staring into my car while on the freeway. I ended up flashing him because it was funny. Then he tried to get me to get off the freeway to exchange numbers. I shook my head no because that would have been real crazy!

Walking into the dressing room, I noticed the normal crowd of girls was not there. The Sunday DJ was working to give his wife another day off. Yeah, they are married. When it was time to start, only five girls were present. Wow. The ones who normally come late didn't. There are like three girls that always come late on Mondays. Oh well.

My Hispanic customer showed up to have lunch. We ordered some tacos from next door. He had shrimp and I had chicken. He stayed for like four hours. Then he gave me another $100 to spend how ever I wanted. I told him, summer clothes for my kids! Yeeessss!!!

It was more dead today than it was Sunday. The five, eight customers that were there talked to the girls, drank the beer, or watched TV. Some would watch the stage every now and then. But they were mostly having conversations.

I didn't care because my customer was taking care of me and I was still tired. Oh well. Some other time. The night shift girls came in and was ready to go. They had a nice amount. I don't know what's going on with the day shift girls. Oh well. Nothing happened all day but the time went by fast!

May 3, 2014
What A WEEK!

Today is Saturday, and boy was I happy to go to work! I have been having car problems since Sunday. I didn't get my car to the shop till Thursday and I had already missed work Tuesday and Wednesday. So I really needed to go to work today.

My car couldn't even get out the yard. Something else was wrong. After having it towed to the shop, it ran fine. I guess I have an issue with the fuel line. It might be clogged. I was already late but I called the manager to see if he would still let me work. I would only be late by an hour. Soon as he said to hurry up and come to work, I was on my way.

When I got there I seen the car of one of the girls who works the night shift. I thought she was getting something but she was there to work. There wasn't too many girls there or customers. I hurried up and got dressed just in time to dance on stage. I was the last on the list.

Now this is what shocked me. I think it was my second or third time on stage, and this one customer who always come, but never sits at my stage, sat down at my stage. I was shocked! He's an older White guy the looks like Uncle Fester. I just danced and entertained him with no problem. When I was done I told him thank you and gave him a hug. He didn't come to the stage anymore after that. I was kind of confused at first but there's a first time for everything.

My Hispanic customer came. I told him how I used the money he gave me last time to take my kids shopping and now he wants to take me shopping. YEAH! We're gonna go on Tuesday morning while my kids is in school. I'm happy. I need some new clothes for the summer. I sat and talked with him till he left. He showed me a small envelope with a lot of money in it that he went to go pick up this morning for a job he did. I didn't really care. It was in his pocket. Not mine.

The time went by fast. It didn't take long for 6:00 to come around. The last thirty minutes I was in the dressing room because my customer left and I wanted to count my money before leaving. Some of the night shift girls were coming in to get ready. I don't know how many there were but I left at six on the dot. My inner thighs were hurting from the pole move I was doing. I'm really good at it now. I didn't have a problem pushing up on the pole while upside down. Tomorrow I want to try another move. Gotta get there early. I hope that not too many girl show up again!

May 4, 2014
What The Hell Happened Sunday?

I was late today because I was flat ironing my daughter's hair. One less thing to worry about after coming home tired. When I arrived, the place was dead. Eight girls showed up and it looked to be like eight customers. The manager cleared his throat. I knew he had an attitude. I just told him, well I could of not showed up. I mean, look around. It's not like there was hella people there and today there were enough girls. I felt that he should have been cool.

No. This man had an attitude. Yes I know I was late but Sundays don't be going down for him to be trippin. And I'm not one of those girls who's always late for him to be getting at me like that. I didn't wanna hear it.

Looking at who was there, I could tell that it wasn't going to be a good day for me. The customers who were there were older White men, who looked like they were retired or would be retiring soon. Then on top of that my MP3 player was acting up so that dulled my mood.

Then I was trying to have a conversation with one of the girls that I was cool with, and she acted like she didn't want to talk to me. I don't know what it was but her vibe was negative. I asked her while she was looking in the mirror how it was going with finding an apartment, and she didn't say nothing. Then she asked who I was talking to. I couldn't believe it. I don't know what the problem was but I wish she would have told me if I did or said something she didn't like. I'd rather talk about it with her than to go through this with her. Normally she talks to me and sits with me but she was very distant. I just left it alone. If that's how she feels then fine with me. I'm not there to make friends and I don't care to loose them either.

I couldn't wait to get off from work. I was in a bad mood from my MP3 player. Can't dance to what I want if that's not working right. And I didn't feel like dancing much. I want Tuesday to hurry up so my customer can take me shopping! Plus I'll have a better week so Sunday doesn't matter. I can slack off if I want.

I was suppose to go to pick up some Cinco De Mayo stuff to wear at work tomorrow. But my car acting up this morning made me forget. So I have to go before work. Then I finds out that one of the Mexican girls is having her birthday party too. I don't want anyone to think I dressed up for her birthday. I don't care for her! I'm trying to be festive!

Cinco De Mayo!

Yes, today was awesome! I went to get me some wearables for today before going to work. I got two necklaces, one hat, and a head band with two chili peppers at the top. The place was decorated real nice. I took my time getting dressed because there wasn't anyone there.

The regular security wasn't there. So while I sat by the door the one who was there talked to me the whole time. We laughed and joked about things. He told me a story about one girl who was coming in for amateur night, and she did something on the pole to where her private area had rubbed against the pole and it was smelling real bad. The girl dancing after her smelled it and had security wipe down the pole. He smelled it and said that she had a problem between her legs. Then one of the customers even smelled it as she danced on stage and he got up to leave.

This is why I keep the wipes and spray. So if even feel un fresh, or just to make sure, I can at least try to do something about it. That girl denied that she was funky. All the towels that place has and soap in the bathroom. I would have asked for a towel and went to wash my stinky, private area.

As him and I were talking, old thang walked in. I was doing so good not seeing. He walked in and gave me a little hug before sitting at the back of the bar. Out of sight. Later on he came over and started talking to me. It was cool. We just talked about random things before I went to the bathroom and he left. I was happy when he did.

I was amped up before I started drinking. I was just excited because I thought we would have been busy. But it was cool and I made good money. Everyone loved my necklaces and my hat. I was the only one who put effort into today. And remember the girl I told you wasn't talking to me yesterday? Well when she came in today, she was talking to me. I was shocked! I even gave her my hat to wear for the night shift when I left.

No, I didn't ask her about why she acted like that. I just figured she was having one of those days. But I'm not holding anything against her. It's not that serious. Long as we aren't going back and forth at each other, I'm happy!

APRIL 7, 2014

Not Bad For A Wednesday

Before I get into the day, I want to talk about my shopping experience with my Hispanic customer. We met at the mall of my choice and went to three stores. I was disappointed because the clothes stores I was looking for were not there anymore. Wish I had went to a different mall when I realized that. But he let me get whatever I wanted. He even asked me about getting something from Victoria Secrets. I got me some more body spray and lotion.

Now back to today. It was dead when I got to the club. No customers inside. Barely any girls. By the time we started the show a few people had came in. All I wanted to do was sit and talk with security. Wait for things to pick up.

I was shocked when I was on the second round of dancing and seen my Hispanic customer at the last stage tipping me. I didn't think I would see him till Saturday. But hey, I was happy to see him! I went and sat with him to talk and drink. When he left I seen another customer come in that I don't get to see too often because he works a lot.

I went on stage to dance and he came to throw me money while I danced. While moving to the second stage I seen him sitting at a table. I went over to give him a hug then continued to the stage. He made sure to turn around in his seat to watch me dance. When I was done I went over to talk to him.

He asked me a question about an experience he went through with an ex. He asked if him and I had a child together, and he had to go to work on the weekend, would I have a problem watching is fourteen year old son, or would he have to get a sitter? I told him I'd watch his son unless I had a serious problem with his attitude towards me. His ex had an issue with his baby mama, and took it out on the kid. Some people. He stayed for a while then left to get some rest for work. It was a nice surprise seeing him. He want to hang out again.

I think what I'll do is hang out with the Hispanic customer in the morning, then maybe hang out with the other customer later that day. Since he's off work. Enjoy my Tuesday and see what fun I have.

After he left, I was dancing on the last stage when old thang came over and started messing with the fan. He knew that was one way to get my attention. He must have taken his sugar mama home. It looked like he might have been in the club with her earlier. He was all in my face now. I went back to the table where I was sitting with the last customer to count my money. He came to the table! Then had the nerve to ask me, "So when we gonna hang out mama?"

I gave him the most confused look I could give. Do I look like I wanna "hang out" with you? How dare he ask me that! I told him, "When I'm on my death bed." He couldn't believe I said that but he started laughing. How can I go hang out with you when I'm happy that I don't hang out with you anymore? SMH. . .

Since it was amateur night, the amateurs started coming in after 8:00 pm. I had already moved my bag in the back dressing room because everyone knows that the amateurs be stealing. Even Rainbow Bright got into it with one. She left her trunk of clothes open, and a girl had put her things on top of her trunk, without closing it. She went off when she seen it. Why would you put your things on top of someone's stuff like that? Don't make sense.

I was happy with the money I made. I hope I can do even better Friday when I show up to make extra money. Got anther Miami trip at the end of the month that should be very profitable with the celebrities showing up at the popular strip club! We shall see!

May 9, 2014
Happy Friday

So I made it to work on time for review. There were over twelve girls. Wow. Well that's better than twenty two. And guess what the best part was? That annoying girl, Ms K, was not there! Yeah super! I got dressed and decided to have a seat till I seen someone worth talking to. There still wasn't too many people in the club. No rush to talk to no one.

I was able to dance on stage and entertain people the first round. After that I sat down at a table looking at people. I really didn't feel like talking to anyone. I didn't have any regulars and there wasn't anyone I wanted to talk to. I was comfortable. One Black guy did come to my table to tip me and talk before he left. He had to get back to work. He spent most of his time talking to the security at the door.

The second round of dancing there was no one at the stage when I started dancing. I was surprised when a few people came to the stage. I did my tricks and entertained. I didn't talk to any customers till one Black dude who's been coming in lately was at the last stage. When I got off I went over to talk to him. I talked for almost thirty minutes. It's fun talking to him. He has a great sense of humor. Then when he left, another dude came up to me and said, "My friend is jealous that you've been over here talking to that dude." I just had to laugh. When I looked to see who he was talking about, it was that one African guy I haven't seen in months. He only comes in on Fridays. I went over to him and sat and talked.

Before I sat with him, I really made a good impression while dancing at third stage. I so love the fact that I can hold myself in the air away from the pole with my arms! There were these young dudes sitting at the stage just loving my moves. They started laying dollars on the bar for me to sit on and pick up with my booty, then shake it and drop it on the stage.

Check it out. So one guy placed a dollar on the bar. I climbed up the pole, suspended myself with my arms so my body was away from the pole while my legs were spread open, I slid down the pole slowly onto the dollar, picked it up with my booty, then shook it out by walking to another pole and suspending myself again and shaking it out. They were loving it! Hell, I was loving that I was doing it!

The day went good. I made some extra money and enjoyed myself. I might work next Friday, not sure. Depends on if I have something to do or how I feel.

May 10, 2014
Dressing Room Day

Today was NOT what I hoped it would be. It was a killer slow day. I would get up on stage and dance like my day had a horrible beginning. I wasn't putting in effort. Then it got to the point that I just stayed in the dressing room because there wasn't anyone to talk to on the floor. And the big shocker, my regular didn't come in like he normally do. I wasn't mad. I was just shocked because he'd come in every Saturday faithfully. Oh well.

Now as I was on stage dancing my last round before getting dressed to leave, this dude had walked up to the stage and just stared at me while he drunk his beer. He didn't tip. Just stared. When I got dressed and went to the bar to turn my ones in for bigger bills, he was sitting there.

He asked me if I was leaving him. I told him yeah, my shift is over. He reached over onto the counter and picked up a stack of one hundred ones. "I was gonna hit you with this money so hard!" I just started laughing. After I was done dancing, he went to the ATM to get $200 out for me. Too late bro. Next time. He was cute. Then he went on to tell me that he would come Sunday, and he would save one stack for me. Yeah right. I'll hold my breath for that one.

When I was in the dressing room getting dressed, there was this one White girl I had never seen before. She didn't look like she should be a dancer. When she was talking to me, she was real ugly in the face. And her front teeth were like three different colors. As if she didn't brush regularly and had some dark fillings behind her upper front teeth. I was trying hard to make a nasty face at her, but it didn't look right. Then she had a little Gucci purse and a Coach purse. Why do you have two different purses like that? Then I remembered seeing her on the floor once. She walks the floor with the little Gucci purse. OMG. SMH.

We didn't have too many girls for Saturday. We also didn't have too many customers either. Things have really been slowing up and changing. I guess they're really gonna be hiring the weirdos now. That's gonna suck.

As I was walking out the door, the night shift girls were on the stages for review. I noticed that one chick who copied my style a few times had some long braids in her hair with blonde streaks. I don't even know why she did that. It did not look good on her. She was also wearing a baseball hat with the brim turned to the back of her head. I just looked at her like, what are you trying to do?

May 11, 2014

Good For Today

My plan to come to work on Mother's Day was a success. Only four girls showed up. I was the only Black girl, one Mexican, and two White. There were a few customers who came and things worked out good. I was mad at first because I didn't stop to get something to eat. I get to work and they're not serving any food. The manager who does the cooking was not there. Dammit! I had to order some chicken tacos from next door.

I didn't put any effort into dancing the first and second round. There was no need. I just kind of walked around swinging my arms, laying the stage watching one of the TVs. But! After the first round, I was asked to sit with a customer who I hadn't heard from in a while. I talked with him and he told me how he's going to Hawaii for ten days to celebrate his birthday, and I could of came with him if we had been in communication. I don't think so!

I danced on the other stages because I didn't want to spend the whole day sitting around. I also wanted to try to get used to the new shoes I got from Miami. Them hurt my feet sometimes so breaking them in was a must. I did good for the time I did wear them.

Once again, I hate when dudes want to talk to me and tell me I don't belong at this club. I could be making more money some where else. Half the time, they want to move me somewhere so they can try to talk me into some other things. Business matters, if you get my hint. Leave me alone with that because I do just fine here. When I got up from the table, I did not go back to them.

Now as I was leaving for the day, this White dude called out to get my attention as I passed by the bar. "You leaving already?" I told him I work day shift. He pulled out some money to give to me, and I opened my top so he could put it in. I wanted to flash him but I was holding my bag with my strong arm and couldn't flash the way I wanted to. Then anther man came up to tip me too. I was so happy I was wearing a cute summer outfit. I knew I looked good!

For tomorrow, we shall see what happens. My period has started but hasn't started heavy like it usually does. I hope it hurries up and come down so I can be worry free! Glad I won't have to worry about it this time in Miami!

May 12, 2014
Where's The People At?

So I went to work Monday not really expecting anything. I was dressed up in my pretty blue dress and blue heels. A lot of the girls were shocked that I came to work all dressed up and didn't go no where or have plans to go anywhere. I got dressed and went out to the floor to see how the day would go.

I sat at a table by the DJ booth on my phone till one of the girls told me that the pictures from Cinco De Mayo were up on the big screen as a side show. I got up and went to look at the screen myself. I seen some of the pictures and was entertained. When I turned around to look at the bar I seen my regular (Hispanic) customer sitting there looking at me.

I went over to him and started talking. He got me a drink and after a while I asked him if he was hungry. I was hungry and wanted something to eat. I was happy when he said he was. I ordered some pizza and wings for us and he took care of the bill. We sat at the bar talking and eating.

Now let me say this. The shift started off so dang slow and remained like that all day. There were like five customers in the club for the whole day shift. Then at one point it was like three. More than half of the girls that showed up didn't have anyone to talk to except each other. They sat at second stage for a while then went to the dressing room to hang out.

The money that I made was mostly from my customer. And I noticed that one of the Black girls who used to work at the club while I was still trying to get in has came back. The last I heard about her was that some White customer really liked her and started taking care of her. She stopped working at the club. I was happy for her. I don't know why she's back but she is. She one of those dark and skinny, skinny girls. She dances good. I even used one of her moves a few times because she was the only one I would see doing it. Then she left.

Nothing happened all day. It was quiet. Some of the girls left early. I stayed till six because I was happy that I was making money. I was even on stage acting a little silly. Just having fun, trying to make the best out of the day with a few drinks in my system.

May 13, 2014
Tuesday Night

When I pulled up to the club the parking lot looked good. I had on a very nice colorful dress and received compliments for it. I was early and hang out till it was time to get dressed. I laid out my beach blanket so when I get tired, I'd have something to lay down on and rest or sleep. There was one Black customer who I started talking to soon as I hit the floor.

He stayed for a few hours and we talked about a few things. There aren't too many girls here so going up on stage was often. Then I noticed one of the Black dudes that came for their friend's birthday. He tipped me while I was dancing on third stage. I had the chance to talk with him before he left. I had spent the first few hours with one customer, I wanted to at least have some time with him.

I was irritated when I went to the dressing room and seen that one of the girls, who I don't really talk to, was laying down on my blanket. I walked in a looked at her funny because she was seriously laying on it, and did not move when she seen in the room! I was trying to count some of my money before going back to dance on the next stage but the next girl was ready to dance. So I put my money back in my purse and went out.

She was a few girls behind me on the list, so while she was dancing on stage I went in the dressing room to change my clothes and I moved my blanket around so it wasn't laid all out. Then when I got tired I stayed in the back sitting on my blanket to keep her off it. Got her dam nerves.

Then one of the other girls came in the dressing room to get ready for a birthday party. She was a little uncomfortable giving the party because she hadn't shaved. She said she was growing out her hair so that she could get a wax before her trip to Vegas. I told her she would be fine as long as she didn't do any close up, leg open moves. I showed her how mine looked because I had canceled my wax appointment for that morning, to wait a few more days so that I can be fresh when I go back to Miami. She asked me, "How do you dance like that?"

I just do my regular stuff. The hair isn't too long to where it looks completely discusting. And it's darker on the floor so it's not too noticeable. Her hairs were barely starting to grow! I can wait till Sunday to get my wax.

Things have slowed down and I'm ready to go home. The manager doesn't want to let me leave at midnight but I'm past tired. I made over $100. I'm happy with that. Now I'm ready to go to sleep. The last dance I had n stage I didn't dance. I just stood around and didn't do much. When I walked off stage that's when these Mexicans wanted to throw a few dollars on stage. I cannot stand that. I didn't dance on the rest of the stages. I stayed in the dressing room. I'm cold now. Don't have the energy to dance. Don't think there's anymore money for me to make. I don't care if there is a bigger crowd out there. I'm done. No more working Tuesday nights because I want to go to sleep when I'm ready for sleep.

A Lot Of Girls

So, on this beautiful Wednesday, we have almost twenty girls, and eight customers. Yes, it's slow at the moment. And we have a new girl that doesn't do a dam thing on stage, except walk around the pole, and she has the fakest booty you could have! All these girls and no customers.

The day went like this. I didn't really talk to anyone all day. There wasn't any customers that I knew. Later on, old thang came in. He never fails to come into the club. We hung out since nothing else was going on. There was one black dude that was there for most of the shift. He was on the Black girl that started working again. The same one I said, who stopped working because a White guy started taking care of her. I noticed that he would tip some of the other girls, but never tipped me. That's cool. I was still making money.

Since I was still trying to get information about dancing at the club in Miami for Memorial weekend, I called one of the other managers who used to work there but now works at another club. He said, how it works is that you have to be there like two weeks before. Working and building up your credentials. Then to work while the rappers are there, they'll charge you up to $500 to work! Naw, I can't do it!

I sent a text to Rainbow Bright letting her know what the system was for the holiday, and she was not trying to go either. I felt relieved because we now knew what to expect. But mostly, I was relieved because I didn't want any issues concerning money with her.

When I got to work Tuesday to work the night shift, I talked with her in the dressing room about the plane tickets. I told her the cheapest I found for one way was $375. This child said to me, that she would give me $200 for the ticket. If it's $375, why would you give me $200? She still hasn't paid me for the last ticket. I'm not giving away free trips to Miami here. I'm trying to make money and you want to tag along to do the same. But you don't have the money to get there. Stay home! Now, the plan is to maybe go to Vegas for the holiday. Let's see how that goes.

The shift was cool. Just boring. And talking to security, he explained how one of the White girls that a handful of girls don't like, is trying to make friends. I understand that she wants to have a little click, but sometimes that shouldn't even be a concern. I was sitting by the door when she walked by me and dragged her hand lightly over my right arm. I didn't like her doing that. I don't talk to her and it felt weird. I told security, if my arm breaks out days after she has touched me, I'm coming back to beat her a$$. She did not have to touch my arm like that, and I have heard about some of the nasty things she does with customers. I don't need any more skin problems.

May 16, 2014
I Feel AWESOME!

Today I got to work late. Just by a few minutes. I got dressed then went to the bathroom to wash the conditioner out my hair then put it up in a high pony tail. When I was done I went and sat down by the front door. There wasn't too many customers there and it was about twelve girls.

When it was my turn to dance in the first round, I danced to my favorite rapper. There were two Black dudes sitting at the stage just watching but looking like they weren't gonna tip. So when a White guy came and sat down I started dancing for him instead. When I untied my top and played with my boobs in his face, this tall, bald, Black dude came over from the bar and showered me with HELLA money. I got up on the stage and started dancing, then did a pole trick. He came back over and threw MORE money. When the song was over I just looked around thinking, now where do I start picking this money up at? Security came over with my purse and helped me stuff it in my purse.

I had to hurry to the next stage to dance then I went over to him and told him "thank you", and gave him a hug. I went over to the next stage to finish dancing. When I was done I wanted to go talk to him but he was talking to another girl. I didn't want to be rude so I just chilled. I had a good $100 in ones so I was happy.

As time went on, things really got busy. My Hispanic customer came in and spent some time with me. We couldn't even sit at the bar because there were so many people there.

Now this is funny to me. I believe it was the second round of dancing when it happened. Maybe third. I was dancing on stage and stuff all happy. When the song was over, a Hispanic customer whispered in my ear that I had a piece of tissue stuck on my. . . private area. I knew exactly what he was telling me. My tampon string was hanging out.

I went to the bathroom and sure enough, a tiny piece of the string was hanging out from my panties. I had cut the string but not short enough. All I could do was laugh. I wasn't mad nor embarrassed. I still made enough money from that one customer to be happy for the rest of the day. I now had enough money to by my plane ticket for Las Vegas! I went to the dressing room and cut the string some more then went back to finish my stages.

It was a good day. I decided to flat iron my hair and buy a long pony tail to wear for my trip. That way I can save some money instead of going to the shop. Do it my dam self. Rainbow Bright wants to change her hair again. She showed me where the long braids she had pulled out her edges. She has some black hair almost like what I had wore to Miami. She still wants to wear some long, twenty two inch hair. We'll see how it comes out.

A customer was telling me to try dancing in Arizona because they would love to have me out there. I never thought about that stage before. But it is closer to home. I'll give it a shot after some online research of the clubs.

MAY 17, 2014
Not Today

The first thing about today was the constant ear ache. Light, but annoying. People were telling me that I might have an ear infection. Just great. I came to work with my pony tail I bought yesterday and I loved it. A few people thought I was a new girl. Changing in the dressing room, one girl took her shirt off to change and two girls in front of her instantly grabbed her boobs to feel on them. I don't care how big a girl's boobs are, I am not touching on them! Real, fake. NO!

The whole day was slow. I made some money but the customer population was low. My regular said he would come in Sunday instead. His work site was not close to the club. That's okay, no problem.

I went to sit with a customer I had never met before but he was tipping. He was having a mini celebration because he had took a test he felt he passed. I talked with him till I had to dance. When I moved to the next stage one of my customers who I haven't seen in a minute came to tip me. I finished dancing then went to talk to him. For some reason, I was suppose to keep in touch with him. It goes both ways. I'm not trying to keep up with none of these customers. He didn't stay long. I was surprised to see him in the day time.

I did good dancing with my hair. I was worried that it might fly or fall off when I went upside down. But it was cool, no problems. Just had to be mind full of it. Felt good to feel some long hair down my back again!

One of the girls who don't work often anymore because of her track meetings showed up. Before it was time to leave he asked me why I didn't invite her to Miami. I quickly asked her, "How often do you work here?" How am I going to invite you to something when you don't come to work often? Then she went into a rant about how Rainbow Bright wasn't a good person to have went with me because she isn't a hustler. Got that right. I told her next time I go I'll let her know. I don't want to be worried about the person with me making money or not. Came too far to play round.

The day went by kind of fast. I sat and talked with Hairy today. He even got me some food. I just wish he didn't like Japanese so much. I'm not familiar with that food so much. I just got some chicken to keep it simple. Miss Stiffie made sure to come stand right in between him and I to eat. Knowing dam well her cock blocking a$$ could have taken her food and sat down somewhere. I just ate my food till I was called to the stage.

I hope tomorrow will be a better day. I might even go to work Tuesday night to try to scrap up some more money. I'm not sure.

What A Day

This morning was a pain. My car wouldn't start. I had to cancel my wax appointment since I couldn't make it on time. Then the guy who was suppose to look at my car couldn't come to the house. I mean I was super frustrated. Then finally it started after hours of trying. I called the job to see if the manager would allow me to come late. There were only four girls there at the time so I was given the okay to show up.

I hurried up to shave under my arms and made a wax appointment at different location on the way to work. Took care of that then made my way. When I got there, I made a total of seven girls. I gave the manager a $10 tip since he let me work. I didn't want him to think he was doing me a favor. I need to make money. He needs girls. We both have a part to play. I even told him that next week I can't make it because I'll be late after my plane lands. He said it was okay because he don't want to be short of girls. Okay.

The shift was okay. I was shocked that people were tipping me on the stage. I still become surprised at times when they tip me because I don't be expecting it to happen when it happens. I danced to my rap music and was careful with this hair piece on my head.

Then the last hour, these Black dudes came in. No, they didn't tip me. I made my money from the Mexicans and White men. Fine with me. I made $60 and that was appreciated. Long as I made my stage fee ($10) back and a little extra. I'm happy.

I told the security that when I go to Vegas, I might dance at least one night. Just to see how it is out there and how good I would do. He called his contact he has out there to let him know that there's a girl who's interested in dancing out there. He was out of town so he's waiting on a call back. I'll have to bring a pair of shoes just in case I do dance. Can't pass up a chance to make money even if it is on vacation.

MAY 22, 2014

Let's See Here. . .

I have to catch you up on what happened Tuesday. It was a pretty interesting night. I showed up a little behind the time I wanted to get there. Traffic was a b-word on the freeway. I was happy that one of the girls I don't get to work with often was there. I got dressed and took a seat at the bar to wait for things to get started.

I knew I'd have to be on my A Game to make enough money for my trip. The place didn't have too many customers there. The guy who was at the bar when I sat down talked to me for a little before he left. When he did this older Black guy who was sitting on the other side of the bar came over to talk to me.

When he walked up to me, he asked me my name to make sure I was the one he wanted to talk to. As we were talking he asked when was I next to dance on stage. I told him I wasn't sure then he said, "The guy told me there were two girls ahead of you." That let me know he had asked someone about my place on the dance list. I was shocked. I always see certain customers come in and look at the list to see who is here and when they dance next. I didn't think anyone would be curious about me since I never was told about it.

I went on stage to dance then sat down to talk more with him when I was done. He was cool to talk to. I had to laugh at myself because he started talking to me about how he would love to be my Sugar Daddy, but he has "issues" at the moment. He had surgery at the beginning of the year that has left him unable to "perform" how he would want to perform with me. I didn't laugh in his face. Hearing him say that didn't even bother me. I'm used to hearing men talk about wanting to have sex with me. I'd never heard one say that to me before.

Anyway, there was this one table by the wall next to the stage where three dudes were sitting. I wasn't paying them any attention because they weren't tipping the two times I went on stage. The one time I was walking by them, one called me over so they could look at my booty. The one dummy who called me over asked if he could touch on me. I told him I don't mind as long as he tip me. His cheap self tells me, "Oh, I'll just wait till I see you at the grocery store." What does that mean? You want me to punch you in the face at the grocery store for grabbing my booty? All the bastard had to do was give me two bucks and I would have been happy. I pulled my hand away and walked over to the other guy who also wanted to see my booty. He was light skinned and thick. Thick like big arms and broad shoulders. Kind of cute.

He was getting on me about not coming over to their table to talk to them. So I had to let him know who the hell he was talking to. He seen me sitting with a customer. He seen him giving me money. Why would I leave him to talk to you, when you ain't pulling out no money? I played around with him for a few minutes giving him an attitude. Then I went back to my customer.

At some point, the waitress got into it with the cute, buff customer. I had just walked away from the older guy to go change my clothes when the argument started. Now, from my understanding, the waitress kept making her rounds asking people at the table if they needed anything. The buff guy got mad when he found out that we sold food. I don't know how he found out but it wasn't because of the waitress telling him. When he did find out about the food, he made a comment that "That b*tch didn't tell me that ya'll sold food." That started it. They were yelling and going back and forth. I had just started walking to the dressing room when they went at each other. I do feel that she should have been telling the customers, who are drinking, that we sell food. It helps to make a little more money, keeps the food from going to waste, and makes the hungry customers happy. Security calmed things down and the customer stayed for a little longer before leaving. The waitress was bothered for a while

The night was going by good. I talked with that one customer for hours. It reached a point when I wanted to lay down. My stomach was acting up and I had to keep going to the bathroom for a number two. Laying down made me feel better. I was happy when he left so I could stay in the back and relax.

I almost forgot! When I was done with my first round of dancing, the chick who be taking my style came over to me to talk about my pony tail. She told me that it was it, and she had been looking for her one, and where did I get it from. All I wanted to do was roll my eyes at her. Why would you want to put a pony tail on your head, with all that hair you already have? I couldn't believe it. Just like when she had them dam braids in her hair. What be going through her head? Some stuff is not for everybody.

I knew she was gonna have something to say when she seen me walking with that hair swinging against my back.

Now, I think it was the last hour. I was at the bar because old thang was sitting there with his friend, and my home girl was standing with him. It was the four of us. One of the other girls walked up to us. I'm cool with her, but my home girl is very annoyed with her. The girl is the same one who asked old thang about me and he told her I'm not his girl anymore. She came over and was talking to us. I forgot that my home girl was annoyed with her, so when she told me to go to the bathroom I thought she had something to tell me about the dude. She started talking about the girl! "Why did she have to bring her a$$ over there with us? She always trying to get attention. Nobody called her over there. She get on my nerves." All I could do was laugh.

I had reached the point that I didn't want to dance on the last stage. It was slow, no one was tipping me, and the music the other girl was dancing to sucked. I went to the dressing room to count my money when I should have been dancing. When the song was almost over, security came to the back and told me that the manager wanted me on the stage. I told him okay, but stayed in the back because the song was over. A few minutes later, the manager came to the back looking for me! He asked me what was going on and I told him I wanted to stay in the back to count my money. He fussed at me about missing the stage. I mean, all I was gonna do was stand in the corner not dancing. But as long as the customers have something to look at, I guess he'd be happy. I couldn't believe that he came from behind the bar to talk to me! Was someone looking for me? If not, what's the dam problem?

Then when it was my last round of dancing, I decided to dance to an old hip hop song to end the night right. There wasn't too many people still there when I walked out. I didn't care. It was time to get ready to go home. I had made good money for the night and I was excited. Soon as the music started playing and I walked out onto the stage, this Hispanic guy threw some money up in the air. I was like dang! Already? I got into dancing and a little crowd of people formed at one end of the stage. I'm shaking my booty and licking my pierced nipple with my pierced tongue, and being real sexual. It was fun. And their reactions helped fuel my performance. They were throwing money and putting it inside my panties. Security wasn't trippin and neither was I. let's end this night with fun!

And the girl who likes attention came over and joined the crowd. It didn't bother me. She was getting the crowd going and that should never be a problem. When I got off the stage there was one more girl to dance after me but he didn't show. So the attention girl was told by the DJ to grab a female customer and take her to the stage. More fun and dancing. Yes, I enjoyed this Tuesday night.

I was annoyed at how old thang was asking me about going out to eat with him. I do not want to do that! You are still messing with the old, White woman. I don't want to be in a love triangle. I've been there, not doing that again. He went back to her, so take her out to eat. Spend your money on her since she's letting you drive her car. Leave me alone and find happiness with her. That's all I'm saying.

Yesterday, May 21, 2014. Wednesday. Another good day for me. I decided to wear my pink fish net body stocking. I haven't worn that in a while. I was trying to be careful about putting it on since my nails were still wet from getting them done before work. I didn't want to be late for work so I hurried out the shop. But I was able to get dressed without messing them up bad.

My Hispanic customer showed up to spend time. We ordered some Chinese food. Rainbow Bright called me over to her because she realized that he faithfully comes to see me weekly. She asked what am I doing, and I told her, I give him the affection he wants. That's why I'd tell the girls he's a biter. I'd let him bite or kiss on me as long as he wasn't leaving any marks. He tips well! Can't complain too much. She said she needs to get her one like him who comes weekly. All she do is sit and talk with them. Sometimes them men want to feel your touch.

When he left, I sat with security telling him about Tuesday night.

May 25, 2014
I Almost Lost It

Sunday. I made my early morning flight from Vegas back home. I was able to make it to work. I was dog tired but didn't want to miss out on any more money. I wasn't able to work in Vegas so I didn't want to miss out on any more money. I had called the job and there were four girls at the time. By the time I showed up a few more had arrived. So it wasn't going to be one of those days when we dance more often than usual.

While I was in Vegas, one of the girls sent me a picture of the girl who copies my hair styles. She had the long pony tail in her hair. I had to laugh because everyone would know where she got it from. It wasn't high up on her head like I wore mine. Coming back to work, I had to change my hair style and wear my hair down. I knew I had to flat iron it so I got ready while my flat iron got hot.

There was one other girl in the dressing room with me. She was laying down chilling in the back while I got ready. I was almost done with my hair when Miss Stiffie walked in and said, "Oh, it smells like burned hair." The girl and I didn't say anything because it should have been clear that I was the cause of the smell. After a little while went by she opened her mouth again. "It smells like dirty hair." I still didn't say anything because I wasn't in the mood for her attitude. Her and I had been cool for a minute and I figured she was having a bad day already.

When she walked out, I picked up my soda cup, went to her trunk, and dropped some soda where she was sitting on top of her trunk. I wanted to make her mad and give her a real reason to talk some shit. She came back in a little later and repeated what she said about my hair.

"Okay, we heard you the first time. You Don't have to repeat yourself."

"Oh you did? Maybe I should say it again. It smells like dirty hair in here."

"You know what? You're pissing me off. There's been times when you had it stinking in here too."

"No I haven't."

"Yes you have. Whatever that stinky food you had in here before that had everyone wanting to throw it in the trash."

She looked at me with narrow eyes and shook her head side to side in disagreement.

"Well, I don't care."

As she walked out she said something else but I didn't hear her. I was pointing my flat iron at her as I talked. I wanted to put it down and walk over to her and punch her in the face. She really has the Devil inside her. And I think she gets mad when she says something and no one responds to it. I finished getting ready and went out to the floor to get my shift going.

The day went good. There were some people there for a birthday so they sat at the front of the stage. They tipped me good. I was shocked because I wasn't sure if they would like my dancing or not. But when I seen the ten dollar bill and five dollar bills from them on the table, I smiled even more at them. It wasn't dead and it wasn't busy. It was cool.

When I seen the girl I'm cool with come in, I went to tell her what happened earlier. She was shocked that Miss Stiffie said those things to me. Then later on she told me about two girls, who I'm cool with that be in the back "sniffing" before work. I was shocked! That would explain why one of the girls be up there moving hella fast when she dance. I was uncomfortable. I don't like being around people who do those kind of drugs. That's what makes them start to trip.

Now check this out. As I was getting dressed to leave, Miss Stiffie was complimenting me on my hair. Asking if I trimmed it, the color looks nice, blah blahh blah. I didn't even look at her. I just told her thank you and kept putting my clothes on. I wanted her to stop talking to me.

I was happy with the money I made. It was all from dancing on stage. I didn't sit with any customers. Wasn't anyone to talk to. It was a good day for me.

May 28, 2014
A Lot Of Catching Up. Dam.

Today is Wednesday and I have to catch ya'll up on Monday and Tuesday. So here I go!

The first thing I will say about Monday was that it sucked. I decided to come in to work to make some money because I thought it would be busy. That was so not the case. It was dead. I really wished I would have stayed home. The customers that did show up was not feeling me. I only made about $30. I didn't bother turning in the ones. I knew I had a few things to do the next day so why bother.

I left early it was so slow. I was happy to leave. Can't stand when it's slow.

Now Tuesday night was much better. When I got to the club my potna was working. I was happy to see her so we could share some laughs. I sat at the bar with the day shift security. He was chilling and having a drink. He offered me one so we sat drinking together. The manager gave me a shot of a new spiced rum. It was cool.

While I was sitting with security, guess who walked out from the back looking right at me with her pony tail behind her head? Yup! Lord I'm so happy I was wearing my hair down. My potna couldn't stop laughing all weekend. Everyone knows who you got the idea to wear a pony tail from, ya dam copy cat. I looked at her then looked back at security as I kept talking. Didn't even bother me. I got over it.

Security told me he was getting ready to go sit with one of his old customers from when he had his town car business. (He would drive customers around who needed to be chauffeured around) I just followed him over to the table to see if it was okay to sit with them. The customer said it was cool so we all moved to the back corner by the DJ booth.

It was cool sitting with them. We talked and laughed about things. When someone was dancing on stage to some cool music, security moved the table back so that I could give his customer a little dance. I sure did it. I was tipped a few dollars and a twenty dollar bill. Yes, I was happy. I just had to remind myself that I wasn't in Miami and not to take my clothes off.

Now while we were sitting down, my potna was behind me at a table with an Asian guy on her lap top. I guess he was doing something to it for her. There's a girl she don't like that I'm cool with who came to the table to talk and hang out. She's white, but according to my potna, the girl wants to be black so bad. I never looked at her like that. But you know how sometimes when people say something, it gets you to thinking.

Another dancer was with her. They both were off work just hanging out. I hadn't noticed at the time, but the other girl had a boob job. I don't know why some of these girls get their boobs done, and they work at a small place like this. But hey, if it makes them happy. It's not like it's my money they used.

When I went to the dressing room to situate my money, I was looking for a ten dollar bill I had put in my purse that a customer had tipped me. After taking all the money out looking for it I couldn't find it. All I had were three twenty dollar bills and ones. So I guess what I thought was a ten was really a twenty. And where did the third one come from? Oh well. I'm not mad.

The night went by cool. I didn't really sit with anyone. I was doing good getting tipped on stage. I was annoyed when the copy cat seen my potna talking to a guy at the bar, and she walked up behind him and started talking to him. My potna just walked off. She knows that he has money and went for him in such a rude fashion. That made me mad. I'm sick of her desperate ass.

Even when I was dancing on stage, she came over to throw me some money that came from him. I didn't even go over to tell him thank you because she was still there in his face and I didn't want to see her. Then I remembered that he is the same dude who came that Saturday at the end of my shift talking about, "I was about to hit you hella hard with this money." Then my potna told me he used to mess around with one of the girls who don't work here any more. Oh, I really don't care to talk to him now.

Later on, I was walking to the bathroom when I noticed an Indian guy looking at me. I smiled at him and he smiled back. When I came back from the bathroom he was still sitting at the bar by himself. So I went over and sat on him lap. He was so surprised that I did that. But I wanted to get the money he had. So he hurried up and pulled his ones from his pocket and started to tip me. It worked out fine.

I spent a little time in the dressing room. Not as much as I normally do. When it was time to leave I didn't waste time putting my head scarf on and taking out my contacts. I wanted to be comfortable and ready for bed. Some of the other girls were talking about how I made them wanna tie up their hair. So, what you waiting for?

May 28, 2014
Bad Day For Me

Not what I expected it to be. A pretty normal day. My regular came in and spent some time with me. He's getting ready to leave for Texas to visit some family June 5 for about a week. He asked me about us hanging out next Tuesday, and buying me some jewelry. I told him I'd let him know if I'm free. Not sure if I want him to do that. He might start asking for more. He already mentioned about me giving him a private dance. I rolled my eyes at the idea.

There was a surprise for me when I came back from the bathroom. I told him I was going to the restroom. I think it was the drink I had. The bathroom was a frequent trip every ten minutes. When I came back from the bathroom, the girl who gets on stage and does nothing was talking to him. I just walked up calm and stood on the side of her, waiting for her to move. When she seen I had walked up, she picked up her purse and left. I sat with my customer and kept the conversation going. No problem. I know security was watching because he knows how I am about certain stuff.

Most of the customers were white today. So tipping was slim for me on stage. Even when I thought I was doing good, everyone else was getting tipped but me. So I started slowing down on my dancing. I went and put my shirt back on for the last dance because I was leaving an hour early. I can be somewhere else enjoying myself if I'm not gonna get paid.

Now this is what I'm talking about. Rainbow Bright came to work today but left early to go spend some time with her boyfriend. What? You talking about needing money, but look at what you doing. No. Next time I get ready to go out of town, it's not gonna be with her. As it was explained to me, she is young and doing what young people do. From what she was talking about in the dressing room, she had already spent time with her boyfriend. Now she's missing work to spend more time? No no no. But that's her. I don't care. But I am taking notes.

Before I left, one of the girls came into the dressing room. Drunk as a skunk. Skinny little thing. She laid down but got up in about ten minute to puke in the trash can. I went to the bathroom then told security the trash needs to be changed in the dressing room. He was not happy about that. When I went back in, she was talking about how she had seven shots of tequila. Now you know yo tiny butt had no business drinking that many shots. Fool almost killed herself.

Good For A Saturday

Today was good. I got to work and enjoyed myself. I bought a short wig. I mean it's like an inch of hair on this wig. I wanna see if that chick will try to copy this short style. If not, then I can wear it for a minute. And I wanted to try something different. A lot of people liked it.

Things went good. I was surprised when my regular was standing at the bar. I went and sat with him. He gave me $100 to take my kids out to eat or do something for the weekend. Then he told me, "You don't know what you do for me." Oh boy. This is why I'm not sure about letting him buy me expensive jewelry Tuesday. I'm still thinking about it.

I did talk to new customers today. Well, customers I never talked to before. I did something different. It worked out for my benefit. I even talked with the one guy who tips fives then moved on to another customer. There was one customer I didn't get to sit with because my regular had showed up. I was kind of bothered by that.

When it was time for the shift change, I went to the back to count my money and talk with the girls for a while. I was upset when one of my potnas told me that she had been dancing to one of my songs. I didn't like that. Get your own songs. Now that's two songs of mine she's danced to.

See, when you get to pick the songs you want to dance to, you feel like certain ones are your signature. Especially when no one else has danced to it before. That's why some songs I like to play from my MP3 player so they can't ask what song is it. Get your own music!

I made sure to hang around the stage when all the girls were doing review, so that the copy cat could see my short hair. I wonder how she felt. Oh well. I might work next Saturday night and she'll see it them for sure.

June 1, 2014
What A Sunday!

I went to work feeling good. Wasn't sure how the day was going to go. I had got the movie tickets for my kids before going into work so whatever I made would go towards food.

There wasn't too many girls that showed up. Good thing for starters. I was feeling so good I even danced on the other stages to maximize my money making. I was having fun. Then I noticed a customer I hadn't seen in a while. The one that tips me twenties. I saw him when I was on fourth stage sitting at the bar.

When I was done dancing, I got off stage, stopped to spray on some perfume, then when I was gonna walk over to him, Miss Stiffie beat me over there. I mean, she ran off the stage straight over to him! I didn't even know that she knew him. And what makes her think he wants to talk to her? She just as old as he is. Plus he likes to touch. They were just sitting there talking.

When I went on stage again, he came over to my third stage to watch me dance. Getting off the stage, I followed him back to the bar and sat with him. We talked about things as I rubbed his back. He gave me $40 and I added that to the pot. He's getting ready to go to DC this week for a family visit. Then he'll be coming to the club on Fridays since the school year for him has ended already.

And you know what he told me that shocked me? He told me that Miss Stiffie told him, she thinks people are out to get her. What? Like, seriously? Did she mean to say that karma is out to get her? Sometimes I think she tried to throw herself a huge pitty party. Smh. . .

Things went smooth. I made some good money and was happy about that. I'm building up my money and hopefully I can find a place and move. Still having issues regarding my credit and proof of income.

June 2, 2014
Still Trying To See

Monday. I'm here at work trying to make something shake. Of course it's slow since things just started. I'm sitting in the dressing room trying to give time to pass and customers a chance to show up. No big whoop.

Today there's a lot of Hispanic construction workers coming in. You see all the highlighter orange and yellow shirts. They sit down, order drinks, and watch the shows. No tipping. Or if they do, it's a dollar or two. The club was still pretty dead even with them in there.

I decided to sit down with two customers who come in regularly. Older men who's nice to talk to. The other girls were sitting around waiting for their turn on stage. Wasn't much going on. When it got close to 3:00 pm I felt like I was ready to go home. I didn't want to dance for a bunch of looking Hispanics. I'd rather be on my way home to my kids then getting ready for my pole class the next day.

For the day I made $40. I'll take that and leave. Then some of the men at the bar had the nerves to ask where I was going when I came out the dressing room dressed and with my bags. Why you care? Yo behind didn't even look interested in my dancing when I was on stage. So don't worry bout me now. So annoying.

JUNE 6, 2014
Bad Friday It Is

So today is the birthday party of one of the girls. It hasn't really been busy today. Earlier around 1:00 pm there were a few construction guys in here. Hispanic. They were having their beers and watching the show. A lot of girls haven't been getting tipped much. You really gotta be working the floor to make any money. Plus there's almost twenty girls here. So it's even more difficult to make some money.

The second round of dancing is going on and I haven't made squat on stage. There were two Hispanic dudes sitting at the main stage when I was dancing. I noticed in the mirror that they weren't watching me dance. So I moved away from them and danced on the other side of the stage. I'm not dancing for them if they don't care to watch.

When I got on third stage, I just stood there and watched the TV like I did on second stage. I looked over to the girls on the other stages, and they had no money on their stages either. It's sad. As I was coming down the stage, the customer who was playing pool by my stage tipped me. I was shocked! He thought I was having a bad day but I told him it's slow and I'm not working up a sweat for lookers.

I think I'ma sit my a$$ in the dressing room till my next round of dancing. It's now about to be 3:00 pm, so we'll see how different it is outside when I go back out.

Things really didn't change much. Some more people showed up and it got a little better but even the DJ said that other girls were having problems making money. They were sitting with customers trying to make money. Guess they were doing more talking with girls than tipping. I'd rather sit in the back or to myself than chat with them for free.

There was a Black dude that took a liking to me. He came to second stage while I was dancing. I did my tricks and he felt that I didn't have to do all the pole tricks. I had to explain to him that I pride myself on being able to do what a lot of other girls can't do. Makes me look better and makes me more valuable.

By the time I left, I had a good $80. I was okay with that. If that's all I'm walking out with, then I'll be happy with it.

June 8, 2014

Double Saturday

I decided to do a double if there isn't too many girls trying to work. Saturday night should be busy and it would be nice to not have to worry about a bunch of girls talking to the customers while you're dancing on stage. They'll be able to tip you better if they're watching you.

The day shift was dead. The few customers that were there weren't tipping much. I just tried to chill and not be bothered by the slowness. There wasn't too many girls working either. The usual crew didn't show.

It kind of got a little busy by four o'clock. I was able to put some "umf" in my dancing because I felt I had an audience that would appreciate it. Then I seen one of my cool customers who always tip nice sit down in the back. When I was done dancing, I went and sat with him and his friend. I think he was high or on something. His friend kept cracking jokes like he was on something. But he was not a problem. Just really animated.

Then when it was close to the shift change, the copy cat chick came over to my stage when I was on the fourth one talking to a customer. She walked up to the side of him and looked me straight in my face. I knew she was checking out my hair. I just looked back at her and kept talking to him.

The night shift only had eight girls. I was happy. When we did the review, I went over to the third stage to dance where I could be by myself on the stage. Then when we started the actual shift, I had to start on third stage, and some dudes came over to watch me dance. Smart move. Every single girl don't have to be on the same stage.

For the most part, I spent the night shift relaxing. I was laying on second stage, since we weren't using it. I didn't hang in the dressing room like I normally would do. Felt kind of good. There was one guy who came in with his nephews in a wheel chair for his birthday. They sat at the stage before my song ended. One of the nephews liked me. Before they left to get something for him to eat, he came over and asked how long I was going to be at the club. They wanted to come back and see me some more. I felt special.

Then, I was sitting at the bar waiting to be called on stage, and copy cat asked me if my hair was a sew in. I told her it was a wig, and she said, "I been looking for one like that. I want one with a pixy cut." Boom. Now she's gonna come to work with a short wig. And she made my potna upset because she liked the one piece she had on. She told her, that she went online trying to find one like hers and she should just sell it to her. Who would want to wear a one piece that has already been worn? Ewe!

Now, when 11:00 pm came around, it got busy. I was happy because I felt that the money was finally here. Nope. When I got on stage, some people left and I barely made $5. What the f#ck? And I was doing pole tricks and dancing. What did you people want to see? I was done and ready to go home. If this was how the people were going to treat me, I'm not giving anything else. My arm was already hurting and I was tired. I made some cool money and felt satisfied. Time to leave.

Some Kind Of Night

So today was gonna be one of those days when you bring your amo to work with you. I was prepared for copy cat to come into work with a short wig on her head. I went to the beauty supply before work to get another short wig just in case. It was a short cut on one side, and long on the other with some purple hair in it. It's cute.

When I was done dancing on the fourth stage on the first round of dancing, I sat down with a customer. He told me how he came in here and was talking to another customer at the bar. I had told him before how some customers have told me they came just to have a beer when I tried to talk to them. The customer he talked to told him the same thing. He knew then that what I told him before was no B.S. Some people really need to go to a regular bar if they just want a beer. Low lifes.

When I got to work my hair was still tied up because I wanted to wait and see how her hair was first. By the time we started the shift she wasn't there. So I felt she just wasn't coming tonight. But after my first round of dancing, I heard her name called to go on stage.

I waited for a few seconds before I looked at her walking to the stage. Her long, curly hair was swinging down her back. Awesome. I can wear this short cut a little longer. But she might have one by this weekend. That's fine. Just give me a few more days to wear this style longer.

The shift started off slow. A lot of the customers who came were talking to girls or watching the basketball game on TV. So I wasn't tripping about going on stage and being watched. But then this happened. . . .

When I was called to dance on stage for the second round, there were two Hispanic females and males sitting at the stage when I started dancing and when I was finished dancing. As I was dancing, I seen how one of the females didn't look too interested in me dancing. So I stopped dancing in front of them and moved away. Then one of the bartenders, who was off, came over and tipped me.

At the end of my dance, the four people sitting at the stage had not tipped me. So I got up from the stage, looked at them all and said, "Thank you for watching." I smiled, turned to walk away, then flipped them off as

I pretended to scratch the back of my head with my middle finger. How dare you sit at the stage and not tip?! I'd rather you walk away and sit some where else. I felt good after I did that. And come to find out, they the same to a few other girls as well. Bastards left shortly after.

The shift was slow for the night. I didn't really talk to too many people. One guy who was from Europe kept staring at me. I knew he wanted me to come talk to him but I didn't really feel like talking. He eventually came over and started talking to me. He was cool to talk to. He works in the computer field and likes to cook.

The night was pretty much uneventful. It was funny when copy cat started dancing to some Indian music. I knew the Indian guy was here. Another girl was talking about her too. Every time he comes she makes sure she dances to some Indian music. She makes it obvious she's begging for money.

I want to make this clear. It is not hating. When you have time to notice how someone operates, and it don't look effortless, it looks like begging. A few other girls feel the same way about her because it's clear that she's trying too hard to make her money. She doesn't even give the guy a chance to sit down, get a drink, and see if he'd like to talk to some other girls. She hogs him. If you're really up on your game and he's really feeling you, you don't have to do those things. Like with my regular. He comes to see me, and only me. Then there's other customers who tip me well whether I sit with them or not. I'm not pressed for their money.

I was approached by two guys who were looking for girls to work at their club. I was interested because if I can work some where else a few days out the week making more money, then that's what I would like to do. Think I'll swing by Friday night and see what they have going on. And the fact that I can give lap dances there makes me feel that I can make more money from that alone. We'll see how that goes. I'm gonna give them a shot.

I was tired by the time midnight came. But I didn't ask the manager to leave early. I figured I left early Saturday, I'll stay till closing. Wasn't too bad. I didn't make $100 and it felt weird. But I made something more than what I had before.

June 11, 2014
Just Not My Day

I was just hoping that today I could make a nice amount of money. My birthday is coming up on the 15th and it would be nice to have some money for my birthday. But that did not happen.

For one, it was slow. Two, the customers that were there were busy talking to other customers or to girls. Three, they were not feeling me. I wasn't trippin off things. I still felt happy. There was plenty to look at. And to hear.

Remember that one customer I told you cannot stand Miss Stiffie? Well, he came in. He was trying to rush me to come sit with him when he arrived. I had to use the bathroom first. When I finally sat with him he was happy and relieved. He did not want to talk to her at all.

He got to telling me about how she was so drunk while she was messing around with this one football player, that he was using her "other hole", and she did a "number two" on his stomach. It reminded me of the time someone was telling me, that before you have anal sex, it's best to use an enema. Yeah, like someone is gonna stop in the middle of sex and take an enema.

Miss Stiffie started hanging with the men who were sitting right next to me and that customer who can't stand her. After a while, I noticed that she wasn't talking to them any more. She was standing still looking out in front of her. Then a few more minutes later, she was laying her head on the bar. Too many shots from them guys. The customer I was with said that she was going out to dinner with someone later. He didn't think she would make it. She started laying on the customers and one was rubbing her back. She could barely walk straight.

He also told me how the same football player was getting money from her. Wait, did that sound right? They were suppose to get married. She got him a ticket to Vegas, where they were to get married. Her mom and some of her friends were there. Dude didn't show up. Wow. I felt a little bad for her, but just a tiny bit.

Now this was funny. That new Black girl with the blonde hair and big booty that doesn't do nothing on stage? When the customer I was sitting with seen her. He even could tell that her booty was fake. Then when I told him that another customer told me she was from Miami, that confirmed it. Girls get all kinds of plastic surgery done out there. He did not like the way she looked and how she moved.

The day went by kind of fast. I don't even know how much money I made because I still had the money from Tuesday night in my purse. I know I didn't do good.

Explaining To Do

I was going to continue a little longer with my daily experiences, but I think I'm ready to end it for now. I'm ready to take a break from thinking about what I and some of these girls go through to take care of themselves as dancers and mothers. I say these two and nothing else because to me, that's what matters. What you go through as a dancer and mother to take care of yourself and others. That's also how we see it.

If you're a dancer with no kids, then you don't have much riding on making enough money to bring home. If you're a mother, then everything counts. Everything adds up. But at what cost? Even today at work, the DJ seen one of the girls standing up at one of the tables, showing her private area to a customer. Who probably didn't even tip more than $5. Now what was going through her head?

Even with working at a bikini bar there are similarities to working at a fully nude club. Some of the male customers want too much from us dancers for too little. And because some will accept less, they mess it up for others when it comes to paying for the same entertainment. Something we all have to deal with. What matters is how you deal with it.

I can say that a lot of people have the wrong idea about dancers. And when I say dancers, I'm not leaving out strippers. I'm choosing to use the word "dancers" as a whole instead of saying all the names people call us. No mater what we do to make the money, we still do some kind of dance to make it.

Since I started dancing, I have come to see this world as something much more than I could of imagined. And in a good way. It's not all about sex and drugs. Only if you let it or make it about sex and drugs. I have met some nice people who I can call a friend. I'm talking about the customers, just so you know. There are a few who I like to talk to and spend time with.

The creeps that I have met are creeps because they were allowed to be by other girls, or that was their nature. As I said before. Just because you dance, and people have stereo types about dancers, doesn't mean you have to do as the stereo type suggest. You can be your own dancer, stripper, slut or whore you want to be. Long as it's what you want to be. Don't let someone make you be what you don't want to be. They'll do what they let you do.

I'm happy being a dancer. I find it fun, interesting, and I feel healthier with all the moving around and things I do. Yeah, the drinking can be a down side if you do it everyday all the time. But even I don't drink all the time. I'll have a water instead just to give my insides a break. It's not a must to drink every time you work.

Over the past few weeks I have watching everything that has been going on in the club. Pure entertainment for us girls and customers. Since the World Cup has been on, the Mexicans have been plentiful with certain teams. And yes, they just drink their beer and watch the TV. Gay pride was last Saturday and the money was great since only four girls came to work. Counting that $300 was one of the best feelings I had in a long time.

I love being a dancer. Just to be able to have the freedom to work when and how I want. Avoid the people I don't want to talk to. Get my money in hand. Look good and feel good. Dress sexy and not have to worry about it being too sexy. And meeting different people. I met a guy a week ago who has bought my books. That worked out in my favor. There are many benefits to working in such a place if you know how to talk and network.

The other day, there were three guys who were sitting at the main stage. I had two songs to dance to. When the first one was finished I did not see any money from the guys. I was pissed off but something told me not to say anything just yet. When I started the second song, that's when I seen the money they had threw on the floor, trying to throw it on the stage. I let my anger go and danced. They tipped nice and was real excited about my dancing. Especially when I made my booty clap.

Now the other girls were really bothered by them. They said they were saying mean and nasty things to them. A few got attitudes with them because of what they were saying. And of course Miss Stiffie had some choice words for them because they didn't pay her attention nor tipped her for her dancing. For her second dance she didn't come to the end of the stage. She stayed in the back away from them. It was funny.

Sometimes I think about what people say or think about me as a dancer. Some of the mean and nasty things they said to the girls, could have been said to me. How would I have took one of them saying, "Yeah she can dance, but can she f#ck?" I think I would have laughed and gave a smart, humorous remark.

The reason I say that is because, in this business, if you can't handle the sexual nature of men, then you shouldn't be in it. Men, especially when alcohol is in their system, will speak on their thoughts no matter how dirty they are when other men are around. Either you entertain what they said and keep the money coming, or you shut them down and stop the cash flow. This is where that thin line between "disrespecting" and "playing" becomes an issue. At what point do a dancer, or "woman", become disrespected by a customer? Every woman as well as situation, is different. All I can say is, it's disrespect when a woman feels disrespected.

I have had customers ask me if they can touch me. They want to touch my breasts, booty, leg, arms, shoulders, or hands. I tell them yes if they don't look like they will give me a skin rash. Some will just grab for what they want. As I have said before, some men come there for affection. I don't mind as long as they are chill about it. And don't put their hands inside my panties.

Have I ever felt disrespected by a customer? Yes I have. The Indian guy who shoed me away with his hand when I told him he has to tip me if he sits at my stage. Have I felt disrespected sexually by a customer? I sure have. When they stick their hands inside my bottoms trying to finger me. Or trying to stick their finger in my booty. I don't know what goes through some of their minds, but that's how some men are. And they come to places like a bikini bar looking for someone who will let them have their way, either with the money or without. Some girls go for it and some don't. I just tap their hand and tell them don't do that because I don't like it. If they don't respect it, I walk off and leave them alone.

Everything is not about the money. Just because someone is giving you money, does not mean you have to let yourself go just to get it. The moment a person feels disrespected, they should act on it. No matter how much money is evolved. But if a dancer can play the role and at the same time, let the irrespective party know that they need to tone it down, then both sides can still win while feeling good about themselves.

That's all people want to do. They want to feel good about themselves in such a place. But that doesn't mean let them walk over you. There was guy who had a ton of bumps on his face. I don't know what the hell they were. His face was not smooth. This fool wanted me to kiss him on his lips. I told him I do not do that. He looked at me funny when I said it. I told him how nasty that would be if I kissed every customer who wanted a kiss. He told me to have a nice day and I walked off. Happy to be leaving him. How did I feel? Freaking awesome!

Working at a bikini bar has been (and is) a fascinating experience. Even the customers, for the most part, enjoy themselves as much as we do. That's why some of them come in every day, or weekly. I enjoy meeting people and hearing their stories. I enjoy that more than talking about myself. I try to make it more about the customer because sometimes they come in there with problems. Why not help them feel a little relieved?

Remember when I told you Rainbow Bright was made when "her" customer gave the Asian girl $100 for the massage she gave him? Sometimes these men just want the simple things that a woman can give. It's not all about sex. It's about getting from a woman what a man needs or want. Attention. Affection. Motivation. Laughter. Friendship. Stuff like that.

And speaking of Rainbow Bright, let me share this with you. Her birthday is coming up and that means she gets a birthday party since she's been working there for over a year. Last month she was telling one of her friends that work with us how she wants her party. The way she was explaining it, I feel she should have done the party herself. Since she had all these specifics and stuff.

A few days ago, she asked the same friend if she could pass around her birthday card at the bar. Since she works right there close to the customers and they know her. The girl told her, "She's busy and don't want to do it." So Rainbow went to the DJ and told her what happened. The DJ sat her down and told her that there are two kinds of people in this world. Takers and givers. She told her she was a taker. She explained a few other things to her about how she's treated people so she could understand why no one wanted to give her a birthday party. She was actually shocked! How selfish are you to not see or think about how you treat people, then be amazed when no one wants to do something special for you out of an act of kindness? I'm not going to her party. I don't want to be apart of it. I still haven't been paid for that plane ticket.

How you treat people has a great affect on how they treat you. When I have a customer who sits at my stage and tips me, I give them a hug at the end and tell them thank you with a smile. Just so they can feel good about the experience and I show my appreciation. It goes a long way. It will let them know you're nice, you appreciate it, you are friendly, and it's okay to tip you again in the future.

No, I don't want to be like Miss Stiffie. An older lady still trying to dance when she clearly should have stopped a long time ago. I enjoy the freedom I have as a dancer, but I want to be a temporary dancer. Why? Because I don't want to be "stuck" when my time is over. I want to use this time to get myself in a better place that I can relax with my kids and not have any worries. That's what my goal is. Use this time to get to a better place in life. Enjoy it while I can!

Before I bring things to a close, I would like to add an update. Miss Stiffie has been cut off from the customer. Just like he said. I talked with him today and he told her that even though she thinks they might be more than friends, they are only friends. She should not be stuck to his hip and being possesive when other girls are trying to talk with him. I was wondering why yesterday she didn't really care about him coming in. She seemed upset. Oh well.

I haven't seen that girl from Miami with the fake booty in about two weeks. I don't know if she left or if she's taking time off. Don't really care. There has been other girls coming in to work the day shift. So the numbers haven't really dropped.

Rainbow Bright had her birthday party. It went okay. There wasn't too many pictures taken, and when she went on stage to blow out her cake and be rained on by money, there wasn't too many girls who went on stage with here. I looked like five or six. Fridays are busy, and if she had a better attitude with and around people, she might have had more love shown for her. Oh well. Hope she enjoyng Vegas. Feels great not to have her around they few days.

I had a talk with my mom as we were on our way to the casino. I told her about some of the things that go on at the job. I told her how I love dancing, but I don't want to be an old woman still dancing. You know what she asked me? Would I want my daughter to grow up and be a stripper?

I had to catch my breath for a second. I have told me son, when he asked me how would I feel if he wanted to become an assassin. I told him, "All I want you to do, is what will make you happy. You are the only person who is going to have to live your life everyday. I just want you to be happy." He was understanding of my answer.

I became a dancer because I couldn't even get a job to have some kind of income coming in. And now that I have been dancing for a while, I love it because I feel that I am great at it. I love doing the pole tricks. I love amazing people. And I enjoy being on stage. If my daughter ever wanted to become a dancer, all I'd want is for her to be the best dancer she can be. She that she can be happy with herself everyday she has to work, and everyday she doesn't have to work. After all, it's not what you do. It's how you do it.

The date is July 27, 2014 It is 11:16 pm and I am tired. Today was a good Sunday. There were seven girls and things went pretty good. I was happy with the money I made and I wasn't complaining about nothing. I even learned a new trick yesterday that I did on impulse, while being upside down on the pole. Awesome. I will be working for the next three days. Hopefully my regular comes in tomorrow and gives me some money to take my kids to Legoland. I don't know how much he is going to give me, but I'll take whatever! It will help for something if not for the trip.

Dancers/strippers have a bad rep with some people. Take the time to get to know one. Get to know her story. Her background. Not every dancer/stripper is the same. Just like our bodies, personalities, and dance styles. We are all different just like we are suppose to be.